Learning Elixir

Unveil the many hidden gems of programming
functionally by taking the foundational steps with Elixir

Kenny Ballou

[PACKT] open source *
PUBLISHING   community experience distilled

BIRMINGHAM - MUMBAI

Learning Elixir

First published: December 2015

Production reference: 1211215

Published by Packt Publishing Ltd.
Livery Place
35 Livery Street
Birmingham B3 2PB, UK.

ISBN 978-1-78588-174-9

www.packtpub.com

Credits

Author
Kenny Ballou

Reviewers
Ahmed El-Sharkasy
Paulo A. Pereira

Commissioning Editor
Kartikey Pandey

Acquisition Editor
Vinay Argekar

Content Development Editor
Anish Dhurat

Technical Editor
Rahul C. Shah

Copy Editor
Swati Priya

Project Coordinator
Bijal Patel

Proofreader
Safis Editing

Indexer
Hemangini Bari

Graphics
Disha Haria

Production Coordinator
Nilesh Mohite

Cover Work
Nilesh Mohite

About the Author

Kenny Ballou is a life-long learner, developer, mathematician, and overall thinker. He enjoys solving problems, learning about technologies, and discussing new and different ideas.

He graduated from the Boise State University, majoring in applied mathematics, and minoring in computer science. He has been programming professionally for nearly a decade, and is currently working as a software developer for an analytics company in the Boise, Idaho area.

Apart from developing professionally, he is active in the open source community, contributing where he can.

When he is not developing, he enjoys reading, learning, and shredding the local mountains.

You can read more from him on his blog at `https://kennyballou.com`, check out his code on GitHub at `https://github.com/kennyballou/`, and follow him on Twitter at `@kennyballou`.

I stand on the shoulders of those before me. I could not be where I am today without the many that have contributed to my success. Thank you.

I would like to specifically thank Sam Schrader for teaching me to teach myself, Dan Feldhusen, and Dillon Woods for affording me the opportunities to learn more, my parents for encouraging me to always strive for more than even I myself think is achievable, and my closest friends for supporting me through to the end.

I would also like to thank my reviewers and Packt Publishing for the guidance and assistance to shape and improve this book. I'm certain this book would not have been of the great quality it is now without their help.

About the Reviewers

Ahmed El-Sharkasy is a senior software engineer at Onfido (`https://onfido.com/`). Over the course of his life, he joined different start-ups. He worked as a team leader at Byteis (`http://web.byteis.com/`), lead developer at Bkam (`https://eg.bkam.com`), and software engineer at eSpace (`http://espace.com.eg/`) and Shaqa (`https://www.shaqa.com/`). He loves building products that can improve people's lives, and is specifically interested in the knowledge and education sectors. He is the cofounder and CEO of Fretsi (`https://fretsi.com/`), having a mission to deliver knowledge to humanity for free and rewarding people based on their knowledge levels. He has also published a research paper named *TRUPI: Twitter Recommendation based on Users' Personal Interests*.

Paulo A. Pereira is a senior software engineer. He fell in love with Elixir, and has a passion for exploring new technologies and keeping himself up to date with the industry's developments.

He previously worked as a consultant and lead developer for Mediadigital, implementing Grails and Rails solutions. He is currently working at Onfido Background Checks, a London-based tech start-up that is proving to be a key player in the background checking industry.

www.PacktPub.com

Support files, eBooks, discount offers, and more

For support files and downloads related to your book, please visit www.PacktPub.com.

Did you know that Packt offers eBook versions of every book published, with PDF and ePub files available? You can upgrade to the eBook version at www.PacktPub.com and as a print book customer, you are entitled to a discount on the eBook copy. Get in touch with us at service@packtpub.com for more details.

At www.PacktPub.com, you can also read a collection of free technical articles, sign up for a range of free newsletters and receive exclusive discounts and offers on Packt books and eBooks.

https://www2.packtpub.com/books/subscription/packtlib

Do you need instant solutions to your IT questions? PacktLib is Packt's online digital book library. Here, you can search, access, and read Packt's entire library of books.

Why subscribe?

- Fully searchable across every book published by Packt
- Copy and paste, print, and bookmark content
- On demand and accessible via a web browser

Free access for Packt account holders

If you have an account with Packt at www.PacktPub.com, you can use this to access PacktLib today and view 9 entirely free books. Simply use your login credentials for immediate access.

Table of Contents

Preface

This is an introduction to Elixir, a relatively new programming language. We will go through the basics of the language and teach functional programming and other paradigms as we progress. We will study the basics of concurrent and distributed programming through the lens of Elixir and OTP. We will also examine one of the more exciting features of Elixir: metaprogramming, or writing code that writes code.

This book doesn't teach the basics or programming in your first language, but it does teach the basics of Elixir under the assumption that this is a new language.

This book will also discuss a fair amount of Erlang, the predecessor language Elixir derives from, and the runtime Elixir compiles to, which is prevalent to the understanding of Elixir.

What this book covers

Chapter 1, Introducing Elixir – Thinking Functionally, introduces Elixir and functional programming, and provides some of the history and justification of Elixir. It also walks you through installing Elixir.

Chapter 2, Elixir Basics – Foundational Steps toward Functional Programming, introduces the basics of Elixir and its types, syntax, and semantics. This chapter lets you start reading and writing Elixir code.

Chapter 3, Modules and Functions – Creating Functional Building Blocks, lets us extend and expand on the previous chapter by introducing the basics of Elixir code organization into modules and functions. It makes us start our lengthy discussion on pattern matching, one of the coolest features of Elixir.

Chapter 4, Collections and Stream Processing, lets us examine collections and explains how to solve common problems using recursive algorithms. This chapter also lets us introduce Elixir's pipe operator and the basis of collection processing.

Chapter 5, Control Flow – Occasionally You Need to Branch, discusses how to do more traditional code branching, conditional statements using Elixir.

Chapter 6, Concurrent Programming – Using Processes to Conquer Concurrency, explains how to write concurrent code using Elixir. It introduces Elixir processes and the basics of message passing.

Chapter 7, OTP – A Poor Name for a Rich Framework, continues the discussion of concurrent programming with Elixir, more specifically in the context of OTP, which is the framework introduced in Erlang for building robust distributed applications.

Chapter 8, Distributed Elixir – Taking Concurrency to the Next Node, examines how to write Elixir that executes on multiple nodes, distributing the processing over possibly many computers.

Chapter 9, Metaprogramming – Doing More with Less, introduces Elixir behaviours, protocols, typespecs, and macros. Using Elixir macros, we examine how we can accomplish more with less code.

What you need for this book

This book was written against the 1.0.4 version of Elixir, but the code should be compatible with the latest version of Elixir, 1.1.1 (as of this writing).

There are, otherwise, no special requirements, even for the distributed chapter. All the code can be executed on a single computer with Elixir installed.

Who this book is for

This book targets the developers who are new to Elixir as well as Erlang to make them feel comfortable in functional programming with Elixir, thereby enabling them to develop more scalable and fault-tolerant applications.

Although no knowledge of Elixir is assumed, some programming experience with the mainstream object-oriented programming languages, such as Ruby, Python, Java, and C#, would be beneficial.

Conventions

In this book, you will find a number of text styles that distinguish between different kinds of information. Here are some examples of these styles and an explanation of their meaning.

Code words in text, database table names, folder names, filenames, file extensions, pathnames, dummy URLs, user input, and Twitter handles are shown as follows: "If you want an integer type back, you can use the `div` and `rem` functions."

A block of code is set as follows:

```
defmodule MyMap do
  def map([], _) do
    []
  end

  def map([h|t], f) do
    [f.(h) | map(t, f)]
  end
end

square = fn x -> x * x end
MyMap.map(1..5, square)
```

Any command-line input or output is written as follows:

```
iex(1)> IO.puts("Hello, World!")
Hello, World!
:ok
iex(2)>
```

New terms and **important words** are shown in bold. Words that you see on the screen, for example, in menus or dialog boxes, appear in the text like this: "This is the basis of what functional languages call **pattern matching** and is really one of the fundamental things that makes functional programming so different and so exciting."

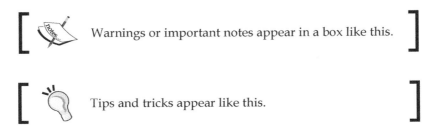

Warnings or important notes appear in a box like this.

Tips and tricks appear like this.

Reader feedback

Feedback from our readers is always welcome. Let us know what you think about this book—what you liked or disliked. Reader feedback is important for us as it helps us develop titles that you will really get the most out of.

To send us general feedback, simply e-mail feedback@packtpub.com, and mention the book's title in the subject of your message.

If there is a topic that you have expertise in and you are interested in either writing or contributing to a book, see our author guide at www.packtpub.com/authors.

Customer support

Now that you are the proud owner of a Packt book, we have a number of things to help you to get the most from your purchase.

Downloading the example code

You can download the example code files from your account at http://www.packtpub.com for all the Packt Publishing books you have purchased. If you purchased this book elsewhere, you can visit http://www.packtpub.com/support and register to have the files e-mailed directly to you.

Errata

Although we have taken every care to ensure the accuracy of our content, mistakes do happen. If you find a mistake in one of our books—maybe a mistake in the text or the code—we would be grateful if you could report this to us. By doing so, you can save other readers from frustration and help us improve subsequent versions of this book. If you find any errata, please report them by visiting http://www.packtpub.com/submit-errata, selecting your book, clicking on the **Errata Submission Form** link, and entering the details of your errata. Once your errata are verified, your submission will be accepted and the errata will be uploaded to our website or added to any list of existing errata under the Errata section of that title.

To view the previously submitted errata, go to https://www.packtpub.com/books/content/support and enter the name of the book in the search field. The required information will appear under the **Errata** section.

Piracy

Piracy of copyrighted material on the Internet is an ongoing problem across all media. At Packt, we take the protection of our copyright and licenses very seriously. If you come across any illegal copies of our works in any form on the Internet, please provide us with the location address or website name immediately so that we can pursue a remedy.

Please contact us at copyright@packtpub.com with a link to the suspected pirated material.

We appreciate your help in protecting our authors and our ability to bring you valuable content.

Questions

If you have a problem with any aspect of this book, you can contact us at questions@packtpub.com, and we will do our best to address the problem.

Introducing Elixir – Thinking Functionally

Let's embark on a journey, let's leave behind the world we know and head to something new and different. We quest to learn a new programming language, Elixir, and new paradigm of programming, functional. We set out leaving behind most of what we know, and attempt to think differently.

Elixir is a functional, dynamic language built on top of Erlang and the Erlang VM (BEAM). Erlang is a language that was originally written in 1986 by Ericsson to help solve telephony problems, including distribution, fault-tolerance, and concurrency, among others. Elixir, written by José Valim, extends Erlang and provides a friendlier syntax into the Erlang VM while maintaining interoperability with Erlang and Elixir without imposing performance costs.

Elixir's roots in Erlang provide some really indispensable functionality for developing distributed and fault-tolerant applications. Developing in Elixir, we can have all that and then some.

That is, Elixir provides and exposes to us the means and tools to create applications that can truly run with nine nines of reliability. Those are a fail-fast by default design of the runtime with the concept of process supervision, which enables strong fault-tolerance, the inherent concurrency of message passing, and a functional language that also enables distribution. We will discuss all of these topics and concepts by the conclusion of this book.

But before we get into these excellent features of Elixir and Erlang, let's take a dive into functional programming and why it's useful in creating a system that has these features.

I assume you're familiar with imperative languages such as Perl and Java. Furthermore, you're likely familiar with the concept of static typing and dynamic typing, as in Python. But what is functional programming? Moreover, why should we care about it?

Why functional?

Functional programming is a paradigm of programming, a means of structuring and reasoning about code. It is, in essence, about composing functions that transform data. That is, when writing functionally, we write simple functions that transform data in a particular manner. Then we later write some other functions that use our previous functions as building blocks for more complicated transformations. This may not sound all too foreign.

In the object-oriented world, programming is about maintaining state in some controlled fashion. We create object hierarchies to define the world and we operate on some methods of those objects to manipulate the world around us. That is, we compose objects to model and, if we're lucky, we solve problems.

These are both methods of and for abstraction. We write simple components and compose. When a simple component is defined, we can forget its details and begin thinking about bigger components that result from the combination of those smaller ones.

However, there are several problems that creep up on us in the object-oriented and imperative worlds. They are subtle and they rarely, if ever, show themselves directly. These are the problems that are hard to find, hard to debug, and hard to fix. Although, we can see their symptoms.

We notice the symptoms when we attempt to conceptualize or interpret our own code using an ideal or imaginary interpreter. We notice the symptoms when we attempt to test large components. We notice the symptoms when we attempt to split execution paths. Something, somewhere, inevitably fails.

Objects and imperative code are usually, relatively easy to understand on paper. So why is this understanding only on the surface and so easily shattered when we dig further?

Imperative code is certainly testable. We can certainly get to correct solutions. But why is it so difficult to write good, testable code? Why are the correct answers so hidden from view?

Clearly imperative code is composable; yet, why is it often difficult to compose objects and existing functions? What is hindering our ability to do this well?

We can also write concurrent, imperative code. Why, then, is it seemingly so daunting and nearly impossible to get correct?

The lurking monster hiding behind our questions is usually the one thing that makes programming actually useful: side-effects or state. Functions in the imperative world usually encapsulate implicit changes to variables, objects, files, and, in other words, changes to state. These changes usually cost nothing to program and may, in fact, be pinnacle to the function they originate from. How useful would printing text to the console be if you were unable to write a stream of bytes to the character device, that is, your terminal?

It is these hidden, out-of-mind side-effects that can make programming so dangerous to understanding, correctness, and composability, not to mention, concurrency. To overcome this, we can't forget the side-effects lurking in our code. That is, when composing components in the object-oriented world, we still fail to release ourselves from the burden of implementation. We must still page the details of our objects to use them effectively. Our escape is functional programming.

Functional programming allows us to escape from these problems by forcing us to confront the issue of changing states. It gives us guidelines for how to construct our components and not to forget that state changes are inevitable and how to handle them appropriately, without compromising on composition, understandability, and testability. Furthermore, well managed side-effect inducing code, is nearly trivial to make concurrent.

The functions implemented in functional languages must return the same output for the same input. Any dependence of the output on the state, outside of what we give the function, must not change the output of the function. Changes of state are handled in a very controlled manner: they must be marshaled through some channel. Most functional languages handle this in similar ways, but this can also depend on the level of **purity** of the language. However, this affords us easy-to-understand and easy-to-personally interpret code, and lets us create well defined modularity and testable components. Also, by restricting changes of state (or disallowing them entirely), making code concurrent is essentially free.

Best of all, functional programming isn't something restricted to a particular language; it's a concept that can be followed and used in any language. It's more of a state-of-mind than being partial to a particular set of languages.

Of course, I can't ethically speak about the benefits of functional programming without also warning you of some potential limitations, particularly of the new learning curve and some performance considerations.

Functional programming can feel very limited to newcomers. It's generally difficult to do anything useful in purely functional programming languages, and often, this isn't helped by examples that only show the functional bits in elementary examples.

When transforming data in purely functional languages, we must create new structures for the modified data. If we could otherwise modify the existing data structures, we would be violating our immutability invariant. Thus, when modifying some data structure, we must usually create a new structure. This has fairly obvious performance issues, namely, the memory copies are required to create the new structure on top of performing the actual modifications.

However, there is hope for both of these concerns. Firstly, with respect to performance considerations, functional programs can typically have more sophisticated tooling because it is not only easier for us to understand as mere mortals, but also the tools we write to parse, compile (translate), and execute the functional code written. Some interesting compiler optimizations can be achieved from the shared nothing, process separation, and message passing processing model enforced by the underlying runtime.

That is, functional code, generally, is easier to parse, both by humans and compilers. Therefore, the compiler and runtime can flatten, unroll, and take our functional code and rewrite it into a safe, optimized form. The runtime can also take advantage of object graph information to decrease the number of copies needed to modify data. The graph can later be checked by the runtime and compressed if necessary; this is the basis for garbage collection.

Secondly, with respect to the learning curve, I hope to teach functional programming through more than elementary or intermediate examples by the conclusion of this book.

Installing Elixir

Before we can truly begin our journey into the depths of Elixir, we need to install it and make sure our environment is sane. I will cover some basic installations for most OSes. As far as hardware requirements are concerned, there really are none. However, if you happen to *not* have a multi-core CPU, you may miss out on the inherent speed benefits of the runtime.

GNU/Linux

Most distributions, today, will have Elixir in their repositories and this is the preferred way to install Elixir. Installing Elixir from your distribution's repositories will also take care of installing Erlang.

If you are using a Red Hat-based distribution of GNU/Linux, you can use the **yum package manager** tool to install Elixir:

```
# yum install elixir

...


Transaction Summary
==================================================================
======
Install  1 Package (+14 Dependent packages)

Total download size: 16 M
Installed size: 31 M
Is this ok [y/d/N]: y
...
Complete!
```

If, on the other hand, you use a Debian-based distribution, you will need to add the Erlang Solutions repository and install Elixir using dpkg and apt-get:

```
$ wget {.deb for your distribution}
$ sudo dpkg -i {downloaded version of erlang}.deb
$ sudo apt-get update
$ sudo apt-get install elixir
...
The following extra packages will be installed:
  erlang-asn1 erlang-base erlang-crypto erlang-inets erlang-mnesia
  erlang-public-key erlang-runtime-tools erlang-ssl erlang-syntax-
tools
Suggested packages:
  erlang erlang-manpages erlang-doc erlang-tools
The following NEW packages will be installed:
  elixir erlang-asn1 erlang-base erlang-crypto erlang-inets erlang-
mnesia
  erlang-public-key erlang-runtime-tools erlang-ssl erlang-syntax-
tools
0 upgraded, 10 newly installed, 0 to remove and 0 not upgraded.
Need to get 12.9 MB of archives.
After this operation, 23.8 MB of additional disk space will be used.
```

```
Do you want to continue? [Y/n] y

...

Setting up erlang-crypto (1:17.5) ...

Setting up erlang-mnesia (1:17.5) ...

Setting up erlang-runtime-tools (1:17.5) ...

Setting up erlang-syntax-tools (1:17.5) ...

Setting up erlang-asn1 (1:17.5) ...

Setting up erlang-public-key (1:17.5) ...

Setting up erlang-ssl (1:17.5) ...

Setting up erlang-inets (1:17.5) ...

Setting up elixir (1.0.4-1) ...
```

 The .deb file you download will be specific to your distribution. The Erlang Solutions download page has as many to choose from.

Or, if you're like me and you're running Arch Linux, you can install Elixir with pacman:

```
$ sudo pacman -S elixir erlang-nox

resolving dependencies...

looking for conflicting packages...


Packages (2) elixir-1.0.4-1  erlang-nox-17.5-1


Total Installed Size:  107.70 MiB


:: Proceed with installation? [Y/n] y

(2/2) checking keys in keyring               [################]
100%

(2/2) checking package integrity             [################]
100%

(2/2) loading package files                  [################]
100%

(2/2) checking for file conflicts            [################]
100%

(2/2) checking available disk space          [################]
100%
```

```
(1/2) installing erlang-nox                    [################]
100%

Optional dependencies for erlang-nox

    erlang-unixodbc: database support

    java-environment: for Java support

    lksctp-tools: for SCTP support

(2/2) installing elixir                        [################]
100%
```

I'm suggesting the non-X (erlang-nox) version as Arch separates the Erlang releases based on whether it has GUI libraries included or not, and we will not need them for this book. If you later decide that you want or need them, you can simply install the regular Erlang package and tell pacman to remove the non-X version.

Apple Mac OS X

For Apple Mac OS X, you are hopefully using Homebrew or MacPorts.

Use the following command to install Elixir via Homebrew:

```
$ brew update; brew install elixir
```

Use the following command to install Elixir via MacPorts:

```
$ sudo port install elixir
```

Windows

If you're using Microsoft Windows, you can download a precompiled binary from the Elixir **INSTALL** (http://elixir-lang.org/install.html) page. Go through the installation wizard to complete the installation.

Manual installation – binary

Manual installation should really be avoided if at all possible, but I'll include it in case your system isn't listed here or on the installation page, or for some other unforeseeable reason.

First, you will need to download and install an Erlang binary provided by Erlang Solution (https://www.erlang-solutions.com/downloads/download-erlang-otp). Next, you will need to download a precompiled ZIP file from Elixir's releases page. Unpack the ZIP folder to the location of your choice. Once unpacked, you should update your PATH variable to include the bin directory of the Elixir release.

Manual installation – source

Another option with respect to manually installing Elixir is to build Elixir from source and, by extension, build and install Erlang from source.

The latest source of Erlang can be found on its GitHub page (`https://github.com/erlang/otp`). After building and installing a satisfactory version of Erlang, download and build the source for Elixir, also available on GitHub (`https://github.com/elixir-lang/elixir-lang`).

Hello, World!

Now that Elixir is installed on your machine, let's fire up the interactive Elixir prompt. Open a shell/terminal emulator and run `iex`.

You should see the following text printed on the terminal:

```
$ iex
Erlang/OTP 17 [erts-6.4] [source] [64-bit] [smp:8:8] [async-
threads:10] [hipe] [kernel-poll:false]


Interactive Elixir (1.0.4) - press Ctrl+C to exit (type h() ENTER
for help)
iex(1)>
```

Before we continue, let's talk about some of the output of running `iex`. The line starting with "Erlang/OTP..." contains the Erlang emulator information tags. Each tag describes something about the underlying runtime VM. Here are some short explanations for each tag shown on my machine:

- `Erlang/OTP 17`: This tells us the current version of Erlang.
- `[erts-6.4]`: This is the version of the Erlang runtime system.
- `[source]`: The Erlang emulator was compiled from source. This is typical if you or your package maintainer built Erlang from source (and didn't use the official precompiled binaries from Ericsson).
- `[64-bit]`: This means the emulator is built to take full control of 64-bit memory addressing.
- `[smp:8:8]`: This tells us how many CPU's and schedulers are available and online.
- `[async-threads:10]`: This gives us the asynchronous threads available to the runtime.

- [hipe]: This tells us that the Erlang emulator is compiled with the high performance extensions enabled.
- [kernel-poll:false]: This informs us that the kernel polling is disabled.

For the majority of these, however, you don't necessarily need to concern yourself with until you get into system and performance tuning, which will be out of the scope of this book. There are also many more options that can be listed here, so you may want to, if you need, look at the Erlang BEAM emulator source (https://github.com/erlang/otp/blob/maint/erts/emulator/beam/erl_bif_info.c). A Stack Overflow question (http://stackoverflow.com/questions/1182025/what-do-the-erlang-emulator-info-statements-mean) has the same information as well, in a, perhaps, more accessible format.

Next, the line following the break tells us the version of Elixir installed, how to quit, and about a helpful command for getting, err, help.

Infamously, we can try typing, "Hello, World!", and we should see it echoed back to the screen:

```
iex(1)> "Hello, World!"
"Hello, World!"
iex(2)>
```

We can also do some basic arithmetic:

```
iex(2)> 40 + 2
42
iex(3)>
```

Best of all, we can get help documentation right in our shell by executing the following command:

```
iex(3)> h


                        IEx.Helpers


Welcome to Interactive Elixir. You are currently seeing the documentation
for the module IEx.Helpers which provides many helpers to make Elixir's
shell more joyful to work with.


This message was triggered by invoking the helper h(), usually
referred to
```

```
as h/0 (since it expects 0 arguments).
```

```
There are many other helpers available:
```

- c/2   — compiles a file at the given path
- cd/1   — changes the current directory
- clear/0   — clears the screen
- flush/0   — flushes all messages sent to the shell
- h/0   — prints this help message
- h/1   — prints help for the given module, function or macro
- l/1   — loads the given module's beam code and purges the current version
- ls/0   — lists the contents of the current directory
- ls/1   — lists the contents of the specified directory
- pwd/0   — prints the current working directory
- r/1   — recompiles and reloads the given module's source file
- respawn/0 — respawns the current shell
- s/1   — prints spec information
- t/1   — prints type information
- v/0   — prints the history of commands evaluated in the session
- v/1   — retrieves the nth value from the history
- import_file/1
             — evaluates the given file in the shell's context

Help for functions in this module can be consulted directly from the command line. As an example, try:

```
h(c/2)
```

You can also retrieve the documentation for any module or function. Try these:

```
h(Enum)
h(Enum.reverse/1)
```

To discover all available functions for a module, type the module name followed by a dot, then press *Tab* to trigger autocomplete. For example:

```
Enum.
```

To learn more about IEx as a whole, just type h(IEx):

```
iex(4)>
```

I'll let you try h(IEx).

To exit the interactive prompt, you can press *Ctrl + C* twice, or you can press *Ctrl +G + Q + Enter.*

As a quick aside, notice the numbers following the methods, for example, h/0. What is the number? The number stands for the arity or number of parameters the function expects. So, h/0 means the h function expects no parameters. This is often how we will see and talk about functions in Elixir (and in Erlang).

Using the IO.puts/2 function

Now we are going to try something else. We are going to continue with some more introductory examples and some code, modules, and functions we will use throughout the book.

Let's fire up our interactive Elixir prompt again:

```
$ iex
iex(1)>
```

This time, we are going to try "Hello, World!" with the IO.puts function:

```
iex(1)> IO.puts("Hello, World!")
Hello, World!
:ok
iex(2)>
```

Well, this is different. What happened? First of all, notice that "Hello, World!" is written to the screen *without* the quotes. Further, what is this :ok thing?

It just so happens that the IO.puts function is a function with side-effects; it writes its parameter's value to the screen. Since Elixir statements are all expressions, every statement must return a value. The value returned in this example, :ok, is an atom, and we will cover exactly what these are in the next chapter. For now, what is important is that this return value signifies to the caller, us, that the operation has been successful. It is very common for Elixir code that either succeeds or fails to return either the atom, :ok, or the atom, :error.

We can try this function with different data and should see similar results:

```
iex(2)> IO.puts(42)
42
:ok
```

```
iex(3)> IO.puts([])

:ok
iex(4)>
```

When we call IO.puts with 42, we get what we expect—the number 42 is written to the screen and we get the :ok return value. But what about the next example? It seems to return an empty string and :ok. What is going on here? Well, as it turns out, Elixir is interpreting the empty list as an empty list of characters. And certainly, we can print an empty list of characters as an empty string. We will discuss this more when we go over lists in the next chapter.

Using the inspect/2 function

Another function we will often use while developing and debugging Elixir code is the inspect/2 function. From the help, type h(inspect/2) in your iex:

```
def inspect(arg, opts \\ [])

Inspect the given argument according to the Inspect protocol.
The second argument is a keywords list with options to control
inspection.
```

We will cover protocols more specifically in *Chapter 9, Metaprogramming – Doing More with Less*. For now, let's check the documentation of the Inspect protocol (http://elixir-lang.org/docs/v1.1/elixir/Inspect.html).

The Inspect protocol is responsible for converting any Elixir data structure into an algebra document. This document is then formatted, either in a pretty printing format or a regular one.

Essentially, the inspect/2 function allows us to peer into our data structures and see what's inside, in a readable format.

The inspect/2 function is a useful function for viewing the internal values or states of some data structures of our programs. These can also be used in print statement style debugging. To some degree, you may think of the inspect/2 function as a to string for most types. However, *do not* use this function for that purpose!

Exercises

Read:

- The Elixir **GETTING STARTED** page (`http://elixir-lang.org/getting-started/introduction.html`)

Do:

- Try out the interactive interpreter (IEx).
- Try some more basic arithmetic.
- Try out the help command some more.
- Try entering `'Hello, World!'` in IEx. What may be the difference between single quotes and double quotes? (No fret, we will cover this in the next chapter!)

Summary

In this chapter, we introduced Elixir as a new and upcoming language; we discussed functional programming and its implications, good and bad; we installed Elixir; and we ran our first few commands in the interactive Elixir prompt.

2

Elixir Basics – Foundational Steps toward Functional Programming

In the previous chapter, we talked about functional programming, installed Elixir, and tried a few elementary examples.

In this chapter, we are going to go into depth on the syntax and basic built-in types and operators of Elixir (and implicitly, Erlang). We are going to explore some more structural elements of Elixir code and begin our discussion of pattern matching.

Everything is an expression

We have hinted at this concept in the previous chapter, but let's discuss it in more detail here.

In Elixir, there are no statements. Everything is an expression. Let's break this down. Statements typically refer to instructions where the programmer specifies to the computer or runtime to perform some action. This action could, for example, add two numbers together and assign the value to a variable. Or, it could instruct the machine to print data—strings, numbers, and bits—to the console. Or, it could instruct the machine to make a remote connection to another machine and request a web page. These actions may have ephemeral results—the value of the variable, output text on the screen, and page data from the request. But in all of these examples, the code, itself, which instructs the performance of such actions, does not necessarily, nor inherently return anything.

To contrast this to expressions, we note that we can still do all of these things, however, each instruction will return something. When we add two numbers and then binding the result to a variable, we still get the value. When we send data to the console, we see a sort of success confirmation symbol. When we request the data from remote connection, we would likely get a success or failure symbol and the response body or the reason for failure, respectively.

More concretely, note that when we add two numbers and assign the value, we still get the result printed:

```
iex(1)> a = 4 + 2
6
```

When we use IO.puts/1 to print data to the console, we see the :ok symbol:

```
iex(2)> IO.puts(a)
6
:ok
```

We'll wait to see the last example, but we can see the idea.

Why does this distinction matter? Are we not accomplishing the same things, regardless of whether a line in the program is a statement or an expression? Yes, we are accomplishing the same things, just with different approaches. However, we gain some distinct advantages if everything is an expression, namely, in terms of composability. That is, with expressions, the concept of program flow and execution becomes more evident because we can compose parts of our programs in a way that is more readable and natural.

Of course, we can write Elixir code, similarly to the way we have written imperative code in the past. However, this will eventually be more painful than to do it the functional way.

We will see this materialize more as our journey progresses.

A short introduction to types

Like most programming languages, Elixir has its fair share of numerical, boolean, character, and collection types. It also has some extra types, namely, atoms and binaries. In this chapter, we will see how all of these types work. However, let's start our discussion with numerical types.

Numerical types

Numerical types include the obvious integers. For example, in the interactive prompt (`iex`), we can enter a few basic numbers:

```
iex(1)> 42
42
```

We can also do some basic arithmetic with numbers, of course:

```
iex(2)> 42 + 5
47
iex(3)> 6 * 7
42
iex(4)> 42 - 10
32
iex(5) 42 / 6
7.0
```

So, addition, subtraction, and multiplication work as we expect. Division, however, did what is typically called implicit type widening or implicit type casting. That is, we took two integer types and converted it into a floating type through division. In fact, the / operator will always return a floating point type. If you want an integer type back, you can use the `div` and `rem` functions:

```
iex(6) div(10, 3)
3
iex(7) rem(10, 3)
1
```

Memory usage

To understand the assumptions of our system and make sure we are using the right types for the job, it's often important to know how big each of our types are. Numerical types are architecture dependent. That is, integers on 32-bit machines will be smaller than integers on 64-bit machines. Integers, on either sized architectures will be 1 word, where a word is defined as 4 bytes or 8 bytes for 32-bit architectures or 64-bit architectures, respectively. This gives us a range of values between -134217729 and 134217728 for 32-bit architectures, and a range of values between -576460752303423489 and 576460752303423488 for 64-bit architectures. Big integers will start at 3 words and will grow to n words to fit.

Floating point numbers should always be double precision, which means they will use 4 words on 32-bit machines and 3 words on 64-bit machines. Furthermore, they will also follow the IEEE-754 specification for memory arrangement and usage. We will talk about IEEE-754 a little more later in this chapter.

Binary, hexadecimal, and octal numbers

Elixir also has some neat shortcuts to represent numbers in different basis. That is, we can represent and convert between different numerical basis nearly trivially. To print a binary number in decimal, we can use the `0b` prefix:

```
iex(1)> 0b1010
10
```

Furthermore, to print an octal number as a decimal, we can use the `0o` prefix:

```
iex(2)> 0o755
493
```

Finally, as the pattern continues, to print hexadecimal numbers as decimals, use the `0x` prefix:

```
iex(3)> 0xFF
255
```

Elixir also supports entering numbers in exponent form. This has some obvious benefits of allowing us to define constants in a more readable form among other uses.

Since these are all still integers, we already know their size in memory.

For example, we can input, say, Newton's gravitational constant in a friendly form:

```
iex(4)> 6.674e-11
6.674e-11
```

 Note that it doesn't convert the exponent form to its full form. [How do we get it to print in the full form?]

Atoms

Atoms, sometimes referred to as symbols in other languages, are literal, constant terms where the name is the value itself. In Elixir, they are always prefixed with a leading colon, :. You may notice, in Erlang, they are not. Here are some examples of atoms we have seen already:

- :ok
- :error

And some we haven't seen yet, but will later:

- :reply
- :noreply
- :stop

But really, any alphanumeric with underscores (_) can be used as an atom. Some examples may include:

- :first_name
- :last_name
- :address1
- :address2

Atoms are really useful for signaling success or failure results, or as keys in a dictionary type. You may also think of atoms as enumerated types from other languages.

In the interactive interpreter, atoms behave very similarly to numbers. For example:

```
iex(1)> :ok
:ok
iex(2)> :error
:error
```

There are also a few internal functions for converting atoms into strings or strings into atoms. For example, here we change the :ok atom to 'ok':

```
iex(3)> Atom.to_string(:ok)
"ok"
```

Or, to convert the other way, we use this:

```
iex(4)> String.to_atom("ok")
:ok
```

We will go into some more detail about the String module shortly.

Atom memory usage

Atoms use 1 word or 8 bytes of memory and are unique. That is, once you define (read use) an atom, it will point to the same memory as all the other occurrences of that atom. Furthermore, they are not garbage-collected, nor are they mutable. The memory used by atoms will never be freed up until the termination of the program.

From the Erlang Efficiency Guide:

> *1 word. Note: an atom refers into an atom table which also consumes memory. The atom text is stored once for each unique atom in this table. The atom table is not garbage-collected.*

Booleans

Booleans, as you expect, are the simple values—either `true` or `false`. Furthermore, boolean expressions have all the expected operators:

```
iex(1)> true
true
iex(2)> true == false
false
iex(3)> 2 < 42
true
iex(4)> 5 > 10
false
```

And as with most languages, we have our typical negation, the AND and OR operators:

```
iex(5)> not false
true
iex(6)> true and false
false
iex(7)> 1 and true
** (ArgumentError) argument error: 1
iex(8)> false or true
true
```

The not, and, and or operators are type strict with their first argument. The second argument can be anything. This explains what happened at prompt 7 here. However, or and and are short-circuit operators, so we can do the following as well:

```
iex(9)> true or error("I will not raise")
true
iex(10)> false and error("I will not raise either")
false
```

Although Elixir provides not, and, and or operators, it also provides non-type strict operators, !, &&, and ||, respectively:

```
iex(11)> !42
false
iex(12)> 1 || false
1
iex(13)> true && 42
42
```

Let's take a quick moment to discuss what is happening in the last two examples. When we try true && 13, we may expect to get either a type error or simply true. Why didn't we?

In Elixir, boolean expressions return the last evaluated value. This is also true in short-circuiting. When we ask Elixir to evaluate 1 || false, we are given back 1 because it evaluates to true and the ||/2 operator is short-circuited. Similarly, an expression like true && 42 returns 42 because the &&/2 operator requires the evaluation of both elements to succeed. Obviously, true will pass. Thus, 42 is returned, because it is the last evaluated value of the two.

On top of the typical boolean operators, we have access to some other operators that allow us to determine types and minor inspection:

- is_boolean/1
- is_atom/1
- is_integer/1
- is_float/1
- is_number/1

 Remember, Elixir functions are described by *{name}/{arity}*.

For example:

```
iex(14)> is_boolean(true)
true
iex(15)> is_boolean(1)
false
iex(16)> is_atom(false)
true
```

Okay, I lied. Elixir doesn't actually have booleans. It turns out that they are just atoms:

```
iex(17)> is_boolean(:false)
true
iex(18)> is_atom(true)
true
```

To fully enumerate our different comparison operators, we have the following:

- `==`
- `!=`
- `===`
- `<` and `<=`
- `>` and `>=`

You are, probably, already familiar with most of these. The `==` operator is used for testing equality, `!=` is used for testing against equality, `<` and `<=` is used to test for less than or less than or equal, respectively, and finally, `>` and `>=` is used to test for greater than or greater than or equal, again, respectively.

But what about `===`? This operator tests equality and equivalence. That is, the values must be equal in value *and* type. This may be easier to see in an example:

```
iex(1)> 1 == 1.0
true
iex(2)> 1 === 1.0
false
```

We can see that `1` shows, semantically, the same value as `1.0`. However, integers are not of the same type as floating point numbers. Therefore, they are not equivalent.

Furthermore, as may be hinted by `1 == 1.0`, the comparison operators can be used across types. We can do something like this, without issue:

```
iex(1)> 1 < :atom
true
```

Since we can compare across types (we can do cool things such as sorting algorithms without care for the types in the collection we are sorting), the `</2` operator will be sufficient for all cases.

The overall ordering of types is `number < atom < reference < function < port < pid < tuple < maps < list < bitstring`.

It's not necessary to memorize this ordering, but you should know it exists.

Strings

Strings in Elixir, as you would expect, are just UTF-8 characters surrounded by double quotes. But they have a few extra qualities that most other languages either don't have or treat differently. For example, strings may contain line breaks, by either including them using escape sequences or by *actually* writing the new line into the string.

We've seen this earlier:

```
iex(1)> "Hello, World!"
"Hello, World!"
iex(2)> "Hello,\nWorld!"
"Hello,\nWorld"
```

But we can also do this:

```
iex(3)> "Hello,
...(3)> World!"
"Hello,\nWorld!"
```

 Note that the `...(#)>` prompt is used by `iex` to denote the continuation of input. It's expecting you to finish your expression.

We can also use the `IO.puts/1` function again to print the newline character:

```
iex(4)> IO.puts("Hello,\nWorld!")
Hello,
World!
```

```
:ok
iex(5)> IO.puts("Hello,
...(5)> World!")
Hello,
World!
:ok
```

UTF-8 strings mean we can also use any character supported by the UTF-8 encoding. So, we can go ahead and write this into our interactive session as well:

```
iex(6)> "こにちは、せかい！"
"こにちは、せかい！"
```

 On Windows, you may have to adjust the output encoding of your terminal or use a terminal that supports UTF-8. You can change the current encoding for the session using `chcp 65001` before launching `iex`.

Elixir strings also have great support for string interpolation. This is accomplished via the #{} character. For example, we can try executing the following command:

```
iex(7)> "Hello, #{:world}!"
"Hello, world!"
```

Furthermore, the `String` module has plenty of functions that we can use to manipulate strings. For example, we can easily reverse strings, determine the length of a string, and pull a single character out of a string:

```
iex(8)> String.reverse("Hello, World!")
"!dlroW ,olleH"
iex(9)> String.length("Hello, World!")
13
iex(10)> String.at("Hello, World!", 6)
" "
```

This, of course, only scratches the surface of the `String` module and I strongly encourage you to read more about it (and other modules) in the documentation.

(Linked) Lists

No language is complete without its own implementation of (linked) lists. Elixir has its own primitive (linked) list type. Elixir lists are heterogeneously typed, meaning they can contain any type at the same time. For example, we can have a list of numbers with an atom somewhere in the middle:

```
iex(1)> [1, 2, 4, :ok, 6, true]
[1, 2, 4, :ok, 6, true]
```

We can concatenate two lists together using the ++/2 operator:

```
iex(2)> [1, 2, 3] ++ [4, 5, 6]
[1, 2, 3, 4, 5, 6]
```

Similarly, we can subtract two lists using the --/2 operator:

```
iex(3) [1, 2, true, false, true] -- [true, false]
[1, 2, true]
```

Note that it removes one for one. The subtraction operator will remove the first element to match and will *not* remove any repeated elements.

Many functional algorithms that process lists will do so in a process head, recursively, process tail. So, it would be nonsense for our functional language to not provide us functions for doing just this. To grab the head of the list, we use hd/1:

```
iex(4)> hd([1, 2, 3, 4, 5])
1
```

And to grab the tail of the list, we use tl/1:

```
iex(5)> tl([1, 2, 3, 4, 5])
[2, 3, 4, 5]
```

Wait! Why did it return [2, 3, 4, 5]? There is a bit of overused terminology here. Often, in other languages, when programmers refer to the tail of lists, they mean the *last element* of the list. However, in functional languages, it is very common for the tail of a list to refer to the rest of the list. Thus, tl/1 returns every element *after* the head.

This is, in essence, the true concept of a linked list. You have a head element that points to the next element. But, more recursively, you have an element, the head, which points to a list.

Furthermore, you may notice that calling `hd/1` or `tl/1` on an empty list is an error:

```
iex(6)> hd([])
** (ArgumentError) argument error

iex(7)> tl([])
** (ArgumentError) argument error
```

A little more about strings

In C, we know strings are really just character arrays. And, `char` is just an unsigned integer. Well, it turns out that we really haven't quite escaped this, even in Elixir.

You may notice that if you put big integers into a list, the interactive prompt will display characters:

```
iex(8)> 'hełło'
[104, 101, 322, 322, 111]
iex(9)> is_list('hełło')
true
iex(10)> [104, 101, 108, 108, 111]
'hello'
```

Why have two different representations for Strings? This is a bit of a historical holdover from the early Erlang days. Erlang was built around telephony switches. Bits and binaries were more important at the time. String handling wasn't important. So many old Erlang libraries did string handling, what may have been the natural way to do it then, as lists of characters (or numbers, really).

Since this is the case, you may find yourself using an older Erlang library that only uses lists of characters, and your representation is an actual string, or vice versa. In that case, there's both `to_string/1` and `to_char_list/1` to help you convert back and forth:

```
iex(11)> to_string('hallo')
"hallo"
iex(12)> to_char_list("hallo")
'hallo'
```

 The `to_string/1` function is more versatile than just converting character lists to strings. You can pass numbers and other types that follow the `String.Chars` protocol and get a string representation out.

Ranges

Similar to lists, we can create number ranges simply with `../2`. For example, to generate a list of numbers from 1 to 100, we would simply use `1..100`. However, typing this into `iex` is less than interesting:

```
iex(1)> 1..100
1..100
```

Actually, this is interesting. Why didn't Elixir expand the range? This is because ranges are considered lazy. The result is not *actually* enumerated until it absolutely has to be. Lazy evaluation enables us to solve problems that are potentially infinite; however, we don't have to worry about that since it turns out that we will only need a tiny subset of the dataset. It turns out, though, that most things in Erlang, and thus, Elixir, are considered eager. We will discuss more about lazy and eager programming in *Chapter 4, Collections and Stream Processing*.

Tuples

Tuples, similar to lists, allow us to collect the elements together into a single structure. Tuples differ from lists in denotion in that they are surrounded by curly brackets— { and }. Furthermore, tuples can hold any value:

```
iex(1)> tuple = {1, 2, :ok, "hello"}
{1, 2, :ok, "hello"}
```

However, the difference between tuples and lists is that tuples store elements contiguously in memory. Lists are inherently linked, and thus, accessing an element of a list by index is a slow, order *n* time, operation. Tuples, on the other hand, enable fast, constant-time element access.

Using the `tuple_size/1` function, we can get the length or size of any given tuple:

```
iex(2)> tuple_size(tuple)
4
```

Using the `elem/2` function, we can access any element of a tuple with an index (indexes start at 0):

```
iex(3)> elem(tuple, 1)
2
```

We can also use the `put_elem/3` function to insert (read replace) elements in a tuple at the provided index:

```
iex(4)> put_elem(tuple, 3, "world")
{1, 2, :ok, "world"}
iex(5)> tuple
{1, 2, :ok, "hello"}
```

Remember, Elixir is a side-effect free language. The `put_elem/3` function does not mutate the existing tuple, but creates a new one.

Tuples or lists

Why have both tuples and lists? Why use one over the other? What's the difference?

It depends. As mentioned earlier, tuples are stored in contiguous blocks of memory, whereas lists are stored as linked lists in memory. The access characteristics of each is given by these two memory layouts. For tuples, accessing arbitrary individual elements is cheap. However, growing and inserting more elements into a tuple is not cheap. For lists, although accessing arbitrary individual elements requires traversing the list. But, prepending elements is cheap, constant time. Appending elements requires traversal.

Binaries

Elixir brings over the binary type from Erlang, and for good reason. The binary type gives us a lot of power over bits and bytes, and does not only enable us to use them effectively, but makes it as pain-free as binary data munging could be.

Binaries, sometimes referred to as bit-strings, in Elixir are enclosed in between `<<` and `>>` and may look a little strange at first:

```
iex(1)> <<1, 2, 4>>
<<1, 2, 4>>
iex(2)> <<255, 255, 256>>
<<255, 255, 0>>
```

What happened at command 2? It turns out, binaries, the disqualified ones, have a maximum value of 255. We must specify to the runtime that it should use more bits to represent our data:

```
iex(3)> <<256 :: size(16)>>
<<1, 0>>
```

The internal representation of each element in binaries will not use values greater than 255. Instead, as we told it to use two bytes (16 bits) for 256, it carried up the extra value into the next byte. See, each element in a binary is actually a byte and the maximum value we can represent with a single byte (unsigned) is 255. To store larger values, we must use more bytes. With 16 bytes, we can represent only up to 65535, unsigned. So, if we try the same trick, we should see 0 again:

```
iex(4)> <<65536 :: size(16)>>
<<0, 0>>
```

We see two elements because we are using two bytes, and Elixir, when printing binaries, prints them in the single-byte representation. Furthermore, we see two zeros because 65536 is out of the range of 16 bits. If we wanted this to fit, we could increase the size:

```
iex(5)> <<65536 :: size(17)>>
<<128, 0, 0::size(1)>>
```

Here, we see something a little different. By increasing the value only by one bit, we are now able to fit the value we want, but the representation of those bits is different.

The runtime is going to try as best as it can to use good-sized word boundaries when it is asked to store non-conforming binaries, that is, bits that do not align (already) to a word boundary.

Even more about Strings

Let's take yet another moment to talk about Strings. This time, we will focus on double-quoted strings, that is, real strings.

Erlang, in its early days, didn't require strings. Erlang code was hardly, if ever, used for user-facing code. Thus, string handling, by manipulation or otherwise, was regarded as secondary. Bit handling, on the other hand, was paramount. It was absolutely necessary to have really good bit and binary manipulation. This is a language that was used to handle telephony data, which is all bits and bytes.

When it came to adding strings and string handling to Erlang, instead of introducing a change that would likely break a lot of systems, it was decided to use the existing types to facilitate. After all, what are characters but a couple of bytes per character (using decent encoding, or they are just one). That is, Strings are either a list of numbers, as we mentioned before, or actually binaries:

```
iex(1)> is_binary("Hello")
true
iex(2)> is_binary(<<"Hello">>)
```

```
true
iex(3)> <<"Hello">> === "Hello"
true
```

Notice that these all say that strings are binaries and vice versa. In fact, `<<"Hello">>` and `"Hello"` are *equivalent*.

We can take this String concept further:

```
iex(4)> <<"Hello, せかい" :: utf8>>
"Hello せかい"
iex(5)> <<"Hello, せかい">>
"Hello せかい"
```

 The `:: utf8` size pattern specification isn't necessary when constructing strings.

Strings in Elixir are, actually, UTF-8 binaries, and there is a nice `String` module that can and will work with UTF-8 binaries. This marks a clear distinction between Elixir and Erlang. String in Erlang refers to a list of characters and there is a `string` module, but it is not UTF-8 aware and will not handle the preceding strings correctly.

Some more built-in types

There are a few more types we should, at least, be aware of before continuing. We aren't going to dive into the real depth of these types just yet, but we are going to introduce them. These are two—functions and PIDs.

Functions

Functions, as mentioned previously, are first-class citizens of Elixir, Erlang, and pretty much any other functional language. This means that we can reference them and pass them around as if they were any other type. We can pass them as parameters to other functions, injecting some sort of functionality into that function, or we can use this function passing as another form of composing programs.

For a quick example, here is a function that squares its input and returns the result:

```
iex(1)> double = fn x -> x * 2 end
#Function<6.90072148/1 in :erl_eval.expr/5>
```

The output tells us how the function was interpreted and saved into memory. Don't mind the details for now, but the take away is that we can now use this as a function as it is. Or, we could pass it to another function to compute some result:

```
iex(2)> double.(2)
4
iex(3)> Enum.map(1..10, double)
[2, 4, 6, 8, 10, 12, 14, 16, 18, 20]
```

In 2, we used `double/1` as a standalone function and doubled the value of the number 2.

In 3, we passed our function, `double/1`, to the function, `Enum.map/2`. The `Enum.map/2` function takes a collection and a function and maps the function over the collection. That is, it processes the collection, passing each element of the collection to our function, and returns the result.

Process IDs

Another built-in type that comes from Erlang is that of **process IDs** (PIDs). These are not to be confused with regular OS PIDs. These are Erlang processes. Most often, when considering processes in the context of Erlang, we mean Erlang processes unless otherwise stated.

PIDs are used for referencing and signaling or message passing between Erlang processes. These are the addresses used to denote each process and its mailbox. Without the mailbox identifier, we have no idea how to send a message to it.

We won't create any processes yet, but we can see all the processes running in the current Erlang VM with `Process.list/0`:

```
iex(1)> Process.list()
[#PID<0.0.0>, #PID<0.3.0>, #PID<0.6.0>, #PID<0.7.0>, #PID<0.9.0>,
#PID<0.10.0>,
 #PID<0.11.0>, #PID<0.12.0>, #PID<0.13.0>, #PID<0.14.0>, #PID<0.15.0>,
 #PID<0.16.0>, #PID<0.18.0>, #PID<0.19.0>, #PID<0.20.0>, #PID<0.21.0>,
 #PID<0.22.0>, #PID<0.23.0>, #PID<0.24.0>, #PID<0.25.0>, #PID<0.26.0>,
 #PID<0.27.0>, #PID<0.28.0>, #PID<0.29.0>, #PID<0.37.0>, #PID<0.38.0>,
 #PID<0.39.0>, #PID<0.40.0>, #PID<0.41.0>, #PID<0.42.0>, #PID<0.44.0>,
 #PID<0.45.0>, #PID<0.46.0>, #PID<0.47.0>, #PID<0.50.0>, #PID<0.51.0>,
 #PID<0.52.0>, #PID<0.53.0>, #PID<0.54.0>, #PID<0.55.0>, #PID<0.56.0>,
 #PID<0.57.0>, #PID<0.59.0>]
```

Note that your output may differ.

This prints all the currently running processes in the current `iex` session.

Invariable variables and pattern matching

One of the most misunderstood concepts in functional programming is that of assignment. Or, said another way, assignment doesn't exist.

Let's try to dispel this misconceived idea. In `iex`, we might see some code like this:

```
iex(1)> a = 2
2
iex(2)> a + 4
6
```

We may be tempted to explain the preceding code snippet with something like, "So we assign 2 to a and then add 4 to a giving us 6." However, in Elixir, this is incorrect. Elixir does not define = as an assignment operator, but rather a *match* operator. That is, Elixir attempts to match the left side of the = operator to that of the right.

In step 1, for Elixir to make the match succeed, we bind the value of 2 to the variable, a. Then later, when we perform the addition, we are substituting 2 for a, yielding an expression that looks like *2 + 4*, which obviously equals 6.

This is a really different way to think about what is going on internally. Take a moment to let it sink in.

Back? Ready to move forward? Good!

If all we are doing is binding, why can we do something like this:

```
iex(1)> a = 2
2
iex(2)> a = 3
3
```

This is because Elixir will rebind values to make the match succeed. Notice, however, you are not able to do this:

```
iex(1)> a = 2
2
```

```
iex(2)> 3 = a
** (MatchError) no match of right hand side value: 2
```

But we can do something like this:

```
iex(1)> a = 2
2
iex(2)> 2 = a
2
```

This is the basis of what functional languages call **pattern matching** and is really one of the fundamental things that makes functional programming so different and so exciting.

Since Elixir will always try to make the left-hand side match the right, we can use this to our advantage to decompose lists, extract elements, or decompose complex structures into simpler variables.

Let's take a look at decomposing lists.

We may define a list as:

```
iex(1)> list = [1, 2, 3]
[1, 2, 3]
```

Then, we may attempt to match it against a, b, c:

```
iex(2)> [a, b, c] = list
[1, 2, 3]
iex(3)> a
1
iex(4)> b
2
iex(5)> c
3
```

So Elixir attempts to create a match between the left side: [a, b, c] and list (which evaluates to [1, 2, 3]). For Elixir to successfully match these two sides, a, b, and c must be bound to the values 1, 2, and 3, respectively. As we see in commands 3-5, this is indeed the case.

Similarly, literal values can be used in the match expressions, using the same list:

```
iex(2)> [a, 2, c] = list
[1, 2, 3]
iex(3)> a
1
iex(4)> c
3
```

Using the underscore

In many functional languages, the underscore (_) is used to denote values we don't wish to bind to any value, or we don't care to use. Using the previous example, perhaps we don't care about the middle value of the list, but we can use the underscore to match against the 2, or whatever it *actually* is:

```
iex(2)> [a, _, c] = list
[1, 2, 3]
iex(3)> a
1
iex(4)> c
3
iex(5)> _
** (CompileError) iex:5: unbound variable _
```

It turns out that the underscore is a bit of a special variable. It allows us to match any expression, for example, _ = list would match successfully, but Elixir never keeps the bound value. This is good for two reasons. Firstly, semantically speaking, when reading any Elixir code, if we see the underscore, we know we can ignore it, and, secondly, the fact that Elixir will not allow us to use it will certainly help ensure that we don't make any mistakes with its actual value.

More pattern matching

Pattern matching has all sorts of uses in Elixir. Let's consider binary data deconstruction using pattern matching. While we're at it, let's learn about IEEE-754, the standard that defines how computers handle floating-point numbers in memory.

IEEE-754

If you're familiar with the IEEE-754 standard, feel free to skip a few paragraphs ahead.

For the sake of the discussion, we will assume we are talking about 64-bit or double precision floating-point numbers. There are other representations, 32-bit/single and 128-bit/quadruple precision, but they usually only differ by the number of bits available.

The IEEE-754 standard, first introduced in 1985, defines a couple of terms we need to become familiar with for our discussion. There is the sign, the exponent, the fraction or mantissa, and the bias.

The sign is denoted by the most significant bit. The exponent is given 11 bits, and the fraction is given 52 bits. The bias is just a constant for the exponent value.

With 11 bits for the exponent, we can store numbers between -1024 to 1023, or without the sign, 0 to 2047. We use the bias to keep the sign bit out of the number; however, we don't gain more precision here, this just has to do with the arithmetic involved. For example, to store a 0 exponent, we would store 1023 or 01111111111.

The fraction or mantissa is given 52 bits. This means that we can represent the fractional bit of a floating point with 52 bits of precision. This gives us a lot of space to represent numbers. However, we can usually give ourselves a little more by assuming that the first bit is, implicitly, a leading 1.

Putting it all together, using the values of each set of bits, denoting integers, we can compute the float saved in memory:

$$sign(1 + mantissa/pow(2,52)) * pow(2,exp - 1023)$$

Or, perhaps a better way to see how IEEE-754 works is to use Elixir to help us match the bits and rebuild it with the preceding equation:

```
iex(1)> <<sign::size(1), exp::size(11),mantissa::size(52)>> =
<<3.14159::float>>
<<64, 9, 33, 249, 240, 27, 134, 110>>
iex(2)> sign
0
iex(3)> exp
1024
iex(4)> mantissa
2570632149304942
iex(5)> (1 + mantissa / :math.pow(2, 52)) * :math.pow(2, exp-1023)
3.14159
```

We don't include the `sign` bit because we already know it's zero and the number is positive.

There are lots of reasons to learn more about IEEE-754, especially if you're computing lots of numerical results. And maybe you won't use Elixir to do those computations, but using Elixir's pattern matching on binaries is a great way to decompose and debug why using *1-tanx* is a bad idea when *x* has values near π/4 and 5π/4.

Elixir structure

So far, we haven't seen much more than tiny snippets, demonstrating a fraction of the syntax of Elixir. Now we are going to go into more detail and look at some more in-depth examples.

We will start with what may be considered a functional language's *real* "hello world", the `map` function.

 Note that this example will use some concepts that we are going to go into more detail in the next few chapters.

The `map` function essentially takes a function and a list, and applies the function to each element in the list. Ideally, the application of one element in the list does not depend or effect any other application of any other element. Thus, this is usually something that *can* be trivial (in concept) to parallelize. However, very few languages make it so easy as the functional languages, and in particular, Elixir.

Using what we know now (and some stuff we haven't covered), here's how we might write our own `map` function:

```
defmodule MyMap do
  def map([], _) do
    []
  end

  def map([h|t], f) do
    [f.(h) | map(t, f)]
  end
end

square = fn x -> x * x end
MyMap.map(1..5, square)
```

Breezing over what we will cover in the next chapter, we have defined a *single* function, `map`, which takes in a list and a function, and then recursively applies the provided function to each element in the collection. After the definition, we define another function that squares its input, and we execute our `map` function with the `square` function and the list `[1, 2, 3, 4, 5]`.

We should expect the output to be a list where each element is squared.

But from the looks of it, there are two functions! Indeed it may appear to be two, however, this is pattern matching showing itself again. When we invoke a function, the runtime takes the given inputs and attempts to match them against the definition. When the runtime finds the match, it executes the given body.

Here we see the `map` function, or the first-class citizenry that functions maintain and the clutter-free cruft of boilerplate code given to us by pattern matching.

Next, let's look at the variation of the `map` function for concurrent programming the parallel map:

```
defmodule Parallel do
  def pmap(collection, func) do
    collection
    |> Enum.map(&(Task.async(fn -> func.(&1) end)))
    |> Enum.map(&Task.await/1)
  end
end
```

Elixir files

Elixir uses two files, `.ex` for compiled code and `.exs` for scripts. They must both be UTF-8 encoded. We will go over `.ex` some more when we introduce mix in the next chapter. But for now, let's discuss `.exs` a little more.

We can write all the Elixir code we have shown so far into a script (we won't though, there is just a small subset) and then we can use the interactive interpreter to load up our script and run it.

For example, we can put the `MyMap` code from earlier into a script:

```
defmodule MyMap do
  def map([], _) do
    []
  end

  def map([h|t], f) do
```

```
      [f.(h) | map(t, f)]
    end
  end

  square = fn x -> x * x end
  MyMap.map([1, 2, 3, 4, 5], square)
```

Go ahead and save it as `mymap.exs`. Launch a terminal and use the `cd` command to navigate to the directory that you saved your script in and then launch `iex`.

Once in `iex`, we will use `import_file/1` to import and launch our script.

In your `iex`, type `h(import_file/1)` to get the documentation of `import_file/1`:

```
iex(1)> h(import_file/1)


                defmacro import_file(path)


Evaluates the contents of the file at path as if it were directly typed
into the shell. path has to be a literal binary.


A leading ~ in path is automatically expanded.


Examples


# ~/file.exs
value = 13


# in the shell
iex(1)> import_file "~/file.exs"
13
iex(2)> value
13
```

Loading our code, we should see something similar to the following:

```
iex(1)> import_file("mymap.exs")
[1, 4, 9, 16, 25]
```

Furthermore, we have access to the `MyMap.map/2` and `square/1` functions we defined in the script. We can now use these in the interactive session to debug or explore the given code:

```
iex(2)> double = fn x -> x * 2 end
#Function<6.90072148/1 in :erl_eval.expr/5>
iex(3)> MyMap.map([1, 2, 3, 4, 5], double)
[2, 4, 6, 8, 10]
```

Here, instead of squaring the number, we double it, and we operate over the same list, `[1, 2, 3, 4, 5]`.

Exercises

Do the following tasks:

- Try modifying the `MyMap` script we wrote
- Play around with the types we covered
- Try more pattern matching, particularly with binaries

Summary

We covered a lot in this chapter, so let's take a quick moment to recap what we went over.

Everything in Elixir is a statement and this has a cool result on composability in the functional world. So, it's easier to compose expressions than statements.

We discussed the basic types of Elixir: numbers (integers, floats), atoms, booleans, Strings, lists, tuples, binaries, functions, and PIDs.

Furthermore, we spent some time covering immutability again and started our exploration of pattern matching.

Finally, we finished up with some discussion on structure, file formats, and scripts.

3
Modules and Functions – Creating Functional Building Blocks

In the previous chapter, we introduced the basic, built-in types of Elixir.

In this chapter, we are going to dive further into functions and properly introduce modules. Furthermore, we are going to continue our discussion on pattern matching.

And, we will now get into some real, nonelementary examples that show how we can solve problems with what we have learned so far.

Modules

If you're familiar with other languages such as Python, modules aren't really a new concept. They define a set of functions and essentially namespace these functions from others. This avoids name conflicts and introduces a level of plugability and reusability throughout. Elixir modules, similarly, follow suit.

A module in Elixir defines a set of public and private functions that can either be used externally or internally. Modules in Elixir are defined with the `defmodule name do block end` construct. In fact, the simplest module we can define is the following:

```
defmodule Foobar do end
```

Of course, this is a highly uninteresting module, but we can define it. In fact, we can even define it in our interactive session:

```
iex>(1) defmodule Foo do end
{:module, Foo,
 <<70, 79, 82, 49, 0, 0, 3, 136, 66, 69, 65, 77, 69, 120, 68, 99,
0, 0, 0, 60, 131, 104, 2, 100, 0, 14, 101, 108, 105, 120, 105,
114, 95, 100, 111, 99, 115, 95, 118, 49, 108, 0, 0, 0, 2, 104, 2,
...>>,
 nil}
```

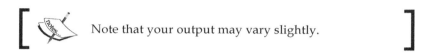 Note that your output may vary slightly.

We've seen this output before, but we have never truly examined it. What is all this?

Well, as you might have already guessed reading the preceding output, it is the VM's internal representation of the module we have just defined. Moreover, it's defined in types we have already seen; we have a tuple whose first element is an atom, :module; second, the name of the module; third, a binary that defines the module; and fourth is nil since the module does not export any public functions.

Notably, this isn't an entirely interesting or useful module though. For a more interesting module, we will need functions.

Anonymous functions

In the previous chapter, we saw that functions are types and first-class citizens in Elixir. We even saw how to define some functions.

Anonymous functions are similar to regular functions except that they are not bound to an identifier.

Furthermore, there are actually two different syntaxes to define anonymous functions. This includes the syntax we saw earlier—fn () -> block end. But there is also a shorter syntax variant—&(block). Let's dive into some examples of both of these syntaxes and general function definitions.

As we saw in the previous chapter, we had the following:

```
iex(1)> square = fn x -> x * x end
#Function<6.90072148/1 in :erl_eval.expr/5>
```

Then we could use it with the following:

```
iex(2) square.(2)
4
```

So what are we doing here (at (1))? We are defining a function and binding it to the name `square`. The function takes a single variable (call it x), and we return the expression, x * x, or, after evaluation, the square of x.

The `#Function<6.90072148/1 in :erl_eval.expr/5>`, after we define the function, is the result of our expression evaluated by the Elixir compiler (where does the number come from?). This return value also tells us something about the function we have defined—it was in-lined by the compiler. Our function is actually translated to Erlang and then compiled by Erlang's compiler, `erlc`, to generate the currently loaded bytecode for our simple `square` function.

Furthermore, we can have, arbitrarily, many arguments, or none at all, if we want:

```
iex(1)> (fn x, y, z -> x + y * z end).(2, 6, 8)
50
```

We also did another trick here, we defined our function and then immediately executed it with the parameters 2, 6, and 8.

We can do the same thing too with the shorter syntax:

```
iex(2)> (&(&1 + &2 * &3)).(2, 6, 8)
50
```

And just to prove that the two syntaxes are the same, we can do the following:

```
iex(3)> square1 = fn x -> x * x end
#Function<6.90072148/1 in :erl_eval.expr/5>
iex(4)> square2 = &(&1 * &1)
#Function<6.90072148/1 in :erl_eval.expr/5>
```

With the shorter syntax, we gain brevity at the cost of named parameters. We can still have as many parameters as we want, we just have to know the order. For most small functions, this order is fine; however, if the anonymous function is long, you may want to opt for the former, longer syntax.

Pattern matching

Like many things in Elixir, anonymous functions support pattern matching! We can define quick functions with the same awesome power of pattern matching as regular functions and binding. For example, we may define a function like the following:

```
iex(1)> area = fn {:circle, r} ->
...(1)> 3.14159 * r * r
...(1)> {:rect, w, h} ->
...(1)> w * h
...(1)> end
#Function<6.90072148/1 in :erl_eval.expr/5>
```

Here, we define an `area` function that can compute the area of either a circle or a rectangle by matching on a tuple with an atom of the shape type as the first element and either the radius or the width and height as the rest of the elements.

We could use this anonymous function like this:

```
iex(2)> area.({:circle, 5})
78.53975
iex(3)> area.({:rect, 5, 5})
25
iex(4)> area.({:triangle, 5, 5})
** (FunctionClauseError) no function clause matching in :erl_eval."-
inside-an-interpreted-fun-"/1
```

Finally, since we didn't define a function for the area of a triangle, we get a match error when we attempt to compute the area for a triangle in (4).

Similarly, we would see a similar error if we attempted to compute the area of a rectangle when only passing the width:

```
iex(5)> area.({:rect, 5})
** (FunctionClauseError) no function clause matching in :erl_eval."-
inside-an-interpreted-fun-"/1
```

Named functions

Named functions, unlike anonymous functions, require a module for definition. That is, to define a named function we must define the function inside a module.

Here, we combine what we learned about modules and anonymous functions a bit, and we define our square function again, though, this time, we define it inside a module named MyMath. Go ahead and create a file called mymath.exs and put the following code into it:

```
defmodule MyMath do

  def square(x) do
    x * x
  end

end
```

Here, we are simply defining a function, square, which takes a single element, and returns the result of x * x. This really looks not much different from our previous versions except for being defined inside a module.

How do we run this module and see whether it works? Well, you might have tried $ elixir mymath.exs but that probably didn't do anything interesting...

The answer lies in importing the module in an interactive session. First, make sure your working directory is the same as the directory you saved mymath.exs. Then, from that directory, launch iex. From iex, we will use the import_file/1:

```
iex(1)> import_file("mymath.exs")
{:module, MyMath,
 <<70, 79, 82, 49, 0, 0, 4, 160, 66, 69, 65, 77, 69, 120, 68, 99, 0,
 0, 0, 113, 131, 104, 2, 100, 0, 14, 101, 108, 105, 120, 105, 114, 95,
 100, 111, 99, 115, 95, 118, 49, 108, 0, 0, 0, 2, 104, 2, ...>>,
 {:square, 1}}
```

Here, we see again the returned tuple, similar to the last time. Here, however, instead of the last element being nil, we get a tuple with the elements :square and 1. This is saying that the module exports a single public function, square/1, which is good because that's what we wanted!

Now, we can use our newly defined square/1 function:

```
iex(2)> MyMath.square(4)
16
```

This is not very different from other languages you may be used to. To invoke a function from a different namespace than the current, you prefix the call with the function's module name.

Private functions

All of the functions we have defined so far are public. That is, they are accessible from outside modules; there is nothing to stop other modules from calling these functions, which, for the most part, we want. But how do we define a function that is internal and should never be directly called from outside?

We can do it the same way we define public functions. We use the `defp` construct, though.

For a simplistic example, we could define a function in a module and then have a private function *actually* perform the named function's work:

```
defmodule MyMath do
  def square(x) do
    do_square(x)
  end

  defp do_square(x), do: x * x
end
```

This isn't notably different to anything we've done so far. We define our function, `square/1`, which returns the result of calling the private member function, `do_square/1`.

Let's see what we get when we import this function into `iex`:

```
iex(1)> import_file("mymath.exs")
{:module, MyMath,
 <<70, 79, 82, 49, 0, 0, 4, 224, 66, 69, 65, 77, 69, 120, 68, 99, 0,
0, 0, 113, 131, 104, 2, 100, 0, 14, 101, 108, 105, 120, 105, 114, 95,
100, 111, 99, 115, 95, 118, 49, 108, 0, 0, 0, 2, 104, 2, ...>>,
 {:do_square, 1}}
```

Everything looks correct. Wait, what about the function tuple? Why does it say `:do_square` and not `:square`? This is because our function is mostly uninteresting, and it is returning an in-lined version of our function. This does not mean that to use this module we need to know the private function name.

We still use the module and function the same way:

```
iex(2)> MyMath.square(2)
4
```

Private functions are really no different from regular functions other than scoping. That is, in private functions we can use the same pattern matching techniques we have already used.

We will see some more examples of private functions soon when we go into some real code examples.

Calling functions

There's another issue I've so far been skirting over—the syntax of calling functions. Specifically, you may have seen some examples around in which calling a function does not use parentheses to denote the function call. For example, from our previous example, these are equivalent:

```
iex(3)> MyMath.square(4)
16
iex(4)> MyMath.square 4
16
```

Why, you ask, is this the case? Why do we have two different acceptable forms? Elixir has a lot of its roots in Erlang. But this is only, so far, as some basic syntax and the runtime. The syntax borrows fairly heavily from Ruby. Thus, there's some Ruby syntactical elements present throughout Elixir, and this happens to be one of the Ruby carry-overs.

As far as when to use one version of the syntax over another is concerned, it depends. I would argue it's mostly a preference of style. If you like to read functions with less braces running around, don't use parentheses to invoke functions. Or, you may like the explicit use as they denote calling a function. Whichever way you choose, you should tend toward consistency.

There are cases, however, where you will have to use parentheses. These cases are usually when the binding of the arguments needs to be explicit, you need to override the default operator precedence order, or you're calling an anonymous function.

For example, when a function has multiple arguments and/or this same function is invoked as an operand to another operator or function. Continuing with the square/1 function from before, are these two expressions equivalent?

```
MyMath.square 2 * 5
```

```
MyMath.square(2) * 5
```

If you're guessing they are not, you would be correct. Function invocation, typically, has less precedence than other operators. Parentheses can help make explicit what your intention is:

```
iex(5)> MyMath.square(2 * 5)
100
iex(6)> MyMath.square 2 * 5
100
iex(7)> MyMath.square(2) * 5
20
```

 My suggestion would be to use parentheses when the code may look ambiguous.

When to use .

There's another syntactical issue I've been neglecting to mention, the use of the . () syntax to invoke (some) functions. This, to me, is probably one of the oddest blemishes of Elixir's syntax. It's slightly confusing, and feels particularly awkward to use. However, it may never go away and we, as Elixir developers, will have to deal with it. The question is, then, when should we use it and when should we not? Fortunately, when to use it is fairly simple, but can often be forgotten when starting out—invoke anonymous functions or function handles grabbed with *&{foo}/{arity}*, otherwise, use the regular syntax (without the . syntax character).

For example, every time we define an anonymous function, we used the . () syntax to invoke it:

```
iex(1)> f = fn x -> x * x end
...
iex(2)> f.(2)
4
```

However, when we define the function part of a module, we use the regular syntax:

```
iex(1)> defmodule Foo do
...(1)> def f(x), do: x * x
...(1)> end
...
iex(2)> Foo.f(2)
4
```

Similarly, using our `MyMap` example from the previous chapter, notice how the function passed in is invoked with the `.` syntax, but calling the `map` function itself isn't:

```
iex>(1)> defmodule MyMap do
...>(1)> def map([], _), do: []
...>(1)> def map([h|t], f) do
...>(1)> [f.(h) | map(t, f)]
...>(1)> end
...>(1)> end
...
iex(2)> MyMap.map([1, 2, 3, 4, 5], &(&1 * &1))
[1, 4, 9, 16, 25]
```

Grabbing functions

Elixir supports passing defined functions as parameters. That is, Elixir's functions are first-class citizens of the type system. But then, how do we pass the existing functions around? We use the `&` operator or function capture operator. Going back to our `MyMath.square/1` function, we could pass it to `Enum.map/2` with the following:

```
iex(1)> import_file("mymath.exs")
...
iex(2)> Enum.map([1, 2, 3], &MyMath.square/1)
[1, 4, 9]
```

Here, we load the module again, for completeness, and then we invoke `Enum.map/2` with the list `[1, 2, 3]` and pass our `square/1` function from `MyMath`. You may wonder why we need to grab the function with the arity. This, if you recall, is because Elixir functions are defined by their name *and* arity or number of parameters. For example, say we define our `square/1` function as `pow/1` instead where, if `pow` is given one function, it assumes we want to raise the argument to the second power, otherwise, there is a `pow/2` that takes the base and the power. It would look something like this:

```
defmodule MyMath do
  def pow(x), do: pow(x, 2)

  def pow(x, p) do
    Enum.reduce(Enum.take(Stream.repeatedly(fn -> x end), p),
&*/2)
  end
end
```

Before we go on, let's take a quick moment to discuss and break apart what this new `pow/2` function is doing.

The `pow/2` function takes the base, `x`, and the power, `p`, and we pass it to a particularly dense function chain. Reading inside out, we are using another internal Elixir module, `Stream`. Specifically, we call `Stream.repeatedly/1` with the argument, `fn -> x end`. This is, of course, an anonymous function that simply returns `x`, our base. `Stream.repeatedly/1` will call this anonymous function as many times as it's required, possibly infinitely!

Moving a step out, we are using another function from the `Enum` module, `Enum.take/2`. This function takes a collection; in this case, the result of `Stream.repeatedly/1`, and a number, `p`, and returns the first `p` elements of the collection.

Moving out again, we are using yet another function from `Enum`, `Enum.reduce/2`. The `reduce/2` function takes a collection, the result from `Enum.take/2`, and a function, `&*/2` (the multiplication operator), and reduces the collection into a single element.

Let's explore this more in an interactive session.

First, let's look at the result of `Stream.repeatedly/1`:

```
iex(1)> repeatedly = Stream.repeatedly(fn -> 2 end)
#Function<24.29647706/2 in Stream.repeatedly/1>
```

Here, we see a function is returned. You might be thinking, "But you said it was a collection!". That is correct, I *did* say the result of `Stream.repeatedly/1` is a collection. However, this is a different type of collection than we've seen before, specifically, the `Stream` module produces `lazy` collections, which are essentially collections that are not realized until it's absolutely necessary.

Next, let's look at the result of `Enum.take/2`:

```
iex(2)> taken = Enum.take(repeatedly, 5)
[2, 2, 2, 2, 2]
```

At this point, we have invoked the function returned into `repeatedly` five times and turned the result into a list, a list of the element 2 *repeated* five times.

Finally, we use the `Enum.reduce/2` function to collapse or fold the list into a single element:

```
iex(3)> Enum.reduce(taken, &*/2)
32
```

Here, we are grabbing the multiplication operator as a function and using it to reduce our list of 2's into a single 32.

That was a long tangent on our new definition of pow/2; let's return to using our new version of the MyMath module.

Reloading the file into our interactive session, we have a choice to map our new function over some list using either pow/1 or pow/2:

```
iex(1)> import_file("mymath.exs")
...
iex(2)> Enum.map([1, 2, 3], &MyMath.pow/1)
[1, 4, 9]
iex(3)> Enum.map([1, 2, 3], &MyMath.pow/2)
** (BadArityError) &MyMath.pow/2 with arity 2 called with 1 argument
(1)
    (elixir) lib/enum.ex:977: anonymous fn/3 in Enum.map/2
    (elixir) lib/enum.ex:1261: Enum."-reduce/3-lists^foldl/2-0-"/3
    (elixir) lib/enum.ex:977: Enum.map/2
```

Oops! Since Enum.map/2 passes each element of our list to the function we pass (and nothing else), the function we pass must only accept a single argument. To use MyMath.pow/2, we must partially apply or curry (https://en.wikipedia.org/wiki/Currying) the function and pass that instead. Since Elixir doesn't have a native syntax for currying, we must resort to simply wrapping it in an anonymous function:

```
iex(4)> Enum.map([1, 2, 3], &(MyMath.pow(&1, 3)))
[1, 8, 27]
```

When patterns aren't enough for matching

So far, we have seen pattern matching very basically in our functions and assignment (reading binding) expressions. However, there's more that can be done when doing pattern matches, particularly when defining functions. When a simple type decomposition pattern isn't enough, we can use *guards* to add an extra layer to our matches.

Guards are simply boolean expressions we can add to our function definitions to make the pattern matches that we define more strict or specific.

Here are some basic examples:

```
iex(1)> defmodule MyMath do
...(1)> def sqrt(x) when x >= 0, do: #implement sqrt
...(1)> end
```

However, we are only allowed a limited set of expressions. The following is a pretty exhaustive list of the available expressions allowed in guard clauses:

- All comparison operators (==, !=, ===, !==, >, <, <=, >=)
- Boolean operators (and, or) and negation operators (not, !)
- <> and ++ as long as the left side is a literal
- The in operator
- All of the following type check functions:

  ° is_atom/1
  ° is_binary/1
  ° is_bitstring/1
  ° is_boolean/1
  ° is_float/1
  ° is_function/1 and is_function/2
  ° is_integer/1
  ° is_list/1
  ° is_map/1
  ° is_nil/1
  ° is_number/1
  ° is_pid/1
  ° is_port/1
  ° is_reference/1
  ° is_tuple/1

  Plus these functions:

  ° abs(number)
  ° bit_size(bitstring)
  ° byte_size(bitstring)
  ° div(integer, interger)
  ° elem(tuple, n)
  ° hd(list)
  ° map_size(map)
  ° node()
  ° node(pid | ref | port)
  ° rem(integer, integer)

- ○ `round(number)`
- ○ `self()`
- ○ `tl(list)`
- ○ `trunc(number)`
- ○ `tuple_size(tuple)`

We won't do examples using *all* of the preceding listed guards, but this certainly gives you an idea of just how much you can accomplish with just guards.

In addition, users may also define their own guards, typically starting with `is_`.

Functional algorithms for everyday problems

Now that we have seen modules, functions, guards, the basic types of the previous chapter, and some basic examples of pattern matching, we essentially have everything we need to start solving problems. Let's take this further and actually write some code!

Let's solve some basic problems such as those you might find in your standard set of interview questions; however, instead of solving them with imperative code, we are going to see how we can solve them using only functional constructs and what we have covered so far.

Iteration versus recursion

Often in functional languages, we will use recursion instead of iteration since iteration, by its very nature, requires side-effects. That is, to use a `for` loop, most languages require that the loop modifies some state (usually, an integer) to keep track of where the loop is in execution.

Functional languages, contrastingly, opt for recursive strategies since these are (or, at the very least, can be) inherently non-destructive.

One may argue, though, that iteration doesn't have the same problems as recursion. Notably, iteration can potentially iterate infinitely, whereas recursion can be limited by the stack. Also, certain algorithms are less space and time complex when solved iteratively versus when solved recursively.

There are some benefits of recursion though too. Chiefly, describing computations with recursion can be simpler to reason about; when defining recursive functions, we are describing the more foundational, even mathematical, model of the concept. Iteration, in contrast, hides this conceptual insight from the programmer.

Additionally, functional recursion can typically overcome the mentioned limitations here. Coming from an imperative world, infinite recursion isn't possible because the program would eventually run out of space on the stack. How would a language like Elixir or Erlang avoid this? The answer is in a concept you may have heard or called **tail recursion**. Tail recursion is, essentially, a way for the runtime to modify the call stack of a well-designed recursive function by collapsing the tailing frames:

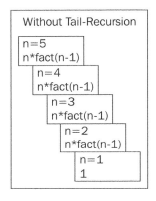

In the preceding diagram, we are given the stack frame of recursively computing factorial of *n* where *n = 5*. We see that each frame is materialized and sticks around until the end when they start popping in rapid succession:

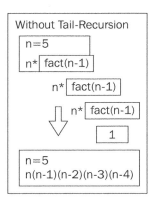

Contrast the last diagram with the preceding one, where we materialize each frame but, instead of hanging onto each frame at each step, the runtime notices that the return value of each frame isn't used other than as a return value of its own. Therefore, we discard each frame and collapse the return values into a single frame or single expression.

To overcome the issue of time and space complexity, typically inherent with recursive algorithms, we usually must think only a little harder and define our recursive solution with an iterative pattern. That is, instead of doing what seems immediately obvious, recursively, we approach the problem with some thought, and what we usually come to is doing the recursion backward. This last issue may be better illustrated through an example.

Let's consider the Fibonacci sequence. The Fibonacci sequence is useful since it has an already recursive definition: $f^n = f^{n-1} + f^{n-2}$ for $n > 2$ and $f^0 = 0$ and $f^1 = 1$.

This definition gives us the sequence we may expect: *0 1 1 2 3 5 8 13 21 ....*

If we wanted to codify Fibonacci in Elixir, we may be tempted to define the following module:

```
defmodule Fibonacci do
  def seq(0), do: 0
  def seq(1), do: 1
  def seq(n) when n > 1, do: seq(n-1) + seq(n-2)
end
```

That is, we define a module with a single function, `seq/1`. This function matches against integers; specifically, if the function is passed `0` or `1`, it will return `0` or `1`, respectively. If it's passed anything greater than `1`, it will return, recursively, the addition of the two previous elements, exactly as the mathematical model defines it.

However, as you may have learned in your introductory algorithms class, this method is awfully slow; in fact, exponentially slow. Tail recursion can't even save us here. Although, it can help, it won't solve the massive duplication of work. How could we write this better still using recursion?

How would we do it sequentially?

Let's take a moment to think about this. If we had sequential constructs available, how could we use them to compute the *n*th number in the Fibonacci sequence?

Let's say, instead of using the definition as stated, let's flip it. Let's use it backward. Instead of starting *at* n, let's start at `1` (or 2, really) and count up.

How would we do this using Elixir? Well, like I noted earlier, we are looking to do the recursion backward. Let's see what this might look similar to:

```
defmodule Fibonacci do
  def seq(0), do: 0
  def seq(1), do: 1
  def seq(n) when n > 1 do
    compute_seq(n, 1, [0, 1])
  end

  defp compute_seq(n, i, acc) when n == i, do: Enum.at(acc,
length(acc) - 1)
  defp compute_seq(n, i, acc) do
    len = length(acc)
    compute_seq(n, i + 1, acc ++ [Enum.at(acc, len-1) +
Enum.at(acc, len-2)])
  end
end
```

Like earlier, we defined our `Fibonacci` module with the `seq/1` function. This function, returns 0 or 1 if n == 0 or n == 1, respectively. But then, instead of computing from the top of the sequence, we start from the bottom of the sequence and build to the result. This takes us from an exponential algorithm for computing Fibonacci to a linear one. Moreover, we haven't necessarily lost the expressiveness of the recursive function. Arguably, there's a little noise from the syntax, but the overall pattern of describing computation with expressions from the definition is still present.

Let's see how this second version compares in terms of performance. In `fibonacci_1.exs`, we will have the following script:

```
defmodule Fibonacci do
  def seq(0), do: 0
  def seq(1), do: 1
  def seq(n) when n > 1, do: seq(n-1) + seq(n-2)
end

IO.puts Fibonacci.seq(50)
```

And in `fibonacci_2.exs`, we will have our second, more iterative version of Fibonacci:

```
defmodule Fibonacci do
  def seq(0), do: 0
  def seq(1), do: 1
  def seq(n) when n > 1 do
    compute_seq(n, 1, [0, 1])
```

```
    end

    defp compute_seq(n, i, acc) when n == i, do: Enum.at(acc,
length(acc)-1)
    defp compute_seq(n, i, acc) do
      len = length(acc)
      compute_seq(n, i + 1, acc++[Enum.at(acc, len-1) + Enum.at(acc,
len-2)])
    end
end

    IO.puts Fibonacci.seq(50)
```

Save both of these files, and we will be able to use the `time` command to get an idea of the difference in running time between the two implementations. Here are the results from my machine:

```
$ time elixir fibonacci_1.exs
12586269025
elixir fibonacci_1.exs   753.42s user 0.07s system 100% cpu 12:32.98
total


$ time elixir fibonacci_2.exs
12586269025
elixir fibonacci_2.exs   0.29s user 0.08s system 115% cpu 0.314 total
```

That's fairly substantial! Notice that we do, in fact, get the same result, but doing it the first way is several orders of magnitude slower. This is a clear win for the second approach. Not only is it functional and recursive, we didn't sacrifice the performance to get it.

Performance considerations

There are a few performance considerations that must be handled when using tail recursion. I mentioned well-designed recursive functions earlier. What does that mean? What are the implications?

Here, well-designed means the runtime is *actually capable* of performing the tail call optimization. If we attempt to use the return of a recursive call in the wrong way, we completely lose the tail call optimization. For example, if we had defined our factorial function from the second diagram as *fact(n-1) * n* instead of *n * fact(n-1)*, we would have lost the tail-recursion optimization completely.

To ensure that we can actually use the optimization, we must take care to define the tail of the function properly. That is, the return can be rolled up into the previous frame *without* breaking the closure that the frame would have created. Returning to the factorial example, using *fact(n-1) * n* breaks the closure created by the current stack frame because we must know what *n* is when we return. Using *n * fact(n-1)* doesn't break the closure because the result can be substituted into current expression.

Tail recursion is a really cool feature and enables some nice optimizations for the runtime. However, like all things, don't abuse it. There will be times when attempting tail recursion will be the wrong way to do something. Take some pragmatism when considering certain algorithms and approaches.

Reverse

Next, let's see how we can easily define a function to reverse a list. In fact, we've already seen the pattern we are going to use to do it too. In the previous chapter, we defined a map function that used [h|t]. This pattern is a way to deconstruct a list (or tuple) into its head component, h, and its tail component, t. We will use this again to construct a function that will reverse a list:

```
defmodule Reverse do
  def reverse([]), do: []
  def reverse([h|t]), do: reverse(t) ++ [h]
end
```

This is fairly straightforward code. We define a pattern for our base case, the empty list, and simply return the empty list. We also define a pattern that allows us to decompose the head and tail of the list. The body of this pattern is then used to build the reverse by appending the head of the list to the recursive call of reverse on the tail.

Let's load this example and see it work:

```
iex(1)> import_file "reverse.exs"
...
iex(2)> Reverse.reverse [1, 2, 3, 4, 5]
[5, 4, 3, 2, 1]
iex(3)> Reverse.reverse 'Hello, World!'
'!dlroW ,olleH'
```

Recall from the previous chapter how single-quoted strings are really simply a list of characters. That is, is_list('hello') returns true. Thus, we can use our reverse function on character lists as well.

Sorting

Another example of pattern matching is implementing sorting algorithms. Quicksort, it turns out, is a bit of a favorite for this since we have nice ways to deconstruct lists:

```
defmodule Sort do
  def quicksort([]), do: []
  def quicksort([h|t]) do
    lower = Enum.filter(t, &(&1 <= h))
    upper = Enum.filter(t, &(&1 > h))
    quicksort(lower) ++ [h] ++ quicksort(upper)
  end
end
```

We define a module, Sort, with a single function quicksort/1. The empty list case simply returns the empty list as we expect. In the nonempty case, we again use the | operator to split the list into head and tail elements. We construct the lower and upper lists using the Enum.filter/2 function. This function takes a collection and an anonymous function and returns the elements that returned true from the anonymous function. In our case, we are using the function, &(&1 <= h), to find elements smaller or equal to h and similarly, &(&1 > h), to find elements strictly bigger than h. After constructing the two lists, we recursively call quicksort on the lower and upper lists, concatenating the results to get our result, a sorted list.

Let's see it in action:

```
iex(1)> import_file "sort.exs"
...
iex(2)> Sort.quicksort Enum.shuffle 1..10
[1, 2, 3, 4, 5, 6, 7, 8, 9, 10]
```

Instead of coming up with some random ordering on a list of numbers, we can just use Enum.shuffle/1 to randomize a list for us. Another example, the worst case, is that we can use our own reverse/1 or Enum.reverse/1:

```
iex(3)> Sort.quicksort Enum.reverse 1..10
[1, 2, 3, 4, 5, 6, 7, 8, 9, 10]
```

Mix – the ladle of Elixir

So far, we have only interacted with simple modules defined in scripts or the interactive prompt. But this will only take us so far. Eventually, we will need more than just scripts. We will need a source tree that encloses our project's code. Moreover, we will need a tool to create the source tree, build the source, test, manage dependencies, and a number of other tasks. That tool is mix.

This tool handles everything we could need from a build tool. It creates projects, compiles code, runs tests, packages projects into distributable units, and even allows us to run our project, importing the necessary files into `iex`.

But enough about `mix`, let's use it and see it in action!

First, like any good command, `mix` comes with the trusty `help` command to give us a good list of what it can do for us:

```
$ mix help
mix                      # Run the default task (current: mix run)
mix app.start            # Start all registered apps
mix archive              # List all archives
mix archive.build        # Archive this project into a .ez file
mix archive.install      # Install an archive locally
mix archive.uninstall    # Uninstall archives
mix clean                # Delete generated application files
mix cmd                  # Executes the given command
mix compile              # Compile source files
mix deps                 # List dependencies and their status
mix deps.clean           # Remove the given dependencies' files
mix deps.compile         # Compile dependencies
mix deps.get             # Get all out of date dependencies
mix deps.unlock          # Unlock the given dependencies
mix deps.update          # Update the given dependencies
mix do                   # Executes the tasks separated by comma
mix escript.build        # Builds an escript for the project
mix help                 # Print help information for tasks
mix hex                  # Print hex help information
mix hex.config           # Read or update hex config
mix hex.docs             # Publish docs for package
mix hex.info             # Print hex information
mix hex.key              # Hex API key tasks
mix hex.outdated         # Shows outdated hex deps for the current
project
mix hex.owner            # Hex package ownership tasks
mix hex.publish          # Publish a new package version
mix hex.search           # Search for package names
```

```
mix hex.user              # Hex user tasks
mix loadconfig            # Loads and persists the given configuration
mix local                 # List local tasks
mix local.hex             # Install hex locally
mix local.rebar           # Install rebar locally
mix new                   # Create a new Elixir project
mix run                   # Run the given file or expression
mix test                  # Run a project's tests
iex -S mix                # Start IEx and run the default task
```

Clearly, mix provides us with a lot of functionality. Furthermore, we can use mix help to get more about a specific task. Since we may want to know how to create projects, let's look at the new task:

```
$ mix help new
```

```
                              mix new

Creates a new Elixir project. It expects the path of the project as
argument.
```

```
┃ mix new PATH [--sup] [--module MODULE] [--app APP] [--umbrella]
```

```
A project at the given PATH  will be created. The application name
and module name will be retrieved from the path, unless --module or -
-app is given.
```

```
A --sup option can be given to generate an OTP application skeleton
including a supervision tree. Normally an app is generated without a
supervisor and without the app callback.
```

```
An --umbrella option can be given to generate an umbrella project.
```

```
An --app option can be given in order to name the OTP application for
the project.
```

```
A --module option can be given in order to name the modules in the
generated code skeleton.
```

Examples

☒ mix new hello_world

Is equivalent to:

☒ mix new hello_world --module HelloWorld

To generate an app with supervisor and application callback:

☒ mix new hello_world --sup

Location: /usr/lib/elixir/lib/mix/ebin

We see that we get the basic command example and some descriptions about the arguments we can specify:

- The --module MODULE argument allows us to create our first module with a different name than PATH. That is, the default will create a folder and module of the same name (with some modifications). However, if we want to change this behaviour, we can use this argument to do so.
- Similar to the --module argument, --app APP allows us to rename the Elixir application created by the project.

The --app argument and the rest of the arguments will make more sense in upcoming chapters and for now, we will mostly ignore them. For now, let's create our first project!

Structure of Elixir projects

Let's start by creating a small project called hello_world:

```
$ mix new hello_world
* creating README.md
* creating .gitignore
* creating mix.exs
* creating config
* creating config/config.exs
* creating lib
* creating lib/hello_world.ex
```

```
* creating test
* creating test/test_helper.exs
* creating test/hello_world_test.exs

Your mix project was created successfully.
You can use mix to compile it, test it, and more:


    cd hello_world
    mix test


Run mix help for more commands.
```

The output of `mix new` tells us of the files it has created, that it created it successfully, and where to go from here.

Let's navigate to our new project's directory and see what's there in it:

```
$ cd hello_world
$ find .
.
./mix.exs
./.gitignore
./config
./config/config.exs
./README.md
./lib
./lib/hello_world.ex
./test
./test/test_helper.exs
./test/hello_world_test.exs
```

This is essentially just another view into the list of files that `mix new` gives us, but it certainly confirms what it says. Let's break each of these files and folders down.

mix.exs

This is the file that describes our project. Unsurprisingly, it's actually Elixir code and defines a module. This is used by `mix` for compiling, testing dependencies, packaging our project, and running our project.

If we open it up, we will see something like the following code:

```
$ cat mix.exs
defmodule HelloWorld.Mixfile do
  use Mix.Project

  def project do
    [app: :hello_world,
     version: "0.0.1",
     elixir: "~> 1.0",
     build_embedded: Mix.env == :prod,
     start_permanent: Mix.env == :prod,
     deps: deps]
  end

  # Configuration for the OTP application
  #
  # Type `mix help compile.app` for more information
  def application do
    [applications: [:logger]]
  end

  # Dependencies can be Hex packages:
  #
  #    {:mydep, "~> 0.3.0"}
  #
  # Or git/path repositories:
  #
  #    {:mydep, git: "https://github.com/elixir-lang/mydep.git", tag:
"0.1.0"}
  #
  # Type `mix help deps` for more examples and options
  defp deps do
    []
  end
end
```

It's not worth going into too much detail here, but we can see that it's really just an Elixir module and it defines a few functions that return information about the project.

.gitignore

There are several files that we will want to ignore when tracking our code with a VCS tool such as git. The mix tool creates this ignore file for us to give us a sane set of default exclusions for starting out, and we do not need to remember this set every time we create a project.

config

The `config` folder contains our project's configuration settings. These are our global, high-level options that our project can reference during execution.

By default, a single file is created for us here—`config/config.exs`. As the file extension might hint, this too is Elixir code. It defines a set of variables we can reference in our project.

README.md

Another default file `mix new` creates for us is a basic `README` file using the markdown markup syntax. This is a good file to have for all the projects as it's a good center place to shortly (or longly) describe your project, how to build and install it, how to use it, and where to go for more information.

Of course, your documentation is only as good as your effort to maintain it. Creating the file with a `TODO` tag isn't going to be enough; before you publish your project, be sure to make a pass through this file and update it.

lib

The `lib` directory, unlike other languages, is actually for your Elixir source. This will be where `mix` will look when building the project.

For this simple project, the `lib` directory only contains one file—`lib/hello_world.ex`. This file defines the so far uninteresting module named `HelloWorld`:

```
$ cat lib/hello_world.ex
defmodule HelloWorld do
end
```

This is what we get to start. Not terribly interesting, but it's something. It doesn't impose a lot, or assume too much. It's a plain module we get to shape as our project matures.

test

The `test` directory, as you may have suspected, is for test code. The `mix` tool will compile and load the modules defined in this folder, and run over the test cases defined therein.

There's initially two files created—`test/test_helper.exs` and `test/hello_world_test.exs`. The former sets up the test harness for the project:

```
$ cat test/test_helper.exs
ExUnit.start()
```

The latter file defines a simple, but passing, module and a test to give us a starting point for writing our tests:

```
$ cat test/hello_world_test.exs
defmodule HelloWorldTest do
  use ExUnit.Case

  test "the truth" do
    assert 1 + 1 == 2
  end
end
```

Compiling a project

Now that we have done a high-level walk-through of the project we have just created, let's see how `mix` can compile this project and turn what we have so far into bytecode for the Erlang VM.

From the root of the project directory, go ahead and run `mix compile`:

```
$ mix compile
Compiled lib/hello_world.ex
Generated hello_world app
```

Elixir found our `lib/hello_world.ex` module, compiled it, and then generated our `app`. We won't concern ourselves with the concepts of Erlang applications for now, but we just acknowledge its existence.

If we list the contents of our directory now, we should see a `_build` directory:

```
$ ls
_build  config  lib  mix.exs  README.md  test
```

Under this `_build` directory will be the `.beam` files of our project and the app file.

Testing a project

Simply to see what testing in Elixir looks similar to, we can go ahead and test our project as well:

```
$ mix test
Compiled lib/hello_world.ex
Generated hello_world app

.
```

```
Finished in 0.02 seconds (0.02s on load, 0.00s on tests)
1 tests, 0 failures


Randomized with seed 27839
```

This tells us a few things: it compiles our source, if it isn't already; runs the tests; times the loading time and computation time of our tests; gives us the result of our tests, pass or fail; and the random seed the test run used.

Running interactively

Finally, if we want to run our code, we can use a special option of `iex` to compile our project, if necessary, and include it into an interactive session:

```
$ iex -S mix
Erlang/OTP 17 [erts-6.4] [source] [64-bit] [smp:12:12] [async-
threads:10] [hipe] [kernel-poll:false]


Compiled lib/hello_world.ex
Generated hello_world app
Interactive Elixir (1.0.4) - press Ctrl+C to exit (type h() ENTER for
help)
iex(1)>
```

This isn't entirely interesting yet. Certainly, we are in an interactive session, but we haven't defined anything in our `lib/hello_world.ex` module; thus, there isn't really anything exciting here for us. Let's correct that by way of revisiting "Hello, world!" quickly.

Open up the `lib/hello_world.ex` file in your favorite editor and add the following function:

```
def hello(name \\ "World") do
    IO.puts "Hello, #{name}!"
end
```

Now, let's return to the interactive session:

```
$ iex -S mix
Erlang/OTP 17 [erts-6.4] [source] [64-bit] [smp:12:12] [async-
threads:10] [hipe] [kernel-poll:false]


Compiled lib/hello_world.ex
Generated hello_world app
```

```
Interactive Elixir (1.0.4) - press Ctrl+C to exit (type h() ENTER for
help)
iex(1)>
```

Now, we can invoke our function from the interactive prompt:

```
iex(1)> HelloWorld.hello
Hello, World!
:ok
iex(2)> HelloWorld.hello "Kenny"
Hello, Kenny!
:ok
```

Files

Let's take a quick moment to revisit Elixir files.

As we have seen again and again, Elixir has two different file types, `.ex` and `.exs`, but what are their differences?

The distinction is actually more conventional and signifies intention. Both files are compiled to bytecode and run by the VM. But the file extension informs the compiler and VM, and ourselves, that a file has a particular purpose.

That is, `.ex` files denote source or project files. The intention of the file is to run part of a project or application. Compared to `.exs` files, whose denoted intention is either scripting, configuration, or testing. These files are compiled the same as the `.ex` counterpart, but the resulting bytecode of these files is ephemeral and discarded after the file's purpose is served.

Mix and beyond

Though we have only touched the surface of `mix` and its capabilities, we will be revisiting `mix` throughout, incrementally building a bigger image around `mix`. Till then, let's play with some more projects and revisit some examples from before.

Building functional projects

We have a lot in our proverbial tool belt so far and we are adding more. Let's take a look at some more examples where we solve some relatively simple problems using Elixir. This time, however, let's use `mix` as well.

Flatten

We will start small, by creating a function to flatten arbitrarily deep, nested lists.

Let's create a project for it using `mix new flatten`:

```
$ mix new reverse
* creating README.md
* creating .gitignore
* creating mix.exs
* creating config
* creating config/config.exs
* creating lib
* creating lib/flatten.ex
* creating test
* creating test/test_helper.exs
* creating test/flatten_test.exs


Your mix project was created successfully.
You can use mix to compile it, test it, and more:


    cd flatten
    mix test


Run mix help for more commands.
```

Now, in the `lib/flatten.ex` file, let's create the flatten function.

Open the file in your favorite editor and add the following `flatten/1` function:

```
defmodule Flatten do
  def flatten([]), do: []
  def flatten([h|t]) when is_list(h), do: h ++ flatten(t)
end
```

In our `Flatten` module, we define our `flatten/1` function with two patterns, the empty list base case, and the `[h|t]` pattern adding that h is a list. When we match against the second pattern, we return the list created by h and append the recursive flattening of t.

Of course, we can go ahead and launch it into `iex` and make sure it works:

```
$ iex -S mix
...
iex(1)> Flatten.flatten [[1, 2], [3], [4, 5]]
[1, 2, 3, 4, 5]
```

Awesome, it works. How could we more quickly try a bunch of different cases and ensure that our function to flatten arbitrarily nested elements does in fact work as we expect? We could write a test.

A small introduction to testing

Testing is an inescapable aspect of software development. It is so essential, most languages now are building it in as part of the language.

Let's take a brief moment to introduce Elixir's testing functionality.

I've already shown you `mix test` and what it does. But let's write a test for our `flatten/1` function.

Writing tests in Elixir, besides syntax, is no different from writing functions. We define a module and a few tests (functions), and assert some results that we expect.

In our case, a third of this is already done! Since we created the project, `mix` helpfully created the `test` folder and stubbed out a module for us to use for testing. Let's open and examine this file.

In your favorite editor, open `test/flatten_test.exs`. You should see something like the following code:

```
defmodule FlattenTest do
  use ExUnit.Case

  test "the truth" do
    assert 1 + 1 == 2
  end
end
```

It is a simple enough module. It defines the module and defines a test, `the truth`, that asserts that *1 + 1* does in fact equal 2.

The string, `the truth`, is the identifier of the test. We can use this to give a good description of the test and its assumptions and/or assertions.

Let's modify this quickly to demonstrate a failing test. Change the assertion statement to:

```
assert 2 + 2 == 5
```

Then, let's run the test and see what we get:

```
$ mix test


  1) test the truth (FlattenTest)
     test/flatten_test.exs:4
     Assertion with == failed
     code: 2 + 2 == 5
     lhs:   4
     rhs:   5
     stacktrace:
       test/flatten_test.exs:5


  .



Finished in 0.03 seconds (0.03s on load, 0.00s on tests)
1 tests, 1 failures


Randomized with seed 800718
```

Since the case fails, Elixir gives us a lot of information about the state and the values that caused the assertion to fail. We can use this information to begin looking at what is causing the failing test.

Moving back to our `flatten/1` function, let's remove this test case and define a new one.

We can go ahead and remove the simple test case. We will start with a simple case of our own:

```
test "return flat list when given nested lists" do
  expected = [1 ,2 ,3 , 4, 5]
  actual = Flatten.flatten [[1, 2], [3], [4, 5]]
  assert actual == expected
end
```

Save the file, and we can go ahead and run the test:

```
$ mix test
Compiled lib/flatten.ex
Generated flatten app

.


Finished in 0.02 seconds (0.02s on load, 0.00s on tests)
1 tests, 0 failures


Randomized with seed 138347
```

As we expect, it passes. However, something smells about this implementation. Let's write a test to sniff out this smell.

Let's add the following new test case:

```
test "return flat list when no nesting" do
  expected = [1, 2, 3, 4, 5]
  actual = Flatten.flatten expected
  assert actual == expected
end
```

Save the test file again, and let's run this:

```
$ mix test

.


  1) test return flat list when no nesting (FlattenTest)
     test/flatten_test.exs:10
     ** (FunctionClauseError) no function clause matching in
Flatten.flatten/1
     stacktrace:
       (flatten) lib/flatten.ex:2: Flatten.flatten([1, 2, 3, 4, 5])
       test/flatten_test.exs:12



Finished in 0.03 seconds (0.03s on load, 0.00s on tests)
2 tests, 1 failures


Randomized with seed 211452
```

This is interesting. We get a no match exception. Looking back to our `flatten/1` function, what could be causing this?

It turns out, we *always* assume that the head of the list will be another list. But we said the function should handle arbitrarily-deep nesting. Zero nesting is arbitrarily deep. We need another pattern.

Let's add the new pattern to our `flatten/1` function and try testing again.

Modify the `Flatten` module to look similar to the following:

```
defmodule Flatten do
  def flatten([]), do: []
  def flatten([h|t]) when is_list(h), do: h ++ flatten(t)
  def flatten([h|t]), do: [h] ++ flatten(t)
end
```

Then, running the tests again, we should get a passing test:

```
$ mix test
Compiled lib/flatten.ex
Generated flatten app

..


Finished in 0.03 seconds (0.03s on load, 0.00s on tests)
2 tests, 0 failures


Randomized with seed 466648
```

We do get that.

The process we just went through isn't too different from TDD or other testing and test development strategies.

More to do about modules

Modules are the enclosing unit of our building blocks. They are the super block to which functions are the blocks. But occasionally, we wish to get data about our modules and metadata on our building blocks. We would probably like to document our code. We would like those following us to be able to read those comments and documentation. Better yet, we would like to have nice tooling around building rich documentation about our code while minimizing duplication, if not entirely eliminating it. Or, instead of documentation, we would like to tag our modules and functions with certain attributes that we could later use for any other number of reasons.

To support these goals, Elixir gives us the ability to give modules attributes, which we can use as developers, or users, or they can be used by the VM. Similarly, we can use attributes as constants.

Attributes are defined in Elixir as `@name`. For example, I could add the `@vsn` attribute to annotate a module named `MyModule`:

```
defmodule MyModule do
  @vsn 1
end
```

That is, I've defined a simple module with a single annotation of `vsn`. Next, let's look at the two most used attributes — `@moduledoc` and `@doc`.

We could define a `Math` module, using the `@moduledoc` and `@doc` attributes appropriately:

```
defmodule Math do
  @moduledoc """
  Provides math-related functions
  """

  @doc """
  Calculate factorial of a number.

  ## Example

      iex> Math.factorial(5)
      120
  """
  def factorial(n), do: do_factorial(n)

  defp do_factorial(0), do: 1
  defp do_factorial(n), do: n * do_factorial(n-1)

  @doc """
  Compute the binomial coefficient of `n` and `k`

  ## Example
      iex> Math.binomial(4, 2)
      6
  """
  def binomial(n, k), do: div(factorial(n), factorial(k) *
factorial(n-k))
end
```

The text between the `@moduledoc` and `@doc` attributes can be Markdown, and the documentation printed to the screen will use this for formatting and printing properly.

Save this module to a file named `math.ex` and let's compile it:

```
$ elixir math.ex
$ echo $?
0
```

If all is well, we should see no output and no exit code.

Next, we can launch `iex` and get the documentation about our new `Math` module:

```
iex(1)> h Math


                           Math

Provides math-related functions

iex(2)> h Math.factorial


                    def factorial(n)

Calculate factorial of a number, n.

Example

▨ iex> Math.factorial(5)
▨ 120
```

That is, we can use the `h/1` function in `iex` to request documentation on even our own functions.

Testing with comments

There's another cool feature of the `@moduledoc` and `@doc` attributes and that is what's called **doctesting**. That is, the lines in our comments that look similar to `iex` sessions can be used as tests where the output return value is the expected result.

Let's return to our flatten project from earlier.

We can add some `@doc` comments to the function, and add what would look similar to an `iex` session of us manually testing the function, but in fact, would be tests run by the `mix` test.

Open the `flatten.ex` file from earlier and add the `@doc` attribute:

```
defmodule Flatten do
  @doc """
  Flatten an arbitrarily nested lists

  ## Examples

      iex> Flatten.flatten [[1, 2], [3], [4, 5]]
      [1, 2, 3, 4, 5]
      iex> Flatten.flatten [1, 2, 3, 4, 5]
      [1, 2, 3, 4, 5]
  """
  def flatten([]), do: []
  def flatten([h|t]) when is_list(h), do: h ++ flatten(t)
  def flatten([h|t]), do: [h] ++ flatten(t)
end
```

Next, open the `flatten_test.exs` file as well and add the following line to the top:

```
doctest(Flatten)
```

Then, when running the `mix` test, we should see that more (of the same) tests are run:

```
$ mix test
Compiled lib/flatten.ex
Generated flatten app
...


Finished in 0.05 seconds (0.05s on load, 0.00s on tests)
3 tests, 0 failures


Randomized with seed 290967
```

Tests in the `@doc` attributes will be combined into a single test when tested this way. So, although we defined two different inputs and outputs, we are only adding a single new test.

Exercises

Do:

- Write tests for `Reverse.reverse` and `Sort.quicksort`.
- Write a function to determine whether the given string is palindrome.
    - Write some tests for this function, considering the length of the string, is it even or odd, capitalization, punctuation, and space.
    - See whether you get an implementation that is just $O(n)$.

Summary

This chapter was also full of material, so let's take a quick moment to recap some of the material we covered.

We discussed how modules are defined, their purpose, and a little about their representation.

We went over functions, more about them as types, more explicitly into how they are defined, and the difference between anonymous (unnamed) functions versus named functions.

Along the lines of functions, we discussed pattern matching more and how it can be used to solve problems.

Using patterns, we also discussed guard statements and what functions or checks are available to us when using guards.

We also introduced Elixir's build tool, `mix`, and how we can use it to create projects, and we started our first few projects.

Along with projects and `mix`, we introduced a few cool features with respect to testing available to us via `mix` and Elixir.

So far, we introduced the functional building blocks required to create programs and applications in Elixir. Next, we will want to see how we can improve some of our building blocks with the new processing techniques.

4
Collections and Stream Processing

Now that we have the syntactical basics of Elixir, we can really start to do exciting things. In particular, we can take some of the ideas mentioned in the previous chapter — recursion and pattern matching — to do some really exciting and cool things. For example, we can introduce one of the coolest operators of Elixir, the pipe operator (| >); start doing something called **pipeline programming**; and borrow an idea from the early days of computing.

Keywords, maps, and dictionaries

However, we should take a quick moment to introduce more collections. We have covered lists and tuples as either linked lists or contiguous blocks of memory similar to arrays, respectively. However, there is another set of types we haven't covered — associative data structures.

Elixir has a few different kinds of associate, key-value structures, keywords, and maps. Both are a type of dictionary, or hash table, although, they have different underlying implementations and performance characteristics.

Keywords

Keywords are a special name for a list of 2-tuples, or pairs, where the first element of each pair, the key, is an atom. For example, we could see the following list:

```
iex(1)> alist = [{:a, 0}, {:b, 2}]
[a: 0, b: 2]
iex(2)> alist == [a: 0, b: 2]
true
iex(3)> alist[:a]
0
```

That is, a list of pairs is the same as a flat list of alternating atoms and values.

There are some very important properties of keywords that make them special and useful:

- Keys must be atoms
- Keys are ordered by the developer or by use (insertion and deletion ordering)
- Keys can be added more than once

We have seen the first one implicitly. The second bullet makes sense with some thought—it's a linked list; the ordering is defined by the ordering of the list structure and therefore, by the developer or the developers call flow. We can do better. Let's examine both the second and third bullet, with examples, of course:

```
iex(4)> alist ++ {:c, 5}
[a: 0, b: 2, c: 5]
iex(5)> {:c, 5} ++ alist
[c: 5, a: 0, b: 2]
```

Again, clearly, we can append or prepend items to a keyword list and get the order we expect.

Moreover, we can add more than one of the same keys:

```
iex(5) blist = [{:a, 1}] ++ alist
[a: 1, a: 0, b: 2]
```

Since keywords are lists, there really isn't any technical reason for Elixir to complain about this. However, since they are lists, we get the same linear performance characteristics of lists; searching for keys and counting elements will take a long time for large lists. If the constant-time performance characteristics are important, use maps, the next type we will discuss.

That said, the `Keyword` module has a lot of functionality for working with keyword lists. For example, if we want to get the values for a repeated key, we can use the `Keyword.get_values/2` function:

```
iex(6)> Keyword.get_values blist, :a
[1, 0]
```

Notice, they are returned in the order they were defined too.

Maps

Maps, as you might expect, create a map from a key to a value. Maps are the de facto type for storing key-value collections. Let's see some examples of maps:

```
iex(1)> my_map = %{'a' => 1, :b => 2, 3 => 5}
%{3 => 5, :b => 2, 'a' => 1}
iex(2)> my_other_map = %{a: 1, b: 2, c: 5}
%{a: 1, b: 2, c: 5}
```

Already, we can see a clear difference between maps and keyword lists, chiefly, map keys can be of any type, and ordering isn't guaranteed. Moreover, we can borrow the syntax of keyword lists of the keys, which are simply atoms.

Accessing elements of a map is the same as for keyword lists:

```
iex(3)> my_map['a']
1
iex(4)> my_map[:b]
2
iex(5)> my_map[3]
5
```

However, maps can only have one-to-one relationships between keys and values. That is, we can't hold multiple values for a single key:

```
iex(6)> Map.put(my_map, 3, 7)
%{3 => 7, :b => 2, 'a' => 1}
```

Furthermore, we can see that the last value, `put`, into the map will the be the last value we get out; in other words, maps are last-write-win data structures.

Dictionaries

Both keyword lists and maps are a form of dictionary. They follow the behaviour of dictionary-like data structures. Of course, they aren't strictly implemented as dictionaries behind the scenes as we saw with keyword lists. However, they allow us to store key-value pairs and read from these stores to retrieve those values if we know or have the key.

There's another module that allows us to manipulate keyword lists and maps—`Dict`. As you might have noticed though, there is no explicit dictionary type. Furthermore, you might have noticed the inherent problem with attempting to manipulate two very different in implementation types. How does the `Dict` module do this?

Although there is not a dictionary type, there is a dictionary protocol that allows us to use a single module to operate on keyword lists and maps. The `Dict` module is a single API that allows us to operate on both keyword lists and maps as if they were the same type.

 Protocols are a way to introduce polymorphism in Elixir, and we will be covering them in more detail in *Chapter 9, Metaprogramming – Doing More with Less*.

Furthermore, the APIs of `Keyword`, `Map`, and `Dict` are generally the same. If you just need a basic dictionary, you can use either keyword lists or maps as the type and the `Dict` module to manipulate the type. Moreover, you may write a module that accepts either keyword lists or maps as parameters, and therefore, the `Dict` module would be the easiest way to operate on those parameters, regardless of the actual type given.

However, there is a time when using the `Dict` module isn't a good idea. For example, if access to repeated keys is needed, you may wish to use the `Keyword` module and keyword lists exclusively. Generalizing APIs to accept either type does add a hidden cost of expectation of the end user and correctness. Therefore, a good set of tests, including both types, would be highly recommended for such a case.

More pattern matching

Of course, we can't introduce another type without discussing pattern matching.

Unsurprisingly, we can create patterns to match against both keyword lists and maps. However, there is a difference in flexibility between the two. Let's look at matching against keyword lists first:

```
iex(1)> my_list = [a: 1, b: 2, c: 5]
[a: 1, b: 2, c: 5]
```

```
iex(2)> [a: 1, b: 2, c: c] = my_list
[a: 1, b: 2, c: 5]
iex(3)> c
5
```

All seems okay so far. What about the following errors though?

```
iex(4)> [a: a] = my_list
** (MatchError) no match of right hand side value: [a: 1, b: 2, c: 5]
```

```
iex(5)> [c: 5, b: 2, a: 1] = my_list
** (MatchError) no match of right hand side value: [a: 1, b: 2, c: 5]
```

This shows us two things about matching with keyword lists. Firstly, it must be a full match, and secondly, the order of the matching is very important.

That is, we can't expect to match partial keyword lists; it's essentially all or nothing. Furthermore, the order of the keys may break an otherwise good match.

To further cement the idea of an all or nothing match, let's see an example of a keyword list match with repeated keys:

```
iex(6)> my_other_list = [a: 0, a: 1]
[a: 0, a: 1]
iex(7)> [a: 0] = my_other_list
** (MatchError) no match of right hand side value: [a: 0, a: 1]
```

Even with a repeated key, keyword lists do not match against a partial keyword list.

Although keyword lists *can* be matched, pattern matching keyword lists is hardly done in practice because when generalizing the preceding rules, the number of elements and order must match, making actual matching difficult.

Let's take a look at matching our other dictionary type—maps.

We will start by defining a basic mapping:

```
iex(1)> my_map = %{:a => 1, :b => 2, 3 => 5}
%{3 => 5, :a => 1, :b => 2}
```

Hopefully, the ordering of the keys should not matter for matching since, as we mentioned earlier, the ordering of keys in maps isn't guaranteed:

```
iex(2)> %{3 => three, :b => b, :a => a} = my_map
%{3 => 5, :a => 1, :b => 2}
```

```
iex(3)> a
1
iex(4)> b
2
iex(5)> three
5
```

Cool, ordering isn't an issue. Let's try some other patterns:

```
iex(6)> %{a: => a} = my_map
%{3 => 5, :a => 1, :b => 2}
iex(7)> a
1
```

As you can see from (6), we can also do partial matching on maps. Let's look at one more match:

```
iex(8)> %{} = my_map
%{3 => 5, :a => 1, :b => 2}
```

Interesting, what is going on here?

Here, we have the empty map, %{}, and we attempt to match it against our map => of three pairs, and the match is successful. This shows any map will match successfully against the empty map. It is essentially the equivalent of using the _ for matching.

Modifying dictionaries

It's unlikely the dictionaries you use will always be write-once, read-many data structures. We need to know how to create new dictionaries from the existing ones.

Mutating a keyword list, we are left using functions from either the Keyword or Dict module. For example, to insert a key into a keyword list, we can use the Keyword. put/3 function:

```
iex(1)> my_key_list = [a: 1, b: 2]
[a: 1, b: 2]
iex(2)> Keyword.put(my_key_list, :c, 3)
[c: 3, a: 1, b: 2]
```

Notice, the Keyword.put/3 function prepends the new key. Let's try using the Dict module to perform the same thing:

```
iex(3)> Dict.put(my_key_list, :c, 3)
[c: 3, a: 1, b: 2]
```

As we might expect, we get the same result. Let's try something a little different:

```
iex(4)> Keyword.put(my_key_list, :a, 5)
[a: 5, b: 2]
iex(5)> Dict.put(my_key_list, :a, 5)
[a: 5, b: 2]
```

Although keyword lists *can* store the same key multiple times, the put/3 functions of Keyword and Dict explicitly state that they will update the key if it already exists. Watch out for these sorts of differences.

Mutating maps is very similar to mutating keyword lists. We can still use the same function, put/3, this time from the Map module as well as the Dict module:

```
iex(1)> my_map = %{:a => 1, :b => 2, 3 => 5}
%{3 => 5, :a => 1, :b => 2}
iex(2)> Map.put(my_map, :c, 4)
%{3 => 5, :a => 1, :b => 2, :c => 4}
iex(3)> Dict.put(my_map, :c, 4)
%{3 => 5, :a => 1, :b => 2, :c => 4}
```

Again, we can also update the existing keys with the same function:

```
iex(4)> Map.put(my_map, :a, 'a')
%{3 => 5, :a => 'a', :b => 2}
iex(5)> Dict.put(my_map, :a, 'a')
%{3 => 5, :a => 'a', :b => 2}
```

This is fine, except that there is a nicer syntax for updating maps:

```
iex(6)> %{my_map | :a => 3}
%{3 => 5, :a => 3, :b => 2}
```

However, inserting *new* keys doesn't quite work:

```
iex(7)> %{my_map | :c => 5}
** (ArgumentError) argument error
```

That is, this more concise syntax requires the key to exist before it works.

Performance considerations

There are some obvious performance considerations when using keyword lists because they are implemented as lists. However, there are even some considerations for maps that must be acknowledged.

That is, maps are a recent addition to the Erlang VM, and it's only a partial addition at that. Therefore, currently as of this writing, Elixir maps only have good performance characteristics with no more than about a dozen keys. To overcome this limitation, Elixir provides the `HashDict` module and structure.

Structures and Hash dicts

Elixir **strucutres** are another type we have yet to discuss, but they are not exactly a new concept from a general programming perspective.

Elixir structures are similar to maps. They keep a name, or key, to a value. However, instead of being freely floating and scoped, they must be defined inside modules. That is, an Elixir structure is defined inside a module. Let's see this in action:

```
iex(1)> defmodule Foo do
...(1)> defstruct bar: 'foobar', answer: 42
...(1)> end
{:module, Foo,
<<70, 79, 82, 49, 0, 0, 4, 228, 66, 69, 65, 77, 69, 120, 68, 99, 0, 0, 0,
99, 131,
104, 2, 100, 0, 14, 101, 108, 105, 120, 105, 114, 95, 100, 111, 99, 115,
95, 118,
49, 108, 0, 0, 0, 2, 104, 2, ...>>,
[bar: 'foobar', answer: 42]}
iex(2)> %Foo{}
%Foo{answer: 42, bar: 'foobar'}
iex(3)> %Foo{bar: "just bar"}
%Foo{answer: 42, bar: "just bar"}
```

Syntactically, structs can be thought of as named maps. Furthermore, they can be accessed and updated similarly to maps:

```
iex(4)> foo = %Foo{}
%Foo{answer: 42, bar: 'foobar'}
iex(5)> foo.answer
42
iex(6)> %{foo | bar: 'bar'}
%Foo{answer: 42, bar: 'bar'}
```

Interestingly, the syntax for updating structs doesn't require the struct name prefix as declarations do. However, there is no harm in specifying it:

```
iex(7)> %Foo{foo | bar: 'bar'}
%Foo{answer: 42, bar: 'bar'}
```

Similar to maps, using the pipe, |, syntax for updating structs will fail if the key doesn't exist:

```
iex(8)> %Foo{foo | foo: 'foo'}
** (CompileError) iex:9: unknown key :foo for struct Foo
```

Furthermore, creating a new structure with a key that doesn't exist will similarly fail:

```
iex(9)> %Foo{foo: 'foo'}
** (CompileError) iex:9: unknown key :foo for struct Foo
```

Yet another dictionary type

As mentioned earlier, if you need to store anything more than a couple dozen keys in a map, you should probably use the HashDict structure. The dictionary of HashDict is implemented using a hashing algorithm for the keys and a structure as the underlying data structure.

Best of all, the interface of using the HashDict structures is remarkably similar to using keyword lists, maps, or the Dict module:

```
iex(1)> my_dict = HashDict.new
#HashDict<[]>
iex(2)> my_dict_2 = HashDict.put(my_dict, :foo, 42)
#HashDict<[foo: 42]>
iex(3)> my_dict_3 = Dict.put(my_dict_2, :bar, 'foo')
#HashDict<[foo: 42, bar: 'foo']>
```

As we can see from the preceding sample iex session, the HashDict module can manipulate the HashDict structures and similarly, the Dict module. Although HashDict isn't *actually* a map, it still defines the protocol or more precisely, what to do if calling certain functions. For the most part, the implementation of the protocol for HashDict is a wrapper around the HashDict module itself.

Again, the reason for this module and structure is to get around the performance characteristics of maps when storing a large number of pairs. Otherwise, they behave very similarly to maps.

Flow-based programming

Let's move on to discuss another topic that isn't necessarily new, but is recently making a stir in the programming world.

Flow-based programming or programming with pipes is a way of specifying and solving particular problems in terms of a flow and a connection of interconnected units. At its basis, flow-based programming defines a sequence of operations that will be performed. Each element in the sequence (of computation) defines a specific computation, and computes and passes to the next in the sequence. Ignoring types for a moment, each unit is independent of each other. Each can be modified without dramatically affecting other components in the flow.

Flow-based programming inherently requires the immutability constructs of functional programming because each element that will be computed over the flow, must be computable without interaction of other elements of the original set. That is, we take some collection of elements, and for each element, pass the element through the flow:

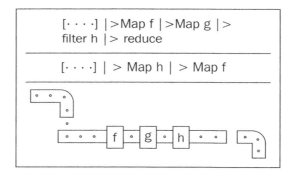

Returning to our discussion of composability. We argued that programming is about creating not only useful outputs, but also composable components. In some languages, these components are objects. However, objects are not really the most composable components. Functions are, by far, more composable than objects.

Flow-based programming is just another great example that shows how unnatural composing objects *actually* is. Think a moment! How would you compose objects to produce a flow or sequence of computation? Further, ponder what it would take to make this easily malleable?

It's certainly possible to create flows with more **object-oriented** (OO) languages; however, as the thought experiment goes, they are usually awkward and brittle.

Compare this to composing and chaining functions. The blocks are already there: `map`, `filter`, and `reduce` are already (usually) defined. In fact, more often than not, when attempting to produce flows in OO languages, after a sufficient amount of time, the solution will resemble the functional `map` and `reduce` version.

Composing functions to create flows turns out to be an easier model to conceptualize too. Each unit, as we described earlier, is just a function, some form of mutation, and is easily tractable. They are not objects and we do not have to mentally unbox the function to track their effects.

Furthermore, we can create a simple mental model about how the computation is performed as well. Mentally traversing a flow's execution, we can imagine a single element passing through each mutation in sequence without the complexities of all the other elements we are processing because, as we stated before, and as inherent with functional programming, the value of other elements does not effect our computation of the current element.

This simple model of execution for flows yields more results too. Since each element's process is independent of the others, this is an easy parallelization point. For example, we could have each stage of the flow be its own process, and each interconnection is just a message passed to the next process. Or, as another example, each element can be processed through the whole flow in its own process.

The other result that is given by independent computability of each element is the ability to compress the computation. Let's discuss loop-unrolling to create an analogy for what we mean by compress. Let's say we write a loop that has several statements that modify or otherwise interact with the element of the current iteration.

For example, the given loop...

```
for x in elements
    x' = f x
    x'' = g x'
```

...might be statically unrolled to something similar to:

```
elements'[0] = f elements[0]
elements'[1] = f elements[1]
elements'[2] = f elements[1]
...
elements''[0] = g elements'[0]
elements''[1] = g elements'[1]
elements''[2] = g elements'[2]
...
```

Each computation of the loop is explicit, and there is no more branching or end-of-loop check. That is, the compiler attempts to optimize the loop by removing the expensive branching patterns of loops at the cost of a larger program binary.

The concept of compressed computation is similar. We have a sequence of mutations, f, g, and h that we wish to perform against an element. We express the sequence in code to maintain the composability of the sequence and each element of the sequence, but our sufficiently sophisticated compiler or runtime will smash the computations together to create an idealized version of our computation; thus, avoid some of the expensive qualities of writing more flexible code. Of course, again, this is only possible if our computations are each independent pieces. If anything in the sequence depends on another element's result, this can no longer be safely applied.

Flow-based programming also has another name—**stream processing**. The analogy is the same as a flow or stream. We are talking about the same thing: a way to process information not only efficiently, but also effectively and compositionally. Constructively, if we can compose functions, we should be able to compose streams. By composing streams, we have yet another block we can create to build bigger blocks.

Stream processing and Elixir

Since Elixir is functional, stream processing in Elixir is quite simple. We have functions such as Enum.map/2, Enum.filter/2, and Enum.reduce/2. Further still, we have a way to express computations inherently as flows, even if we are not (yet) completely taking advantage of flow-based programming.

Simply, the |> operator is a way to express program flow as you read it. Rather than awkwardly writing programs inside out or right to left, we can express our computation naturally from left to right. Let's begin to examine some simple examples of this.

Quickly, let's take a look at our `map/2` function from earlier chapters:

```
iex(1)> defmodule MyMap do
...(1)> def map([], _), do: []
...(1)> def map([h|t], f), do: [f.(h) | map(t, f)]
...(1)> end
{:module, MyMap,
 <<70, 79, 82, 49, 0, 0, 4, 220, 66, 69, 65, 77, 69, 120, 68, 99, 0, 0,
0, 130,
131, 104, 2, 100, 0, 14, 101, 108, 105, 120, 105, 114, 95, 100, 111, 99,
115, 95,
118, 49, 108, 0, 0, 0, 2, 104, 2, ...>>,
 {:map, 2}}
```

So far, we have invoked the map function with some list of integers, and we have either generated a list of squares or doubled the original list. However, the way we invoked it is what we are interested in now. Earlier, we wrote something similar to this:

```
iex(2)> MyMap.map([1, 2, 3, 4, 5], fn (x) -> x * x end)
[1, 4, 9, 16, 25]
```

If we wanted to use a range instead, we would have to expand it with `Enum.to_list/1` and then pass the result to our `MyMap.map/2` function:

```
iex(3)> MyMap.map(Enum.to_list(1..5), fn (x) -> x * x end)
[1, 4, 9, 16, 25]
```

These are functionally equivalent. But the mess of inside-out evaluation is starting to show. To write this better, we change the flow and we use the `|>` operator to piece it all together:

```
iex(4)> 1..5 |> Enum.to_list |> MyMap.map fn (x) -> x * x end
[1, 4, 9, 16, 25]
```

This reads as you might expect: we create a range from 1 to 5 and pass it to `Enum.to_list/1`, passing the result to `MyMap.map/2`.

This is the same as the invocation from (3); however, we can read it with a single scan. Reading (3), if never seen before, can take quite a bit more time. We were even able to drop some otherwise required parentheses.

Elixir's `|>` operator is much like the `|` operator of UNIX. We take the results of some computation and pass it to the next, chaining arbitrarily many times.

How does the |> operator know where to pass the result? The |> operator only returns a single result, the result of the previous operation. This result is always passed as the first parameter of the next operation or function. For example, the result of 1..5 was the first parameter of Enum.to_list/1. Similarly, the result of Enum.to_list(1..5) was the first parameter of MyMap.map/2. If we had defined our map function with the function as the first parameter, we would have been in trouble as we would have to do some extra lifting to ensure we call our map function correctly.

Processing with the Enum module

There is a lot we can do with the Enum module.

Instead of writing our own version of map, we can use the one already defined in the Enum module:

```
iex(1)> 1..5 |> Enum.to_list |> Enum.map fn(x) -> x * x end
[1, 4, 9, 16, 25]
```

In fact, since the pattern on Enum.map/2 is more universal than the one we defined, we can actually drop the Enum.to_list/1 call:

```
iex(2)> 1..5 |> Enum.map fn(x) -> x * x end
[1, 4, 9, 16, 25]
```

If we start looking at more functions from the Enum module, we can actually start asking interesting questions, and finding the solution is just a matter of piecing together the right set of operations.

For some simple problems, let's generate the first 10 odd numbers:

```
iex(1)> 1..100 |>
...(1)> Enum.filter(fn(x) -> rem(x, 2) != 0 end) |>
...(1)> Enum.take(10)
[1, 3, 5, 7, 9, 11, 13, 15, 17, 19]
```

Here, we use the Enum.filter/2 function to produce a list of only the elements that satisfy the condition of the provided function. Here, only odd numbers are desired. Then, since we only want the first 10 odd numbers, we must further reduce our output. Using Enum.take/2, we take only the first *n* numbers we see and discard the rest.

Another way we can generate the first 10 odds is by using Enum.take_every/2 and Enum.take/2:

```
iex(2)> 1..100 |>
...(2)> Enum.take_every(2) |>
```

```
...(2)> Enum.take 10
[1, 3, 5, 7, 9, 11, 13, 15, 17, 19]
```

Let's say we want to find the sum of the first 10 squares:

```
iex(3)> 1..10 |>
...(3)> Enum.map(fn(x) -> x * x end) |>
...(3)> Enum.sum
385
```

Similar to the previous examples of using map and the square function, this time, however, we reduce the number to a single value with the Enum.sum/1 function. However, we could rewrite this to use the Enum.reduce/2 function as well:

```
iex(4)> 1..10 |>
...(4)> Enum.map(fn(x) -> x * x end) |>
...(4)> Enum.reduce(fn(x, acc) -> x + acc end)
385
```

The Enum.reduce/2 function uses the provided function to accumulate the value of the previous calls; this reduces the values of the list into a single value.

Or, maybe we want to find the product of squares:

```
iex(5)> 1..10 |>
...(5)> Enum.map(fn(x) -> x * x end) |>
...(5)> Enum.reduce(1, fn(x, acc) -> x * acc end)
13168189440000
```

In (5), instead of using Enum.reduce/2 we used Enum.reduce/3. The difference between these is the specification of the accumulators starting value, for example, 1 in this case.

Processing with the Stream module

Similar to the Enum module, Elixir has the Stream module. The Stream module is different from the Enum module in one very distinctive way: it is lazy. This means collections created with the Stream module are not realized until they have to be. The result of mapping a function over a Stream module means we won't get the result of the full map until we ask for it explicitly.

Greedy versus lazy

What does it mean for a collection to be greedy and to be lazy?

Simply, greedy collections or enumerations are collections that are realized immediately. That is, generating a list of odd numbers with `1..100 |> Enum.filter(fn(x) -> rem(x, 2) != 0 end)` is greedy since the result is immediately (minus the few microseconds it takes to actually generate) available to use. Lazy collections, on the other hand, are not realized until the latest possible moment. We could write something similar as before; however, all that is returned (instantly) is a promise that it will generate the result we are asking. The result is not given until we ask to realize the promise. Asking to realize a promise often takes many forms, such as reducing, taking, or any operation that requires the entire collection to compute.

The benefits of lazy evaluation of collections are often subtle but profound.

How might a program deal with infinite collections?

How might our sufficiently sophisticated compiler or runtime from earlier *actually* compress the computations?

Using lazy evaluation, working with infinite collections is easy. They do not materialize until we ask them to. By then, we will have filtered or made them finite. Related to infinite collections, perhaps our data is polled slowly from some I/O device, whether that be a file, some device on the Internet, or so on; we can use lazy evaluation to stream the computations through without having to wait for the I/O device to finish reading or for us to finish polling.

The representation of mutations over a lazy collection is actually more accurately represented as a list of functions instead of a list of values. This way, we can tightly compute the results of the mutations when the list is actualized.

Stream examples

First, let's see what the Elixir representation of a stream looks similar to:

```
iex(1)> 1..10 |> Stream.map fn(x) -> x * x end
#Stream<[enum: 1..10, funs: [#Function<45.29647706/1 in Stream.map/2>]]>
```

Dissecting the output a bit, we see that the stream has a reference to our original enumeration, `1..10`. It also has a list of functions that it will apply to the stream.

Let's see how this might look with an additional `map` step:

```
iex(2)> 1..10 |>
...(2)> Stream.map(fn(x) -> x * x end) |>
...(2)> Stream.map(fn(x) -> 3 * x end)
#Stream<[enum: 1..10,
 funs: [#Function<45.29647706/1 in Stream.map/2>,
  #Function<45.29647706/1 in Stream.map/2>]]>
```

It's a little contrived, but as we might have expected, there are now two maps in the `funs:` list.

Let's revisit our examples from the `Enum` section, and see how they would be done using the `Stream` module.

Let's generate the first 10 odds:

```
iex(3)> 1..100 |>
...(3)> Stream.filter(fn(x) -> rem(x, 2) != 0 end) |>
...(3)> Stream.take(10)
#Stream<[enum: 1..100,
 funs: [#Function<39.29647706/1 in Stream.filter/2>,
  #Function<50.29647706/1 in Stream.take/2>]]>
```

That's not a list. We forgot to add a new step in our generation; we need to realize our stream. We can do this with `Enum.to_list/1`:

```
iex(4)> 1..100 |>
...(4)> Stream.filter(fn(x) -> rem(x, 2) != 0 end) |>
...(4)> Stream.take(10) |>
...(4)> Enum.to_list
[1, 3, 5, 7, 9, 11, 13, 15, 17, 19]
```

If all we are going to do after `take` is actualize the stream, we could do this with the `Enum.take/2`, `Enum` functions, which are greedy and will realize our stream for us:

```
iex(5)> 1..100 |>
...(5)> Stream.filter(fn(x) -> rem(x, 2) != 0 end) |>
...(5)> Enum.take(10)
[1, 3, 5, 7, 9, 11, 13, 15, 17, 19]
```

Since the entire enumeration isn't realized, we can pass a very large range, and it should still perform the same. In fact, we can measure the amount of time it takes to generate the first 10 odds using the `Stream` module versus when using the `Enum` module, particularly when passing a very large collection.

We'll start by defining a few anonymous functions:

```
iex(6)> stream_f = fn() -> 1..100000 |>
...(6)> Stream.filter(fn(x) -> rem(x, 2) != 0 end) |>
...(6)> Enum.take(10) end
#Function<20.90072148/0 in :erl_eval.expr/5>
iex(7)> enum_f = fn() -> 1..100000 |>
```

```
...(7)> Enum.filter(fn(x) -> rem(x, 2) != 0 end) |>
...(7)> Enum.take(10) end
#Function<20.90072148/0 in :erl_eval.expr/5>
```

Next, we can use the Erlang `timer.tc` function to time both functions. The result of the `timer.tc` function will be a 2-tuple where the first element will be the number of elapsed *microseconds* and the second element will be the result of the function.

 To invoke Erlang code from Elixir, we prefix the Erlang module with a colon.

To invoke the `timer.tc/2` function, we would do something like `:timer.tc(function, args)`:

```
iex(8)> :timer.tc(enum_f)
{209069, [1, 3, 5, 7, 9, 11, 13, 15, 17, 19]}
iex(9)> :timer.tc(stream_f)
{141, [1, 3, 5, 7, 9, 11, 13, 15, 17, 19]}
```

In this case, enumerating the whole list was a lot of wasted effort.

Koolaid

Streams are pretty neat and are a great way to improve certain stream computation performance. However, there are occasions you should avoid them.

The nature of streams can be, in certain circumstances, actually slower than full enumerations. That is, asking for a promise and then asking to fulfill that promise requires time: the time spent in a circle of asking for a promise, and asking for fulfillment. If the size of the list is small, or the latency of the promise-fulfillment cycle is larger than the latency of the data itself, use the `Enum` module. The `Stream` module lends itself more appropriately to I/O bound tasks. Asking for data from a file or a web service is a perfect use of the `Stream` module.

Graphs

Simple graphs have some interesting properties or structures that we can usually query or search. Such properties are things such as shortest path, minimum spanning tree, and so on.

A small introduction to graphs

Graphs from mathematics are structures that describe a set of nodes or vertices and a set of connections or edges. Adjacent nodes are nodes connected by a single edge.

Representing a graph in memory can be accomplished with an adjacency matrix. Each row and column of the matrix corresponds to a node in the graph, and each element of the matrix is either 0 or 1 to denote that the nodes are connected.

For example, the graph in the following diagram can be represented as the adjacency matrix:

```
    A B C
A   0 1 1
B   1 0 1
C   1 1 0
```

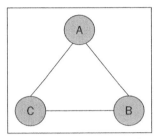

A simple graph is a finite graph without cycles or multiple edges. Such graphs can be represented as adjacency lists. That is, we can take the previous graph, and instead of using a matrix, we can just use the following list to represent the graph:

```
[{:b, :c}, {:a, :c}, {:a, :b}]
```

This is a list of tuples. We are implicitly indexing the elements in order. The neighbors of **A** are defined in the first element, the neighbors of **B** are defined in the second, and those of **C** are defined in the third element. We can both continue to use a list *and* make explicit whose neighbors are whose using keyword lists:

```
iex(1)> k3 = [a: {:b, :c}, b: {:a, :c}, c: {:a, :b}]
[a: {:b, :c}, b: {:a, :c}, c: {:a, :b}]
```

 We call the graph k3 because it is a K_3 or complete graph with three nodes.

In terms of pure semantics, this isn't technically a list, but this is, in some respect, a better representation because we can use nice, explicit syntax for getting the neighbors or a particular node:

```
iex(2)> k3[:b]
{:a, :c}
```

Another type of graph typically encountered in computing is the **directed acyclic graph (DAG)**. Directed means that there is a sense of direction in the edges connecting a graph, whereas earlier, an edge was bidirectional. Acyclical refers to the lack of cycles present in the graph. That is, no pattern of vertices can be visited and returned to the starting vertex.

Similar to simple graphs, we can represent DAGs using adjacency lists as well. The difference would be that some nodes will be considered sinks since they will have no adjacent nodes, and other nodes might be considered spouts or sources because they will not be a neighbor to any other node (check this verbiage...).

For example, we can represent the DAG in this diagram with the following list:

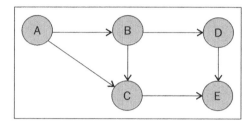

```
iex(1)> dag = [a: {:b, :c}, b: {:c, :d}, c: {:e}, d: {:e}, e: {}]
[a: {:b, :c}, b: {:c, :d}, c: {:e}, d: {:e}, e: {}]
```

In this case, node **A** would be considered a source and node **E**, a sink.

Node ancestors

A common problem when using directed graphs is getting the ancestors of the nodes, or, more often, the least common ancestor of any two arbitrary nodes. This is a problem Git often has to compute.

Let's start simple and try to just create a structure for the nodes' ancestors. We will use the DAG we have defined in the preceding diagram. That is, we will use the following structure:

```
[a: {:b, :c}, b: {:c, :d}, c: {:e}, d: {:e}, e: {}]
```

The structure we would like as a result is the following:

```
[b: {:a}, c: {:a, :b}, d: {:b}, e: {:c, :d}]
```

Note that we lost the :a node. Ideally, we would still have it and it would be represented in the latter list as a: {} since it has no ancestors. However, this is a bit of a corner case, tends to be irrelevant, and adds too much noise to this example.

Instead of giving you the stream all at once now, we will construct it, iteratively, together. We'll start by defining our DAG in an interactive session:

```
iex(1)> dag = [a: {:b, :c}, b: {:c, :d}, c: {:e}, d: {:e}, e: {}]
[a: {:b, :c}, b: {:c, :d}, c: {:e}, d: {:e}, e: {}]
```

No surprises here, we have just created our adjacency list of nodes using a keyword list.

Our first step will be to invert the relationship of the nodes. We will do this by mapping a particular function over the nodes. This function will extract the nodes' neighbors, convert them to a list of nodes, and finally, map another function over the neighbors to get a pair for each child and parent.

We will use a new function from the `Tuple` module—`Tuple.to_list/1`. This function simply converts tuples to linked lists. This is required since tuples do not implement the Enumerable protocol:

```
iex(2)> dag |>
...(2)> Enum.map(fn({node, neighbors}) ->
...(2)> neighbors |> Tuple.to_list |> Enum.map(fn(child) -> {child, node}
end)
end)
[[b: :a, c: :a], [c: :b, d: :b], [e: :c], [e: :d], []]
```

The result is, well, nested. It's a list of nested keyword lists. Since we are using two maps, we might expect it to be. This does not look fun to work with though. We can pass this result to yet another function, `List.flatten/1`, to get a single keyword list. Let's see what that gives us:

```
iex(3)> dag |>
...(3)> Enum.map(fn({node, neighbors}) ->
...(3)> neighbors |> Tuple.to_list |> Enum.map(fn(child) -> {child, node}
end)
end) |>
...(3)> List.flatten
[b: :a, c: :a, c: :b, d: :b, e: :c, e: :d]
```

It gives us exactly what we wanted. We get a flat keyword list that has all of the inverted node relationships. If this was an acceptable data structure to work with, we could stop here. But, since we said we want a structure similar to the graph adjacency list itself, we must convert the structure back.

To convert our flat keyword list to our graph keyword list of tuples, we must gather the nodes together. This is the most involved step because we do not want to use temporary variables.

The first stage of this process will be to create a tuple with a list of the keys—child nodes—and the current structure. This function would look similar to the following:

```
fn(nodes) -> {nodes |> Keyword.keys |> Enum.uniq, nodes} end
```

Let's add this to our stream so far:

```
iex(4)> dag |>
...(4)> Enum.map(fn({node, neighbors}) ->
...(4)> neighbors |> Tuple.to_list |> Enum.map(fn(child) -> {child, node}
end)
end) |>
...(4)> List.flatten |>
...(4)> (fn(nodes) -> {nodes |> Keyword.keys |> Enum.uniq, nodes} end).()
{[:b, :c, :d, :e], [b: :a, c: :a, c: :b, d: :b, e: :c, e: :d]}
```

 Notice the trailing, `.()`. If this was omitted, we would get an error because we would be attempting to pass our keyword list to the result of *defining* an anonymous function. The trailing, `.()`, ensures that we *execute* our anonymous function.

We pass the keys through `Enum.uniq/1` because `Keywords.keys/1` only naively grabs the keys, regardless of whether we've seen the key before, similar to doing something like `Enum.take_every(collection, 2)`.

In the next pass, we can collect the values and produce our original structure. This will involve creating another special function that will internally map over the keys, extracting the parent(s) from the existing structure, and returning our desired structure. The function itself will look similar to the following:

```
fn({keys, nodes}) -> keys |>
                   Enum.map(fn(key) ->
                      {key, nodes |>
                          Keyword.get_values(key) |>
                          List.to_tuple} end)
   end
```

Let's append this to our stream so far:

```
iex(5)> dag |>
...(5)> Enum.map(fn({node, neighbors}) ->
...(5)> neighbors |> Tuple.to_list |> Enum.map(fn(child) -> {child, node}
end)
end) |>
...(5)> List.flatten |>
...(5)> (fn(nodes) -> {nodes |> Keyword.keys |> Enum.uniq, nodes} end).()
|>
...(5)> (fn({keys, nodes}) -> keys |>
...(5)>                       Enum.map(fn(key) ->
...(5)>                         {key, nodes |>
...(5)>                           Keyword.get_values(key) |>
...(5)>                           List.to_tuple} end)
...(5)>  end).()
[b: {:a}, c: {:a, :b}, d: {:b}, e: {:c, :d}]
```

This is the exact structure we were seeking! We could then go on to create walks, a sequence of nodes in the graph, to compute the least common ancestor between two nodes. Moreover, we could make this all a function and pass arbitrary graphs at it and see what it produces.

Put the following code in graph.exs:

```
defmodule Graph do
  def ancestors(graph) do
    graph |> Enum.map(fn({node, neighbors}) ->
      neighbors |> Tuple.to_list |> Enum.map(fn(child) -> {child, node} end)
    end) |> List.flatten |>
    (fn(nodes) -> {nodes |>
                   Keyword.keys |>
                   Enum.uniq, nodes} end).() |>
    (fn({keys, nodes}) -> keys |>
                   Enum.map(fn(key) -> {key, nodes |>
                                   Keyword.get_values(key) |>
                                     List.to_tuple} end)
    end).()
  end
end
```

Then, in an `iex` session, we can try it out:

```
iex(1)> import_file "graph.exs"
{:module, Graph,
 <<70, 79, 82, 49, 0, 0, 8, 188, 66, 69, 65, 77, 69, 120, 68, 99, 0, 0,
0, 120,
131, 104, 2, 100, 0, 14, 101, 108, 105, 120, 105, 114, 95, 100, 111, 99,
115, 95,
118, 49, 108, 0, 0, 0, 2, 104, 2, ...>>,
 {:ancestors, 1}}
iex(2)> [a: {:b, :c}, b: {:c, :d}, c: {:e}, d: {:e}, e: {}] |>
...(2)> Graph.ancestors
[b: {:a}, c: {:a, :b}, d: {:b}, e: {:c, :d}]
iex(3)> [a: {:b}, b: {:c, :d}, c: {:e}, d: {:e}, e: {:f, :g}, f: {}, g:
{}] |>
...(3)> Graph.ancestors
[b: {:a}, c: {:b}, d: {:b}, e: {:c, :d}, f: {:e}, g: {:e}]
```

To test if our function *really* works, we can pass an undirected graph, and we should receive the same graph back:

```
iex(4)> [a: {:b, :c}, b: {:a, :c}, c: {:a, :b}] |> Graph.ancestors
[b: {:a, :c}, c: {:a, :b}, a: {:b, :c}]
iex(5)> [a: {:b, :c, :d}, b: {:a, :c, :d}, c: {:a, :b, :d}, d: {:a, :b,
:c}] |>
...(5)> Graph.ancestors
[b: {:a, :c, :d}, c: {:a, :b, :d}, d: {:a, :b, :c}, a: {:b, :c, :d}]
```

And, for K_3 and K_4, we do.

We could even time the function like we did when comparing `Stream` with `Enum`:

```
iex(4)> dag = [a: {:b, :c}, b: {:c, :d}, c: {:e}, d: {:e}, e: {}]
[a: {:b, :c}, b: {:c, :d}, c: {:e}, d: {:e}, e: {}]
iex(5)> :timer.tc(Graph, :anestors, [dag])
{22, [b: {:a}, c: {:a, :b}, d: {:b}, e: {:c, :d}]}
```

Remember, `:timer.tc/3` returns *{Time, Value}* where time is measured in *microseconds*.

The syntax used for `:timer.tc/3` is a result of the new atom syntax Elixir uses. In Erlang, atoms are simply the atom, without the colon; thus, occasionally, we have some oddities to have them interoperate.

Exercises

Try:

- Using the `stream` module for our graph problem. Does it work? Try timing it; is it faster or slower?

Summary

We didn't cover as much material as we did in the previous chapter, but the power of the contents of this chapter is nothing to be underestimated.

We discussed the dictionaries of Elixir, namely, keyword lists and maps. We also discussed the general dictionary protocol.

We introduced flow-based programming or stream processing, using the |> operator. The examples used may have been slightly contrived, but the flexibility and readability afforded by the |> operator is easy to see.

In the end, we introduced graph structures and examined how we can use stream processing to collect information about the structures.

Control Flow – Occasionally You Need to Branch

We're nearly half way through the book, and we will just be getting into control statements, otherwise known as branching statements. This again speaks to the power and flexibility of pattern matching and stream processing available in Elixir. We can write a number of algorithms without even an `if then else` structure. We have programmed `quicksort`, we just recently reversed a graph structure, and we will do more without these control structures. But, occasionally, we will need a branching structure. For those situations, we will use expressions, such as `if true do "something" end`, or a number of other possibilities given to us by the branching constructs built into Elixir.

Branching with Elixir

A lot of languages have a staple in their language as the traditional branching structure, some form of "IF some condition is true THEN perform some statement ELSE do some different statement". Typically, then, `if` and `else` become *keywords* of the language; they are reserved and can only be used in the formation of branching statements.

Programming `if` condition then `else` is simply a way to express a fork in the execution path. We are saying, based on some condition, we should either execute one set of instructions or another. But as we saw before, pattern matching is quite expressive to this end. Based on structural or value matching, we can execute one version of a function, or another. What motivation, then, is there for expressions such as `if true do x = 42 end`? The expressiveness of pattern matching is occasionally too high-level when expressed in terms of functions. We need something that is closer together, but still expressively simple and easy to reason about. That is not to say pattern matching is inherently limited to use when defining functions. As we will soon see, we pattern match all the way down.

if and unless

Elixir, like other languages, has its own version of `if` and `else`. Elixir also has a logically inverted `if`: `unless`. However, these constructs in Elixir are very simple and can only test for a *single* condition; there is no way, currently, to create `if else if` chains. But this tiny limitation tends to not be an issue, as we will later see.

We've already seen a very simple example of `if`, let's look at some more. Go ahead and launch an interactive session and let's try some more `if` statements in `iex`:

```
iex(1)> x = 42
42
iex(2)> if x > 0 do
...(2)> x * -1
...(2)> end
-42
iex(3)> if 1 > 2 do
...(3)> "this won't be returned"
...(3)> end
nil
```

First, we bind the value of `x` to be `42` and then we test whether it is greater than `0`, which, of course, it is. After that, we simply express `x * -1`. The interactive shell then prints `-42`. In `(3)`, we tested whether `1` is greater than `2`, which, of course, it isn't, and the expression returns `nil`. Why?

Remember, everything is an expression, even branching statements. That is, even though we fork the execution path based on some condition, the last expression of the branch will be implicitly returned. For example, if we chain a series of expressions together, the last expression will be returned:

```
iex(4)> if true do
...(4)> x = 42
...(4)> y = x + 8
...(4)> z = x + y - 42
...(4)> z
...(4)> end
50
```

In this example, the expression is clearly the same as if we didn't use the `if` statement. However, instead of returning a value for each expression, we only return the last statement. Furthermore, the last expression inside the `if` statement is an idiomatic way of making explicit the value we are returning. Otherwise, it's completely unnecessary since the result of binding a value to a name is the value itself.

Even using `else`, the expression will return the last value of the forked path:

```
iex(5)> if false do
...(5)> "nope"
...(5)> else
...(5)> "I will be returned"
...(5)> end
"I will be returned"
```

Since the condition evaluated to `false`, we execute the expression in the `else` block, which is just returned and printed.

Since the expression must return a value, we could even pattern match on the returned expression:

```
iex(6)> 42 = if true do
...(6)> 42
...(6)> end
42
```

Since this is a trivial example, we will expand on it soon.

The `unless` is very similar to `if`. In fact, it's actually implemented as a reversed `if`. It evaluates the first block *unless* the condition is `true`; otherwise, it evaluates the second block (or `nil`):

```
iex(1)> nil = unless true do 42 end
nil
iex(2)> 42 = unless false do 42 end
42
```

Additionally, similar to `if`, `unless` *can* have an `else` block:

```
iex(1)> "true" = unless true do 42 else "true" end
"true"
iex(2)> "false" = unless false do "false" else "true" end
"false"
```

Really, using `unless` is equatable to writing `if not condition ...`:

```
iex(3) "false" = if not false do "false" else "true" end
"false"
```

Note that `(3)` is just `(2)`, except that it uses `if not ...` instead.

The new else if

Since we can't easily and reliably chain together the `if else if` expressions, we need a way to safely reason about multiple predicates and conditions. This is what `cond` allows us to do. Not only can we test multiple variables, but we can also test multiple conditions, and we can match against the first one as the order we define the conditions matters. Otherwise, `cond` is very similar to `if` and `unless`:

```
iex(1)> cond do
...(1)> 2 + 2 == 5 -> "For big values of 2"
...(1)> 2 * 2 == 3 -> "For poorly sided squares..."
...(1)> 1 + 1 == 2 -> "Math seems to work."
...(1)> end
"Math seems to work."
```

This may look similar to some C-based languages' `switch` statements. Notice, however, there is no "fall through" behaviour like the `switch` statements of C or Java:

```
iex(2)> cond do
...(2)> 2 + 2 == 5 -> "For big values of 2"
...(2)> 1 + 1 == 2 -> "Math seems to work."
...(2)> 2 * 2 == 3 -> "For poorly sided squares..."
...(2)> end
"Math seems to work."
```

Another thing to mention in regards to condition ordering is to put more generic tests *last*. Said another way, a condition that almost *always* evaluates to `true`, should either not be a condition or evaluated last in the chain as it will mask the result of the conditions below it. For a simplistic example, notice how the first statement here is the *only* thing that will ever return, always:

```
iex(3)> cond do
...(3)> true -> "Always"
...(3)> true -> "Never"
...(3)> false -> "Similarly never"
...(3)> end
"Always"
```

Thus, take care of the ordering of your conditions when writing the
cond expressions.

Although the syntax of the previous examples may seem to imply that cond can *only*
execute a single-line expression, this is not the case. We can put as many lines in the
result of a cond condition as we feel comfortable. Remember, of course, that the last
line or value will be what is returned when that path is executed:

```
iex(4)> x = 7
iex(5)> y = 2
iex(6)> cond do
...(6)> x + y > 8 ->
...(6)>     y = x - y * div(x, y)
...(6)>     x = y - x
...(6)> x - y < 0 ->
...(6)>     x = y - x * div(y, x)
...(6)>     y = x - y
...(6)> true -> "Else"
...(6)> end
0
```

The expressions are grouped together between the conditions by ->, and we can
use as many expressions as we feel comfortable reading. Another thing to note is, in
this cond expression, we have a last true condition: if no condition is met in a cond
expression, it results in an error:

```
iex(7)> cond do
...(7)> false -> "This is never returned"
...(7)> end
** (CondClauseError) no cond clause evaluated to a true value
```

Thus, it is a common practice to add the true condition as an else expression. This
way, we can handle the unmatched condition ourselves if it makes sense to do so.

Furthermore, since everything is an expression, we can bind the *result* of a cond
expression to a name:

```
iex(8)> result = cond do
...(8)> 2 + 2 == 5 -> "For large values of 2"
...(8)> 2 * 2 == 3 -> "For oddly shaped squares"
...(8)> 1 + 1 == 2 -> "Because math works"
...(8)> end
```

```
"Because math works"
iex(9)> IO.puts(result)
Because math works
:ok
```

Further still, we can also pattern match against the result of cond, similar to any use of =.

Obviously, the cond expression is useful, particularly since it allows us to test against multiple conditions, but it is actually hardly used in practice. Instead, it is much more often the case that we use case.

Elixir case expressions

The case expression is similar in structure to the cond expression, except that its behaviour is more similar to that of pattern matching. We use case to more locally test and branch different blocks of code, based on a single value. In this way, it will feel more like C or Java's switch statement.

Since case is very much like pattern matching, we can use it as if it was pattern matching:

```
iex(1)> mylist = [1, 2, 3, 4]
[1, 2, 3, 4]
iex(2)> case mylist do
...(2)> [a, 2, c, d] ->
...(2)>     "Second element is 2"
...(2)>      a + c * d - 2
...(2)> _ -> "Second element was _not_ 2"
...(2)> end
11
```

Moreover, since case is more akin to pattern matching, we use more syntax and semantics from pattern matching than conditions. That is, similar to our else statement for cond being true, for case, we use the underscore (_) for our match. This gives us the similar behaviour as an else clause for our case statements.

Here's is another example of case:

```
iex(1)> x = 1
1
iex(2)> case 10 do
```

```
...(2)> ^x -> "Won't match
...(2)> end
** (CaseClauseError) no case clause matching: 10
```

 Pattern matching is great, but what good is it if we can bind a value but never test *against* that value? Elixir gives us the ^ operator so that we can test if a *value* is equal to some *bounded* value. That is, we can execute code such as x = 1, then later somewhere test x with something like ^x = 10. If the values were the same, everything would be happy; however, in this case, we get a match error since 1 and 10 are *not* the same nor equal.

Examples using branching

Now that we have gone through some of the basic syntax and ideas of our branching structures, let's attempt some problems that use these different expressions.

FizzBuzz

Nothing is complete without "Hello, World!", nor is anything complete without some variation of the FizzBuzz problem.

The FizzBuzz problem, if you're not familiar with it, is a small problem, interview question, or small programming exercise. It asks the programmer to iterate over the numbers 1 to 100, and print Fizz if the number is divisible by 3, print *Buzz* if the number is divisible by 5, print FizzBuzz if the number is divisible by both 3 *and* 5, or simply print the number.

If you've never heard of this problem, take a moment and try it before continuing.

We are going to quickly implement this in Elixir. We'll create an EXS file, aptly named fizzbuzz.exs. In it, we will create our FizzBuzz module, and define a print/0 function to perform our task:

```
defmodule FizzBuzz do
  def print() do
    1..100 |> Enum.map(fn(x) ->
      cond do
        rem(x, 15) == 0 -> "FizzBuzz"
        rem(x, 3) == 0 -> "Fizz"
        rem(x, 5) == 0 -> "Buzz"
        true -> x
      end
```

```
      end) |> Enum.each(fn(x) -> IO.puts(x) end)
    end
  end
```

In our `print/0` function, we start a stream and map an anonymous function over it. Our anonymous function simply tests the remainder value for 15, 3, and 5, and emits the correct text for each value, or, returns the number itself. After this `map` step in the stream, we have the output we need to print. We use the `Enum.each/2` function to print the results.

> Why not use `Enum.map/2`? The critical difference between `Enum.map/2` and `Enum.each/2` is the purpose and result. `Enum.map/2` returns the result for each element in the stream, whereas `Enum.each/2` only returns `:ok`. That is, the results are discarded. This is a perfect function for printing each element as `Enum.map/2` would return `100 :ok` and we have no use for those.

Using a shell in the directory with `fizzbuzz.exs`, we can launch `iex`, import the script, and try it out:

```
$ iex
iex(1)> import_file "fizzbuzz.exs"
{:module, FizzBuzz,
 <<70, 79, 82, 49, 0, 0, 7, 36, 66, 69, 65, 77, 69, 120, 68, 99, 0,
0, 0, 94, 131, 104, 2, 100, 0, 14, 101, 108, 105, 120, 105, 114, 95,
100, 111, 99, 115, 95, 118, 49, 108, 0, 0, 0, 2, 104, 2, ...>>,
 {:print, 0}}
iex(2)> FizzBuzz.print
1
2
Fizz
4
Buzz
...
```

Mergesort

Let's start by implementing `mergesort`. As you may remember, we implemented `quicksort` in *Chapter 3, Modules and Functions – Creating Functional Building Blocks*. Mergesort is slightly different in performance bounds and implementation. Quicksort has a worst case of $O(n^2)$, whereas `mergesort` has a worse case of $O(n\ log(n))$. Moreover, `quicksort` uses partitioning, and is typically performed in place, whereas `mergesort` uses merging, and is typically not done in place.

In this example, we will create a project and do the implementation using `ExUnit`, Elixir's unit testing framework.

Start by creating the project:

```
$ mix new mergesort
* creating README.md
* creating .gitignore
* creating mix.exs
* creating config
* creating config/config.exs
* creating lib
* creating lib/mergesort.ex
* creating test
* creating test/test_helper.exs
* creating test/mergesort_test.exs


Your mix project was created successfully.
You can use mix to compile it, test it, and more:

    cd mergesort
    mix test


Run `mix help` for more commands.
```

Writing tests

In a test-driven-development fashion, we will create our tests first. If you prefer, you may skip ahead and come back and write your tests after.

We will start by opening up the `test/mergesort_test.exs` file in our favorite editor and removing the default test.

Next, we will create tests for the actual `sort/1` method. This should be easy enough. Add the following test to the `test/mergesort_test.exs` file:

```
test "test returns [] when empty" do
  assert [] == Mergesort.sort([])
end
```

Of course, this will fail when we try to run `mix` test because we have not yet defined our `sort/1` function. But before we do that, let's add another quick test:

```
test "test return sorted list when given reversed list" do
  assert [1, 2, 3, 4] == Mergesort.sort([4, 3, 2, 1])
end
```

Again, this will also fail because we have not yet defined the `sort/1` function.

There is another set of tests I would like to write before we go off to implementing `sort/1`, the tests that handle the internal `merge/2` function. This function, typically, is the most difficult to get right and is the heart of the `mergesort` algorithm. However, the test for it is mostly trivial though and could benefit from a fuzz tester or some other way of seeding the test with more data for edge case detection. Let's add the last test:

```
test "merge returns [] when given empty lists" do
  assert [] == Mergesort.merge([], [])
end

test "merge returns side when other is empty" do
  l = [1, 2, 4, 5]
  ^l = Mergesort.merge(l, [])
  ^l = Mergesort.merge([], l)
end
test "merge returns merged list" do
left = [1, 3, 5, 7]
right = [2, 4, 6, 8]
assert [1, 2, 3, 4, 5, 6, 7, 8] == Mergesort.merge(left, right)
end
```

These last three tests test our basic assumptions for the `merge/2` function. The function should return the empty list if it is given empty lists, it will return the other side if one side is empty, and finally, it should return a properly merged list if given two sorted lists.

We will later add some more tests to this file for more cases. For now, let's start implementing our `sort/1` function.

The complete file should look similar to the following code:

```
defmodule MergesortTest do
  use ExUnit.Case

  test "sort returns [] when empty" do
    assert [] == Mergesort.sort([])
  end

  test "sort returns sorted list when given reversed list" do
    assert [1, 2, 3, 4] == Mergesort.sort([4, 3, 2, 1])
  end

  test "merge returns [] when given empty lists" do
    assert [] == Mergesort.merge([], [])
  end

  test "merge returns side when other is empty" do
    l = [1, 2, 4, 5]
    ^l = Mergesort.merge(l, [])
    ^l = Mergesort.merge([], l)
  end

  test "merge returns merged list" do
    left = [1, 3, 5, 7]
    right = [2, 4, 6, 8]
    assert [1, 2, 3, 4, 5, 6, 7, 8] == Mergesort.merge(left,
right)
  end

end
```

Implementing the sort

The sort/1 function itself is actually quite easy. It's simply a recursive function that returns the merged results of each split.

Open the lib/mergesort.ex file in your favorite editor and add the following for the sort/1 function in the Mergesort module:

```
def sort(l) do
  cond do
    l == [] -> []
    length(l) <= 1 -> l
    true ->
```

```
        middle = div(length(l), 2)
        left = Enum.slice(l, 0, middle)
        right = Enum.slice(l, middle, length(l) - length(left))
        left = sort(left)
        right = sort(right)
        merge(left, right)
    end
  end
```

If the list is the empty list, return the empty list. If we are given a list with one or zero elements, return the given list. Finally, if the list has more than one element, the last case, we find the middle of the list, slice the list into a left and a right, recursively `mergesort` each half, and finally merge the result.

The last step may require some more detail. We find the middle index of the list by using the integer division function, `div/2`. Then, using the `Enum.slice/3` function, we create two sublists of the original by taking the 0th element to the middle (exclusive) and then by taking the middle (inclusive) to the end of the list. The reason we use `length(l) - length(left)` is because `Enum.slice/3` expects the third argument to be `count` or the number of elements to take. It works to use middle in the first case because the index of the middle just so happens to *also* be the number of elements we wish to include on the left-hand side of the list. The last three expressions are fairly straightforward; we sort each slice and merge the results.

This is all and good, however, this function won't compile and will not sort. We need to write our `merge/2` function. Next, let's implement the `merge/2` function:

```
def merge(left, right) do
  cond do
    left == [] -> right
    right == [] -> left
    hd(left) <= hd(right) -> [hd(left)] ++ merge(tl(left), right)
    true -> [hd(right)] ++ merge(left, tl(right))
  end
end
```

Here, we define three patterns, the first for if the first list is empty, the second for if the second list is empty, and finally, the last pattern *actually* does the merging. For the final pattern, we separate out the head and tail of each list using the heads for our comparison. In the body of the merge function, we test whether the head of the first list is less than or equal to the value of the second list. If it is, we create a new list placing the head element of the first list in the first position, and recursively calling merge on the tail of the first and second lists. And, if the head of the second list is smaller, we create a new list using the head of the second list, or progressing the same.

Thus, our `lib/mergesort.ex` module should have the following code:

```
defmodule Mergesort do
  def sort(l) do
    cond do
      l == [] -> []
      length(l) <= 1 -> l
      true ->
        middle = div(length(l), 2)
        left = Enum.slice(l, 0, middle)
        right = Enum.slice(l, middle, length(l) - length(left))
        left = sort(left)
        right = sort(right)
        merge(left, right)
    end
  end

  def merge(left, right) do
    cond do
      left == [] -> right
      right == [] -> left
      hd(left) <= hd(right) -> [hd(left)] ++ merge(tl(left),
right)
      true -> [hd(right)] ++ merge(left, tl(right))
    end
  end
end
```

Finally, we should also be able to run our tests and get some nice green tests:

```
$ mix test
Compiled lib/mergesort.ex
Generated mergesort app

.....


Finished in 0.04 seconds (0.04s on load, 0.00s on tests)
5 tests, 0 failures


Randomized with seed 226379
```

As we can see, the tests pass. Further still, we can launch `iex` and more thoroughly test our sort with some custom data:

```
$ iex -S mix
```

```
Erlang/OTP 18 [erts-7.0] [source] [64-bit] [smp:12:12] [async-
threads:10] [hipe] [kernel-poll:false]


Compiled lib/mergesort.ex

Generated mergesort app

Interactive Elixir (1.0.5) - press Ctrl+C to exit (type h() ENTER for
help)

iex(1)> list = Stream.repeatedly(fn() -> :random.uniform(20) end) |>

...(1)> Enum.take(10)

iex(2)> Mergesort.sort(list)

[1, 1, 4, 5, 6, 7, 17, 17, 17, 18]
```

Or, all together:

```
iex(3)> Stream.repeatedly(fn() -> :random.uniform(20) end) |>

...(3)> Enum.take(10) |>

...(3)> Mergesort.sort

[1, 1, 2, 8, 12, 13, 14, 18, 18, 20]
```

We use the `Stream.repeatedly/1` streamed into `Enum.take/2` to create a list of randomly-generated numbers. The `Stream.repeatedly/1` expects a single function that takes no arguments, so we curry the `:random.uniform/1` function into an anonymous function, which takes no parameters.

> The `:random.uniform/1` function is an Erlang function that we use to generate a single random integer over the range *(0,N]*, that is, from *0* exclusive to *N* inclusive.

Now, we could repeat this several times, and with varying lengths, to empirically convince ourselves that our function *actually* works. For example, let's try to sort an odd length, random list:

```
iex(4)> Stream.repeatedly(fn() -> :random.uniform(20) end) |>

...(4)> Enum.take(15) |>

...(4)> Mergesort.sort

[1, 2, 2, 6, 6, 8, 9, 12, 12, 13, 13, 14, 15, 16, 16]
```

Luckily enough for us, it works just fine with odd numbered lists.

Exception handling

You may be familiar with the concept of exceptions from other languages. Thus, you may be tempted to think of them similarly when coming to Elixir. However, like many things we have covered so far, and many things we will cover, we need to forget most what we have learned when learning most concepts of functional programming and Elixir.

Elixir offers some basic facilities for raising and catching exceptions.

First and foremost, exceptions in Elixir are *not* control flow or branching structures. Exceptions are meant strictly for exceptional behaviour, that is, things that should absolutely not happen is happening. Some examples of exceptions are database servers going down, name servers failing, or attempting to open a fixed location configuration file. However, failing to open a file whose name is given by a user is not an exception; this is entirely something we can, as programmers, anticipate failing.

This boils down to the assumptions made about a system when it is programmed, for example, fail early and fail often.

Raising exceptions

To raise exceptions in Elixir, we use the `raise/1` and `raise/2` functions.

The first function allows us to simply specify a message:

```
iex(1)> raise "Failing"
** (RuntimeError) Failing
```

The second form allows us to specify the exception type along with the message:

```
iex(2)> raise RuntimeError, "Flailing"
** (RuntimeError) Flailing
```

There are more uses of the `raise/2` function, and you should refer to the documentation on `raise` for more information.

Error, exit, and throw

In Elixir, we can raise a second type of error using `error`, `exit` and `throw`. These can all be caught and handled with the `try-catch` blocks, which we will see soon.

Handling exceptions

Elixir uses the same `try-catch` block structure found in other languages. It also includes another form called `try-rescue`. The latter form differs from the former in that exceptions catch by `try-rescue` can be used to rescue errors that occur.

The try-rescue blocks

The `try-rescue` blocks work and behave very similarly to the `try-catch` blocks. For example, we could have a block of code that attempts to divide by zero, and instead of letting the error propagate up, we could handle it locally:

```
iex(1)> try do
...(1)> 1 / 0
...(1)> rescue
...(1)> e in ArithmeticError -> e
...(1)> end
%ArithmeticError{}
```

Here, we rescue the process and print the error structure *without* exciting the child process.

The try-catch blocks

Elixir's `try-catch` blocks are similar to its `try-rescue` blocks, but they do have some subtle differences. The `try-rescue` block has the ability to rescue the error and return to the normal flow, whereas `try-catch` blocks generally perform some extra code then exit. That is, the process is not saved, but some extra code is still executed right before the process exits.

Although they are slightly different, the `try-catch` blocks still operate using a form of pattern matching. We can catch `:exit`, `:throw`, or some catch all. Here is an example that catches a `:throw` and the thrown value:

```
iex(1)> try do
...(1)> throw :fails
...(1)> catch
...(1)> :throw, value -> IO.puts :stderr, "Failure in above code:
#{inspect value}"
...(1)> end
Failure in above code
:ok
```

Similarly, we can `catch` and `exit` as well:

```
iex(2)> try do
...(2)> exit :oops
...(2)> catch
...(2)> :exit, code -> IO.puts :stderr, "Exited: #{inspect code}"
...(2)> end
Exited: :oops
:ok
```

We can also use the Erlang `error/1` function with Elixir's `try-catch`:

```
iex(3)> try do
...(3)> :erlang.error "More oops"
...(3)> catch
...(3)> error -> IO.puts :stderr, "Error received: #{inspect error}"
...(3)> end
Error received: More oops
:ok
```

> In all three cases, the child process is closed. We don't see
> this in an interactive session because the failed processes are
> immediately restarted. Note that if an error is thrown, the
> interactive session restarts with the same number as the line
> that threw the error.

Similarly to other languages, with the `try-catch` blocks, if there is no associated `catch` for specific errors, the raise propagates up:

```
iex(4)> try do
...(4)> throw "oops"
...(4)> catch
...(4)> :exit, code -> IO.puts :stderr, "Exit received #{inspect
code}"
...(4)> end
** (throw) "oops"
```

Since there is no pattern in the `catch` that matches `:throw`, `value` or `_`, the thrown value propagates past the `catch` and is caught by the supervising process.

Using exceptions

There are a few situations where it is necessary to actually raise exceptions; otherwise, we should allow errors to propagate to the controlling process (you will learn more about processes in the next chapter). For example, failing to open a file that we expect to always be available for reading would be an exception and we should raise it as such.

Opening files

Firstly, let's consider how we perform file operations and what the results of those operations are.

Elixir provides the `File` module that we can use to open, read, write, and close files.

Let's say we have a file in our current working directory called `hello.txt` with the following content:

```
Hello, World!
```

We could open and read this file with the following:

```
iex(1)> {:ok, hello} = File.open "hello.txt"
{:ok, #PID<0.74.0>}
iex(2)> IO.read(hello, :all)
"Hello, World!\n"
iex(3)> :ok = File.close hello
:ok
```

Or, we could do all of those steps with the convenience function, `File.read/1`:

```
iex(4)> {:ok, contents} = File.read "hello.txt"
{:ok, "Hello, World!\n"}
```

Either of these blocks allows us to open, read the entire contents of the file, and close the file. Which we prefer is usually a matter of flexibility and control. With `IO.read/2`, we have more control with *how* the file is read than we do with `File.read/1`. However, the first example requires more steps, whereas `File.read/1` does and abstracts those steps for us.

Now, what happens when we fail to open a file? Or, what happens when we try to open a file that does not exist? Let's try it:

```
iex(1)> File.open "some_file_that_does_not_exist.txt"
{:error, :enoent}
```

We get a tuple back, but the first element is :error and the second is :enoent. Clearly, this isn't a good result, but it takes some references or good memory to know what the :enoent atom symbolizes. As we might expect though, :enoent means one of these three things: the path isn't found, the file isn't found, or there are no more files. To find these symbols, you may occasionally need to look into the Erlang documentation.

Now that we know some basics of opening files, we will see how we can use the results to do different things.

We can use the case expression from earlier in the chapter to do different things, depending on the success or failure of a file read operation:

```
iex(1)> file_name = "some_file_that_does_not_exist.txt"
iex(2)> case File.read file_name do
...(2)> {:ok, contents} -> IO.puts contents
...(2)> {:error, reason} -> IO.puts :stderr, "Couldn't open file
#{file_name} because: #{reason}"
...(2)> end
Couldn't open file some_file_that_does_not_exist.txt because: enoent
:ok
```

Here, we try to read a file that doesn't exist. If the file did exist, the {:ok, contents} tuple would match, and we would have printed the contents to :stdout (the default device for IO.puts/1). Since the file *doesn't* exist, we match the tuple, {:error, reason}, and the result being we print an error message to :stderr and provide the reason.

 Notably, this is an awful error message to present to the user unless that user is comfortable with Erlang/Elixir. User messages should be more friendly than this!

However, if we assume the file will *always* be available, we could rewrite the preceding code using a raise/1 call instead:

```
iex(3)> case File.open "config_file" do
...(3)> {:ok, config_file} -> parse_config(config_file)
...(3)> {:error, reason} -> raise "Failed to open config file:
#{reason}"
...(3)> end
** (RuntimeError) Failed to open config file: enoent
```

We do the same thing as earlier; we attempt to open and parse a configuration file; however, if the file fails to be opened via `File.open/1`, we raise an exception with the reason.

Another option is to allow Elixir to raise the exception for us, that is, to raise a match error:

```
iex(4)> {:ok, config_file} = File.open("config_file")
** (MatchError) no match of right hand side value: {:error, :enoent}
```

Although, this method isn't always the easiest to debug, it is usually sufficient for a while. But there's a better option—`File.open!`. The trailing, `!`, is an Elixir convention that denotes that the function will raise an exception on error instead of returning the tuple, `{:error, reason}`:

```
iex(5)> config_file = File.open!("config_file")
** (File.Error) could not open config_file: no such file or directory
    (elixir) lib/file.ex:969: File.open!/2
```

This way, we don't have to do anything special *and* we get a good error message.

Exceptions recap

Although exceptions and the use of `try-catch` and `try-rescue` can be used to do *some* code branching, these are not strictly code branching constructs. Here, in fact, the few sections about catching and handling exceptions should be ignored. It is the philosophy of Elixir to treat errors literally. Most often, the function in Elixir's standard library and the code you write will return a tuple with the first element being `:ok` or `:error` and the value or the reason, respectively. It will be up to you, the programmer, and the assumptions of your system to decide whether an `:error` is truly exceptional. Beyond that, we will extensively use pattern matching or `!` functions to raise and propagate errors to control processes.

We will see in *Chapter 7, OTP – A Poor Name for a Rich Framework*, how we gracefully handle propagated exceptions and how this enables us better stability through the system.

Determinism

There is a lot of emphasis on the results of these branching expressions returning a value. This is a natural result of Elixir's functional nature.

Like with functions, we can more easily grok and reason about branching code if the code itself is deterministic. If it always returns a result, the branches are tractable. Our mental compilers are able to trace the code and see the result without much extra thought.

The branching examples we have done don't nest either. This arises because it is often unnecessary in functional languages to nest conditions. The syntax often lends itself to allow a single level of branching. If there's more branching, it's in another function, or implicit with pattern matching, or both; we only mentally page the branch depth that we need.

Mental easiness aside, there is also a technical reason for branch determinism in Elixir.

To more easily explain this technical aspect, let's look at another, very common, runtime environment—the **Java Virtual Machine** (**JVM**). Java's branching expressions are not inherently deterministic; they may never return a result or exit. Furthermore, an `if then else` clause in Java doesn't inherently return a result either. These expressions, quite literally, fork the execution path. However, the JVM does something to improve performance around these execution paths—it can and will assume certain paths are the *only* path of execution.

An execution path in the JVM that is common and highly exercised is one that the JVM will optimize by flattening the instructions and taking a shortcut around the expressions that branch the code. However, this optimization isn't free. If the path it assumes is *incorrect*, the JVM must backtrack its assumptions and go forward, unoptimized. This is called a **branch miss** (prediction), and they are often very expensive.

The **Erlang Runtime System** (**ERTS**) does not inherently use this optimization. Instead, it sacrifices this speed boost for safety guaranteed by the type system and runtime. ERTS will *never* branch miss; it simply cannot.

 That is not to say ERTS cannot have better performance either, though. The **High Performance Erlang** (**HiPE**) extension will compile certain modules and functions to native code ahead of time.

To enable the ERTS to never branch miss, the code it executes has to be correct and deterministic. The assumption that all the paths of execution lead to a result that enables the compiler and runtime system to be better equipped for ahead of time optimizations and ensures both that the code is correct and will not lead to a failed branch. That is, we can have the compiler tell us about bugs before we execute them while the code executed is still performant.

References

Comparison of ERTS and JVM (`http://ds.cs.ut.ee/courses/course-files/To303nis%20Pool%20.pdf`).

Exercises

Do:

- Write a test for odd length lists.
- Practice our pattern matching and rewrite our `mergesort` to use pattern matching.
- Rewrite our `quicksort` example from *Chapter 3, Modules and Functions – Creating Functional Building Blocks*, using `if`, `case`, and `cond`.
- Advanced: Write a test for our `mergesort` that uses our `Stream.repeatedly...` pipe and `Enum.sort/1` to make sure our `mergesort` really, *really* works. The result of this would be a step in the right direction for fuzz testing.

Summary

In this chapter, we discussed the branching semantics provided to us by Elixir. We went through examples using `if else`, `unless`, `case`, and `cond`.

We briefly discussed Elixir's exception facilities and how infrequently they should be used.

Furthermore, we looked at the deterministic nature of the Erlang runtime and how branches in Elixir, too, must return values.

6

Concurrent Programming – Using Processes to Conquer Concurrency

We have gone through most of the basic syntax of Elixir; we covered modules, functions, types, branching, recursion, and pattern matching. If that's all there was, we would be done. We would know enough of the language to be able to do most things, although, not very elegantly, but we would be finished. However, there is another world emerging, and it has been emerging for some time now—concurrent processing.

Chip manufacturers are no longer focusing on how frequent we can make a chip cycle (hertz, now measured on the Giga scale), they are more interested in how many *cores* we can put onto a chip. Dual core chips weren't common 12 years ago, but now, we are looking at machines with 4, 8, and even 12 cores, being common among desktops and laptops. These core counts were usually only available in high-end servers, but are now the norm, even for phones!

But this is where our problem as developers appears—current languages are designed, usually, with a single thread, a single path, and a singular context of execution. Most languages don't expose good facilities for utilizing multiple cores well, and this is where the ERTS and Erlang/Elixir really set themselves apart. Concurrency is cooked into the language; it was and is the first constraint of the language. If it doesn't handle concurrency well, the language has failed.

Thus, we start our journey into the workings of concurrent processing with Elixir. Over the next three chapters, we are going to cover the basics of concurrent processing, process execution in Elixir, the available abstractions Erlang/Elixir provide, and distribution.

Parallel computation and concurrent computation

These two concepts are often confounded and otherwise used interchangeably (this book even does it!). But this is a mistake; they are different, although subtly, but it is an important distinction.

I'll use the word *context* to talk about threads or processes. These are, obviously, not the same thing, but they do share in concept with respect to parallel versus concurrent.

Parallel processing is simply the execution of two or more contexts *simultaneously*. Visually, this may look similar to the following diagram:

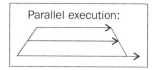

The contexts are executing at the same time, there is no switching or other interruptions between the execution.

Concurrent processing is subtly different. It can appear to be parallel, and in fact, *be* parallel, but there is no guarantee that it *actually* is parallel. For example, two contexts could be attempting to execute, but contend the CPU. The scheduler is then executing between the two, based on some criterion (cache miss, deadline priorities, branch miss, and others). We can see a similar visual representation of concurrent execution in the following diagram:

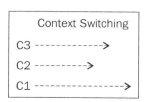

In concurrent execution, processing appears parallel, but the CPU may, in fact, be rapidly switching between the tasks.

A single core machine running multiple processes is a great example of concurrent execution at work. Each process *appears* to be computed simultaneously, but is, in fact, being interrupted, suspended, and resumed multiple times, even thousands of times a second.

When we add cores to this hypothetical machine, the machine is able to execute more processes in parallel, but it is still doing thousands of things concurrently.

Erlang processes and OS processes

When discussing processes in the context of Erlang, we are usually referring to Erlang processes and not OS processes. There is a subtle but very important distinction between the two. OS processes are scheduled and controlled by, well, the operating system, or more correctly, the kernel. The kernel is tasked with queuing, dequeuing, marshalling data, memory allocation, and many other tasks required for smooth process execution. Erlang processes, on the other hand, are processes local to the Erlang VM (BEAM). ERTS is the proverbial kernel in this regard. It is in charge of the scheduling and management of these processes.

Another important distinction between these two is a question of weight. Typically, when thinking of OS processes, these are heavy, clunky objects to deal with, and forget about inter-process communication. Erlang processes are, in contrast, extremely lightweight. In fact, it is not uncommon for a single Erlang VM to have many thousands to millions of processes running at once.

Parallel map

Let's take a look at a small example to show the featherweight of Erlang processes. We implemented map a hundred times, so this will appear to be very similar, but with one major difference; we will compute the map in parallel.

We will create a module and define a function, pmap/2:

```
defmodule MyMap do
  def pmap(collection, f) do
    collection |>
    Enum.map(&(Task.async(fn -> f.(&1) end))) |>
    Enum.map(&Task.await/1)
  end
end
```

We are taking some shortcuts, but this gives us a parallel mapping function. We take the collection, pass it to `Enum.map/2` with a wrapped `Task.async/1` function. Finally, we wait for the entire collection to finish and that is the result returned to the caller.

We can execute this inside an interactive session:

```
iex(1)> import_file "pmap.exs"
{:module, MyMap,
 <<70, 79, 82, 49, 0, 0, 6, 64, 66, 69, 65, 77, 69, 120, 68, 99, 0,
0, 0, 133, 131, 104, 2, 100, 0, 14, 101, 108, 105, 120, 105, 114, 95,
100, 111, 99, 115, 95, 118, 49, 108, 0, 0, 0, 2, 104, 2, ...>>,
 {:pmap, 2}}
iex(2)> MyMap.pmap(1..10000, &(&1 * &1))
[1, 4, 9, 16, 25, 36, 49, 64, 81, 100, 121, 144, 169, 196, 225, 256,
289, 324,
 361, 400, 441, 484, 529, 576, 625, 676, 729, 784, 841, 900, 961,
1024, 1089,
 1156, 1225, 1296, 1369, 1444, 1521, 1600, 1681, 1764, 1849, 1936,
2025, 2116,
 2209, 2304, 2401, 2500, ...]
```

After importing our module, we get the first 10,000 squares. Amazingly, this happens so fast, and we don't notice that we actually just launched *10,000* processes and used all of the cores in our machine. We will do more expensive work and watch it pin the cores in a bit.

Basics of Elixir process

Elixir processes are self-contained abstractions. The context of each process is isolated from the contexts of other processes. Messages are required to share information between the processes. This is considered the actor-model. Each process is an actor, capable of sending and receiving messages from other actors. Based on the contents of a message, an actor may perform certain actions. This is the foundation of Elixir processes: self-contained actors operate on information sent to them, and the result is often sent back to the calling process.

Of course, if that's all there was to it, we would be essentially done. But concurrent programming is never that simple.

There are several functions automatically available to most Elixir modules and inside an `iex` session, and these will be the majority of the discussion of this chapter.

Self

We have seen process identifiers before, but now it's time to explain the numbers involved with the numbers shown.

If we start an interactive session and type `self`, we will get some response that may look similar to the following:

```
iex(1)> self
#PID<0.60.0>
```

The response to the `self/0` function is a process identifier. This is the identity of the current process (the REPL, in this case). The numbers in the identifier are the process address. The first number, `0` in this case, tells us the Erlang node the process exists on. We will discuss Erlang nodes in *Chapter 8, Distributed Elixir – Taking Concurrency to the Next Node*, but for now, this will always be 0, the special address for the local node. The second number, `60`, in this case, is the first 15 bits of the process number, part of the process index. Finally, the last number, `0`, in this case, is the rest of the process index address, typically 16-18 bits. These three numbers give us the full address to any process. We can use this reference identifier as an address to send messages.

Sending messages

Intuitively, we can use the `send/2` message to send messages between the processes. For now, we can send messages to ourselves to be later received:

```
iex(1)> me = self
#PID<0.60.0>
iex(2)> send me, :ping
:ping
```

We created a reference to ourselves, called it `me`, and then we sent a `:ping` atom to ourselves using `send/2`. The `:ping` atom that is returned is simply the message of `send/2` being evaluated locally. We are not sending computation, we are sending the result of some computation.

Sending messages turns out to be very easy. Receiving messages is generally easy, but there are cases to look out for.

Receiving messages

To receive the message we sent ourselves, we need to use the `receive` block. Perhaps unsurprisingly, the `receive` block may feel like a special form of case, where the variable being matched against is sent from another process (or ourselves!). Let's receive our ping:

```
iex(3)> receive do
...(3)> x -> IO.puts("#{inspect x}")
...(3)> end
:ping
:ok
```

We receive the atom, `:ping`, and the expression of printing the atom returns `:ok`. This is pattern matching showing its beautiful self again. However, in this case, if any other process sent another message *before* we sent `:ping`, we would receive that message first. The message is simply queued.

Sending a message to a process doesn't interfere with the process it is sent to, it is placed in that process' message queue. There, the message will sit until the process decides to check its queue. If the receiving process never checks the queue and many messages are sent, the process can and will crash because messages take space, the space that is never reclaimed during the process' lifetime. The size of the message queue is fairly large and the number of messages allowed to be queued does depend on the size of each message as well.

Since we can queue a number of messages before receiving them, we can create a process that talks to itself:

```
iex(4)> 1..5 |> Enum.map(&(send(me, &1 * &1)))
[1, 4, 9, 16, 25]
iex(5)> receive do
...(5)> x -> x
...(5)> end
1
```

Here, we sent the first five squares to ourselves and we received the first one. We can keep going and retrieve the next four squares; however, this gets incredibly tedious in its current form. Thus, the `flush/0` helper function may be very useful when testing message passing in the interactive session. We can dump the rest of the messages in the current process mailbox:

```
iex(6)> flush()
4
```

```
9
16
25
:ok
```

Plus, a process that is able to talk to itself via `send/2` and `receive` isn't terribly exciting. Let's look at creating our own processes!

Spawn

The Elixir `Kernel` module provides us with the `spawn/1` and `spawn/3` functions for creating processes. These can be used to create separate processes that compute some result and send back the result, or really, can perform any sort of work we can imagine.

The `spawn/1` function takes a 0 argument function and executes the function inside a new process:

```
iex(7)> spawn fn -> 6 * 7 end
#PID<0.95.0>
```

Notice that the process identifier of the new process is returned, not the result of the computation. Furthermore, using the `Process.alive?/1` function, we can see that the process is actually dead:

```
iex(8)> pid = spawn fn -> 6 * 7 end
#PID<0.97.0>
iex(9)> Process.alive?(pid)
false
```

The process exits as soon as the function returns. The spawned process has nothing left to do; the result is dropped and the process and its context is marked for cleanup and is discarded. If a process exits for a non-normal reason, an error is raised, for example, it does not affect or notify the parent process:

```
iex(10)> spawn fn -> raise :oops end
23:45:55.643 [error] Process #PID<0.102.0> raised an exception
** (RuntimeError) oops
    :erlang.apply/2
```

The message is logged and life goes on.

If we want the result of a spawned process, we will need to tell the process to send it back when it's done computing it:

```
iex(1)> parent = self()
#PID<0.60.0>
iex(2)> spawn fn -> send(parent, 6 * 7) end
#PID<0.63.0>
iex(3)> receive do
...(3)> x -> IO.puts("#{inspect x}")
...(3)> end
42
:ok
```

We create a reference to the parent (current) process, and we spawn a new process that sends the result of 6 * 7 to the parent process. Notice that we can't use self/0 in-line here because it would be evaluated to a *different* process ID if we did. Finally, from the parent, we receive the result and print it to standard out.

Again, these sort of manual steps of sending messages between the processes is tedious and unwieldy though. Thus, we use the spawn/3 function.

Both spawn/1 and spawn/3 are in-lined by the compiler. Furthermore, Erlang only has a spawn/3 function, and the parameters to Elixir's spawn/3 are the same for Erlang; and it was done this way for consistency between the languages.

The spawn/3 function requires us to specify the function in the older Erlang syntax, but allows us to better create the processes that do more useful computations.

The older Erlang syntax is to specify the module, function, and arguments, even if none, in the form of a triple. That is, if we wanted to launch the do_work/0 function of the Worker module, we would pass the following to spawn/3:

```
spawn(Worker, :do_work, [])
```

Fortunately, this is consistent throughout the spawning functions.

Let's actually create the Worker module and have it compute our squares for us.

In a file, worker.exs, we can define the following module and single function:

```
defmodule Worker do
  def do_work() do
    receive do
```

```
        {:compute, x, pid} ->
            send pid, {:result, x * x}
      end
      do_work()
    end
  end
```

Our function is relatively uninteresting, but we are more interested in the basic structure for the moment.

Once started, our function waits for a message in the form of a triple, {:compute, x, pid}, where :compute tags the message, x is the number we wish to square, and pid is the sending process ID to send the return result. Once this process receives a triple, it sends the result to the calling process and launches into an infinite loop.

Tagging messages is common practice so that we can easily distinguish the message, how to parse, what action to perform, and others.

Infinitely looping like this is actually more common than you might think. Many languages and frameworks behave this way. Elixir, however, makes this explicit to the programmer.

In an interactive session, we can import the module and spawn it in another thread:

```
iex(1)> import_file "worker.exs"
{:module, Worker,
 <<70, 79, 82, 49, 0, 0, 5, 52, 66, 69, 65, 77, 69, 120, 68, 99, 0,
0, 0, 96, 131, 104, 2, 100, 0, 14, 101, 108, 105, 120, 105, 114, 95,
100, 111, 99, 115, 95, 118, 49, 108, 0, 0, 0, 2, 104, 2, ...>>,
 {:do_work, 0}}
iex(2)> pid = spawn(Worker, :do_work, [])
#PID<0.67.0>
iex(3)> Process.alive?(pid)
true
```

Our worker process is waiting for another process to provide it work; let's give it something to do:

```
iex(4)> send pid, {:compute, 4, self()}
{:compute, 4, #PID<0.60.0>}
```

We should now have the result in our inbox:

```
iex(5)> flush()
{:result, 16}
:ok
```

Furthermore, checking to see if our worker process is still alive should yield that it is in fact still running and should still be accepting more work:

```
iex(6)> Process.alive?(pid)
true
iex(7)> send(pid, {:compute, 16, self()})
{:compute, 16, #PID<0.67.0>}
iex(8)> flush()
{:result, 256}
:ok
```

The `Worker` module isn't very resilient, though. It's trivial to think of an example that will bring it down:

```
iex(9)> send(pid, {:compute, "square this", self()})
{:compute, "square this", self(
17:42:10.396 [error] Process #PID<0.67.0> raised an exception
** (ArithmeticError) bad argument in arithmetic expression
    iex:6: Worker.do_work/0

iex(10)> Process.alive?(pid)
false
```

In this case, we might actually want to be notified that the process exited so that we know not to attempt to send messages to it or to resurrect it before sending more messages. We could spend some time thinking of a way to do this with just `spawn/3` or we could look at `spawn_link/3`, which solves this problem for us.

Process links

Process links create relationships between the processes and enable another channel of communication to be used between the two. The channel allows processes to be signaled when another process dies. It might not be obvious that cascading process death would be useful, but it turns out to be very useful, especially with respect to the fail-fast philosophy.

For complicated systems, there will be many processes working together to model and compose the system. Many of these processes will be interrelated and possibly codependent on each other for results. When a process dies, because there is no longer a question of if, the programmer will have to make a decision: should the programmer attempt to conceive of all the possibilities and state when a process dies, or kill all the dependent processes and restart the failed processes in a clean state?

The former strategy is an alluring trap and often chosen for naive reasons such as the number of failure cases is thought to be small or that certain things, for, example, hardware failure or some other seemingly uncommon cause, will never happen. However, many of these reasons for choosing this route are based on assumptions that are, at best, misguided.

The overall design of the system becomes easier when the assumptions are limited, and the steps to take on failure are clear. That is, the system becomes easier to reason about, and when the assumptions are limited and clear, the failures explicit.

Process links serve the purpose of enabling the cascading failure of dependent or downstream processes when an upstream process fails. What to do *after* this has happened will be the topic of monitoring processes and part of the next chapter.

Spawning with links

Instead of spawning a child process and *then* adding a link between the parent process and the child process, we could spawn the child process *with* the link already established. This is accomplished with spawn_link/1 and spawn_link/3.

Using spawn_link/1 in place of spawn/1 works the same as you expect; in fact, they are no different if we use the same example as well:

```
iex(1)> spawn_link fn -> 6 * 7 end
#PID<0.62.0>
```

However, the difference of creating a link right away is that the parent process is notified if the child process fails during its startup steps. For example, if we spawn a child process that immediately fails, the error is propagated correctly to the parent process:

```
iex(2)> spawn_link fn -> raise "failing" end
#PID<0.62.0>
iex(2)> spawn_link fn -> raise "failing" end
** (EXIT from #PID<0.60.0>) an exception was raised:
    ** (RuntimeError) failing
        :erlang.apply/2
```

```
Interactive Elixir (1.0.5) - press Ctrl+C to exit (type h() ENTER for
help)


23:34:05.758 [error] Process #PID<0.64.0> raised an exception
** (RuntimeError) failing
    :erlang.apply/2


iex(1)>
```

 Note that your output order may differ.

A linked process doesn't always kill the parent, however. The propagation of the errors is related to the *reason* the child processing is terminating.

For example, we can create a more robust version of our worker process from the last section to also receive the `exit` signals. The new version might look similar to the following code:

```
defmodule Worker do
  def do_work() do
    receive do
      {:compute, x, pid} ->
        send pid, {:result, x * x}
      {:exit, reason} ->
        exit(reason)
    end
    do_work()
  end
end
```

Save the preceding code in either a new version of `worker.exs` or the same version as earlier. Then, we could import and spawn it in an interactive session:

```
iex(1)> import_file "worker.exs"
{:module, Worker,
 <<70, 79, 82, 49, 0, 0, 5, 160, 66, 69, 65, 77, 69, 120, 68, 99, 0,
0, 0, 96, 131, 104, 2, 100, 0, 14, 101, 108, 105, 120, 105, 114, 95,
100, 111, 99, 115, 95, 118, 49, 108, 0, 0, 0, 2, 104, 2, ...>>,
 {:do_work, 0}}
```

We will be using the `spawn_link/3` function instead of `spawn_link/1`. The former requires the same syntax as `spawn/3`, so there is nothing surprising about the next line of code:

```
iex(2)> pid = spawn_link Worker, :do_work, []
#PID<0.67.0>
```

Of course, we can still send work to the process using the usual message:

```
iex(3)> send pid, {:compute, 4, self}
{:compute, 4, #PID<0.60.0>}
iex(4)> flush
{:result, 16}
:ok
```

But we can also kill the process without causing a failure in the parent process:

```
iex(5)> Process.alive?(pid)
true
iex(6)> send pid, {:exit, :normal}
{:exit, :normal}
iex(7)> Process.alive?(pid)
false
```

The child process was running and then we sent the `exit` signal. After that, the child process was no longer running and the parent process was left unaffected. However, we could have sent a strong `exit` signal since we are requesting the reason for exiting, and therefore, such a reason can bubble up to the parent process. There are two standard exit reasons in Elixir, `:normal` and `:kill`. Any other atom can also be used, and there are few processing rules for how they are handled. For more information on this, see the help of `Process.exit/2`.

Process monitor

Process monitoring is slightly different from process links, but are fairly similar. Monitors are special, stackable, and unidirectional links.

Links were bidirectional and facilitated the cascading death of many processes. Two processes where the failure of one makes the other useless is a great example of where using a process link is ideal. However, maybe a process simply needs to know the state of another process and not necessarily the other way around. Furthermore, since monitors are stackable, removing a monitor doesn't remove *all* of the other monitors. Unlinking two or more processes will do exactly this; it will remove every link, in a cascade, ruining the assumptions the links provide.

This is exactly where process monitors stand apart from process links. They enable the monitoring process to receive messages about the state of the monitored process. To accomplish this, we use `spawn_monitor/1` and `spawn_monitor/3`. These work exactly as you might expect, same as `spawn` and `spawn_link`. However, instead of simply returning the PID of the child process, they return an atom of the child PID and the reference to the monitor. The monitor reference can be used for removing the monitor, if need be:

```
iex(1)> {pid, _} = spawn_monitor(fn -> :timer.sleep(500) end)
{#PID<0.64.0>, #Reference<0.0.3.82>}
iex(2)> Process.alive?(pid)
false
iex(3)> flush
{:DOWN, #Reference<0.0.3.82>, :process, #PID<0.64.0>, :normal}
:ok
```

Using a process monitor is very similar to using a link, however. Instead of a process failure or normal termination resulting in a cascading termination of processes, the monitoring process receives a regular message in its inbox about the death of the monitored process. The monitoring process can receive this message and is given the opportunity to perform some action, based on the receipt of these messages.

Storing state inside processes

Elixir processes are great. Well, they are great, so far, as long as you don't need them to remember anything. This quickly becomes a problem when we attempt to extend the uses of the Elixir processes and we need a way for a process to remember or store data.

It turns out, though, this is relatively easy to solve with `spawn/3` and friends. The third argument of the three arity versions could be considered the initial state of the process. The process, then, could begin running using its initial state. Then the question becomes, how does it update its state? Elixir data is immutable, so how does the process modify this data? The answer is in the tail-recursive infinite loop. In each invocation of the loop, the state of the process is passed, with changes and all, to itself.

Let's create a simple key-value storage process to demonstrate this. The overall design will be a module that accepts the `:put` and `:get` messages:

```
defmodule KV do

  def start_link do
    spawn_link(fn -> loop(%{}) end)
```

```
    end

    defp loop(map) do
      receive do
        {:put, key, value, sender} ->
          new_map = Map.put(map, key, value)
          send sender, :ok
          loop(new_map)
        {:get, key, sender} ->
          send sender, Map.get(map, key)
          loop map
      end
    end
  end
```

The start_link function is a convenience function for spawning our KV process; it simply starts the looping portion with an initially empty map. The preceding receive do loop is fairly straightforward. We match against two different kinds of messages, :put and :get. If we are given a :put message, we update the map (our internal state) with the new key using the Map.put/3 function and then we send the calling process, the :ok message. Finally, we recurse using the updated map. If we are given a :get message, we send the value, or more precisely, the result of Map.get/2 to the calling process and loop with the existing map.

Save the module definition to a file and let's try it out in an interactive session:

```
iex(1)> import_file "kv.exs"
{:module, KV,
 <<70, 79, 82, 49, 0, 0, 7, 16, 66, 69, 65, 77, 69, 120, 68, 99, 0, 0, 0,
 99, 131, 104, 2, 100, 0, 14, 101, 108, 105, 120, 105, 114, 95, 100, 111,
 99, 115, 95, 118, 49, 108, 0, 0, 0, 2, 104, 2, ...>>,
 {:loop, 1}}
iex(2)> pid = KV.start_link
#PID<0.73.0>
iex(3)> send pid, {:get, :a, self}
{:get, :a, #PID<0.62.0>}
iex(4)> flush
nil
:ok
```

Of course, since the map is initially empty, our use of the `:get` message returns `nil`. But, at least it doesn't crash the KV store. Let's add something and attempt to retrieve it again:

```
iex(5)> send pid, {:put, :a, 42, self}
{:put, :a, 42, #PID<0.60.0>}
iex(6)> send pid, {:get, :a, self}
{:get, :a, #PID<0.60.0>}
iex(7)> flush
:ok
42
:ok
```

 Remember that the final `:ok` in `flush/0` is the return value of `flush/0`, and not part of the messages returned from the message queue.

After inserting a key into the KV store, we are able to retrieve it as well.

This is an essential pattern for state in processes. We have some map structure and the process will store data. Modifications to this structure are persisted by passing the new version into the loop. We will, in fact, see this pattern in the next chapter as well.

Naming processes

After a while of using process IDs, the requirement to have the PID reference becomes overbearingly tedious. Thus, there is a simpler mechanism for referencing a process if desired—process registration. Instead of referring to the process by the PID reference object, we can register an atom to use for the process ID.

For example, using our key-value store from the previous section, we can register the PID for the process and then refer to it by the atom for all the messages. This is accomplished with the `Process.register/2` function:

```
iex(1)> import_file "kv.exs"
...
iex(2)> pid = KV.start_link
#PID<0.62.0>
iex(3)> Process.register(pid, :kv)
true
```

Now, we can use `send/2` just the same, but instead of passing `pid`, we will pass `:kv`:

```
iex(4)> send :kv, {:put, :a, 42, self}
{:put, :a, 42, #PID<0.60.0>}
iex(5)> flush
:ok
:ok
iex(6)> send :kv, {:get, :a, self}
{:get, :a, #PID<0.60.0>}
iex(7)> flush
42
:ok
```

The code here is the same as before; we are just using the `:kv` process name to reference the running KV store instead of the raw process ID.

Process module

We have used a few functions already from the `Process` module, namely, `Process. alive?/1` and `Process.register/2`. But there are many more, very useful functions in the `Process` module. I highly recommend going through some of the functions in this module.

Applications

Now that we have most of the basics of processes in Elixir, let's try out some examples and applications.

There will be a progression through these examples. We will start pretty small and grow in complexity.

Ping pong

Let's start with a very basic example where one process sends a `:ping` message to another process. The receiving process will send a `:pong` message in response.

We will start with a module that looks very similar to the module we created for storing state in a process, except that we have no need for state, this module will only listen for the `:ping` messages and return `:pong`:

```
defmodule PingPong do
```

```
def start_link do
  spawn_link(fn -> loop() end)
end

defp loop do
  receive do
    {:ping, sender} ->
      send sender, {:pong, self}
  end
  loop
end
end
```

We start with the `start_link/0` function that spawns a new process context and kicks off our internal loop. From the loop, we block with the `receive do` expression. Once the process receives a `:ping` message, it sends back the `:pong` message to the caller. Once this is all complete, it recurses into itself, waiting for the next `:ping` message.

We can load this module up into an interactive session and send it a message to try it out:

```
iex(1)> import_file "pingpong.exs"
{:module, PingPong,
 <<70, 79, 82, 49, 0, 0, 7, 196, 66, 69, 65, 77, 69, 120, 68, 99, 0, 0,
0, 99, 131, 104, 2, 100, 0, 14, 101, 108, 105, 120, 105, 114, 95, 100,
111, 99, 115, 95, 118, 49, 108, 0, 0, 0, 2, 104, 2, ...>>,
 {:loop, 0}}
iex(2)> pid = PingPong.start_link
#PID<0.70.0>
iex(3)> send pid, {:ping, self}
{:ping, #PID<0.60.0>
iex(4)> flush
{:pong, #PID<0.70.0>}
:ok
```

So far, this example is fairly uninteresting. We are only able to interact with it via the interactive prompt and it's not terribly exciting as we have already done a lot of this, for example, this is a simpler version of the `Worker` module from before.

Let's make it more interesting by adding state and making it more like a heartbeat process.

Heartbeats, in terms of distributed computing, are the concept of pinging or monitoring a process or machine. If the machine does not respond in an acceptable interval, the process or machine is considered dead.

We will develop this version of our `HeartMonitor` module in stages. We will start with defining the messages the `HeartMonitor` process should be listening for, for example, we should definitely receive and handle the `:pong` messages. Another message that should certainly be handled is a message for adding, and, related to it, a message for removing monitors. We should also consider a message for peering into the current monitors, so let's also add a message for `:list_monitors`. Related to listing the current monitors, users of the heartbeat monitor may be curious of what processes are alive and similarly what processes are dead, so we can add patterns for those messages as well. That certainly should be enough messages for a simple heartbeat monitor.

So, we have the following for our internal loop:

```
defp loop(state) do
  receive do
    {:pong, sender} ->
      loop(handle_pong(sender, state))
    {:monitor, pid} ->
      loop(%{state | :monitors => [pid] ++ state.monitors})
    {:demonitor, pid} ->
      loop(%{state | :monitors => state.monitors -- [pid]})
    {:list_monitors, sender} ->
      send sender, {:reply, state.monitors}
      loop(state)
    {:list_alive, sender} ->
      send sender, {:reply, state.alive}
      loop(state)
    {:list_dead, sender} ->
      send sender, {:reply, state.dead}
      loop(state)
  end
end
```

For the `:pong` message, we loop with the result of calling another internal function, `handle_pong`, a function we will get to soon.

When we receive a `:monitor` message, we add the passed `pid` to our internal list of monitors. Similarly, receiving a `:demonitor` message, we remove the given `pid` from our list of monitors.

Finally, all of the `:list_` messages respond to the calling process with the requested list in a `{:reply, list}` tuple.

Moving to the `handle_pong/2` function, what do we need this function to accomplish? An easy answer is it certainly must return an updated version of the state map since the internal loop expects it. But obviously, it must do more. The heartbeat process will send out pings to each of the monitored processes. In this step, we may create a list of outstanding pings. Thus, the `handle_pong/2` function should resolve the outstanding ping. Furthermore, we will maintain the list of alive processes; during the handling of a `:pong` message, we need to ensure the responding process is in the alive list. Similarly, it should be removed from the dead list if it was there earlier.

To remove a process from our list of currently dead processes, we will use something similar to the following line of code:

```
dead = state.dead -- [sender]
```

If the process is *already* not a member of the dead list, this set difference will return the dead list, unchanged.

We do a similar operation on the outstanding pings, however. Since the outstanding pings will end up being a map, we can't do the *exact* same thing:

```
pending = Map.delete(state.pending, sender)
```

We will need the list of alive processes locally if we wish to change it:

```
alive = state.alive
```

Moreover, if the current responding process *isn't* in the alive list, we should add it:

```
unless sender in state.alive do
  alive = [sender] ++ alive
end
```

 Remember that this reads as "if sender not in alive, then ...".

Finally, we need to update our state map:

```
%{state | :alive => alive, :dead => dead, :pending => pending}
```

This maintains the rest of the current state, and we update the lists we (potentially) touched.

Thus, the `handle_pong/2` function in full is:

```
defp handle_pong(sender, state) do
  dead = state.dead -- [sender]
  pending = Map.delete(state.pending, sender)
  alive = state.alive
  unless sender in state.alive do
    alive = [sender] ++ alive
  end
  %{state | :alive => alive, :dead => dead, :pending => pending}
end
```

We are close to having a working, albeit simplistic, heartbeat monitoring process; there are only a few more steps involved.

Next, we need to be able to update our dead list and add processes that haven't responded. An approach to accomplish this would be to check, during heartbeat stage, whether the process has *already* been added to the outstanding list. If the process is already in the outstanding list, it hasn't responded to the first ping. A more relaxed version would be to wait until the process is added to the outstanding list for the *third* time. That is, it hasn't yet responded twice and we are attempting to contact it again. At this point, it may be safe to mark the process as dead. Although this approach is very dependent on the length of time between heartbeat pulses, it should be safe for us to use for now.

We will start by sending pings and updating the outstanding map. This will look something like the following lines of code:

```
pending = state.monitors |>
Enum.map(fn(p) ->
  send p, {:ping, self}
  Map.update(state.pending, p, 1, fn(count) -> count + 1 end)
end) |>
Enum.reduce(%{}, fn(x, acc) ->
  Map.merge(x, acc, fn(_, v1, v2) -> v1 + v2 end)
end)
```

We map over the current monitors, send a ping to each process, and update or insert the process key into the outstanding or pending map. Since this is a stream, we actually create a new pending list for *every* monitor. Thus, we must reduce and merge the updated versions. This is accomplished by passing the resulting maps to `Enum.reduce/3` using `Map.merge/3` as the reduction. The merge simply adds the two values together. To convince you that this merge works the way you might expect, let's try it with more simplistic example:

```
iex(1)> a = %{:a => 1, :b => 2, :c => 3, :d => 4}
%{a: 1, b: 2, c: 3, d: 4}
iex(2)> b = %{:a => 4, :b => 3, :c => 2, :d => 1}
%{a: 4, b: 3, c: 2, d: 1}
iex(3)> [a, b] |> Enum.reduce(%{}, fn(x, acc) ->
...(3)> Map.merge(x, acc, fn(_, v1, v2) -> v1 + v2 end) end)
%{a: 5, b: 5, c: 5, d: 5}
```

Here, we create two maps, a and b. The a map has its values increasing from the first key to the last key. And, the b map, using the same keys, has its values decreasing from the first key to the last key. The result of merging these two maps should yield a map where the values are all the same.

Next, we need to update the dead process list, based on the result of our new outstanding list. This is accomplished by filtering the processes in the outstanding list that are greater than some threshold, say 2, and adding it to the dead list:

```
dead = (pending |>
Enum.filter(fn({p, c}) -> (not p in state.dead) and c > 2 end)
Enum.map(fn({p, _}) -> p end)) ++ state.dead
```

This process is more straightforward. The filter will only yield tuples from the pending map that have been inserted more than twice and are not already marked dead. The final map strips the count because the dead list is simply a list. Finally, we also want to keep the existing list, so we append the existing list as a final operation.

 There are extra parentheses here because of the binding of ++/2.

Putting together our send_ping/1 function, we have the following code:

```
defp send_ping(state) do
  pending = state.monitors |>
  Enum.map(fn(p) ->
    send p, {:ping, self}
    Map.update(state.pending, p, 1, fn(count) -> count + 1 end)
  end) |>
  Enum.reduce(%{}, fn(x, acc) ->
    Map.merge(x, acc, fn(_, v1, v2) -> v1 + v2 end)
  end)
  dead = (pending |>
  Enum.filter(fn({p, c}) -> (not p in state.dead) and c > 2 end)
  |>
```

```
Enum.map(fn({p, _}) -> p end)) ++ dead
  %{state | :pending => pending, :dead => dead}
end
```

The final step of the function is to return the new state object, similar to `handle_pong/2`.

Recall the line from `handle_pong/2`, `pending = Map.delete(state.pending, sender)`. We simply remove the entire record of the process. Since, even if we were waiting for it for a while, it responded and thus, it is no longer dead. Note that this is *different* from healthy, however.

The final step in putting this process together is *actually* sending the heartbeats. From the perspective of the message blocking interpreting loop, we have nowhere to put this step as part of the process loop. The loop blocks, waiting for a message, possibly receive a message, respond, and recurse. It's possible that the blocking step is the most expensive part. We should do something other than block, for example, send pings.

It turns out that this is a common problem with `receive do` in general. What is a `receive` loop supposed to do if it *never* receives a message? Thus, there is another clause for `receive` that allows us to do something else if the `receive` clause hangs for too long. This looks similar to the following code:

```
receive do
  _ -> 42
  after 5000 ->
    -42
end
```

If we enter this same expression into `iex`, we have actually created a sleep timer:

```
iex(1)> receive do
...(1)> _ -> 42
...(1)> after 5000 -> -42
...(1)> end
-42
```

Notice, once you enter `end`, the prompt hangs for about 5 seconds and then returns -42. This is because the process blocked, waiting for a message, but failed to receive one after 5 seconds, thus executing the expression for the `after` clause.

We can use this exact concept for our heartbeat process. We will add this step to the end of our `loop/1` function:

```
{:list_dead, sender} ->
  send sender, {:reply, state.dead}
```

```
    loop(state)
  after 3000 ->
    loop(send_ping(state))
  end
```

At the end of the message patterns, we insert an `after` clause that will execute our `send_ping/1` after the process fails to receive a message for 3 seconds.

Of course, we will need to add a `start_link/0` function to kick off the whole process:

```
def start_link do
  spawn_link(fn ->
    loop(%{:monitors => [], :alive => [], :dead => [], :pending =>
%{}})
  end)
end
```

This is also straightforward; we spawn a link, seeding the default state map of the process.

So the entire `HeartMonitor` module should look similar to the following code:

```
defmodule HeartMonitor do

  def start_link do
    spawn_link(fn ->
      loop(%{:monitors => [], :alive => [], :dead => [], :pending
=> %{}})
    end)
  end

  defp loop(state) do
    receive do
      {:pong, sender} ->
        loop(handle_pong(sender, state))
      {:monitor, pid} ->
        loop(%{state | :monitors => [pid] ++ state.monitors})
      {:demonitor, pid} ->
        loop(%{state | :monitors => state.monitors -- [pid]})
      {:list_monitors, sender} ->
        send sender, {:reply, state.monitors}
        loop(state)
      {:list_alive, sender} ->
        send sender, {:reply, state.alive}
        loop(state)
      {:list_dead, sender} ->
```

```
        send sender, {:relpy, state.dead}
          loop(state)
        after 3000 ->
          loop(send_ping(state))
      end
    end

  defp send_ping(state) do
    pending = state.monitors |>
    Enum.map(fn(p) ->
      send p, {:ping, self}
      Map.update(state.pending, p, 1, fn(count) -> count + 1 end)
    end) |>
    Enum.reduce(%{}, fn(x, acc) ->
      Map.merge(x, acc, fn(_, v1, v2) -> v1 + v2 end)
    end)
    dead = (pending |>
    Enum.filter(fn({p, c}) -> (not p in state.dead) and c > 2 end)
|>
      Enum.map(fn({p, _}) -> p end)) ++ state.dead
    %{state | :pending => pending, :dead => dead}
  end

  defp handle_pong(sender, state) do
    dead = state.dead -- [sender]
    pending = Map.delete(state.pending, sender)
    if sender in state.dead do
      IO.puts("Process #{inspect sender} was dead but is now
alive")
    end
    alive = state.alive
    unless sender in state.alive do
      alive = [sender] ++ alive
    end
    %{state | :alive => alive, :dead => dead, :pending => pending}
  end

end
```

Simplistically, we should be able to load this up into an interactive session and try it out:

```
iex(1)> import_file "heartmont.exs"
{:module, HeartMonitor,
```

```
  <<70, 79, 82, 49, 0, 0, 27, 72, 66, 69, 65, 77, 69, 120, 68, 99, 0,
0, 0, 99, 131, 104, 2, 100, 0, 14, 101, 108, 105, 120, 105, 114, 95,
100, 111, 99, 115, 95, 118, 49, 108, 0, 0, 0, 2, 104, 2, ...>>,
  {:handle_pong, 2}}
iex(2)> heart_pid = HeartMonitor.start_link
#PID<0.67.0>
iex(3)> Process.alive?(heart)
true
```

Now that the heartbeat process is alive, we can begin monitoring processes and watching the alive process list change. For example, we can start by monitoring the REPL process:

```
iex(3)> send heart_pid, {:monitor, self}
{:monitor, #PID<0.60.0>}
```

You should begin to see messages pile up into the REPL inbox:

```
iex(4)> flush
{:ping, #PID<0.67.0>}
{:ping, #PID<0.67.0>}
{:ping, #PID<0.67.0>}
{:ping, #PID<0.67.0>}
{:ping, #PID<0.67.0>}
{:ping, #PID<0.67.0>}
{:ping, #PID<0.67.0>}
:ok
```

We can also request to see which processes are dead:

```
iex(5)> send heart_pid, {:list_dead, self}
{:list_dead, #PID<0.60.0>}
iex(6)> flush
{:ping, #PID<0.67.0>}
{:ping, #PID<0.67.0>}
{:ping, #PID<0.67.0>}
{:reply, [#PID<0.60.0>]}
:ok
```

We are still receiving pings because the REPL process is still being monitored. We could, at this point, also send back a :pong message:

```
iex(7)> send heart_pid, {:pong, self}
Process #PID<0.60.0> was dead but is now alive
{:pong, #PID<0.60.0>}
```

As far as the heartbeat process is concerned, the REPL process is alive again because it is responding to the pings. However, after 9 seconds, that will no longer be the case.

Let's create a separate process by which we can have the heartbeat process monitor.

 If you are going to keep your existing iex open, be sure to demonitor the REPL: send heart_pid, {:demonitor, self}.

The new process will be similar to the worker, but it will be specific to the heartbeat process. That is, it must know how to respond to the :ping messages. However, all the other messages are free:

```
defmodule NewWorker do
  def start do
    spawn(fn -> loop() end)
  end

  defp loop do
    receive do
      {:ping, sender} ->
        send sender, {:pong, self}
        loop()
      {:compute, n, sender} ->
        send sender, {:result, fib(n)}
        loop()
    end
  end

  defp fib(0), do: 0
  defp fib(1), do: 1
  defp fib(n), do: fib(n-1) + fib(n-2)

end
```

Our worker here accepts two messages, :ping and :compute. The :ping message is as we expect and the :compute message requests the computation of the nth digit of the Fibonacci sequence.

Let's hook it into the heartbeat process:

```
iex(1)> import_file "heartmon.exs"
...
iex(2)> import_file "newworker.exs"
...
iex(3)> heart_pid = HeartMonitor.start_link
#PID<0.130.0>
iex(4)> w1 = NewWorker.start
#PID<0.137.0>
```

After importing the two modules and starting the processes for each, we can add the worker to the monitoring process:

```
iex(5)> send heart_pid, {:monitor, w1}
{:monitor, #PID<0.137.0>}
```

We should see the process now in the `alive` list:

```
iex(6)> send heart_pid, {:list_alive, self}
{:monitor, #PID<0.123.0>}
iex(7)> flush
{:reply, [#PID<0.137.0]}
:ok
```

Next, we can send compute messages to the worker to see it perform some work for us, and we can see that the monitoring process doesn't really mind:

```
iex(8)> send w1, {:compute, 5, self}
{:compute, 5, #PID<0.123.0>}
iex(9)> send w1, {:compute, 20, self}
{:compute, 20, #PID<0.123.0>}
iex(10)> flush
{:reply, 5}
{:reply, 6765}
:ok
```

Asking for alive processes again should still show the worker process:

```
iex(11)> send heart_pid, {:list_alive, self}
{:list_alive, #PID<0.123.0>}
iex(12)> flush
```

```
{:reply, [#PID<0.137.0>]}
:ok
```

Now, let's try having the worker compute out the sequence a bit:

```
iex(13)> send w1, {:compute, 40, self}
{:compute, 40, #PID<0.123.0>}
iex(14)> flush
:ok
...
Process #PID<0.137.0> was dead but is now alive
```

It takes a while to compute the 40th digit of the Fibonacci sequence, occasionally longer than 9 seconds. Thus, we see a message from the heart monitor process about the process being marked dead and then coming back to life later:

```
iex(15)> send heart_pid, {:list_alive, self}
{:list_alive, #PID<0.123.0>}
iex(16)> flush
{:reply, [#PID<0.137.0>]}
:ok
```

Once the worker has finished and stabilized, we should see it now listed in the alive list.

As a sort of disclaimer, this heartbeat monitoring process we have just developed is very incomplete and will likely not do well for production use, or, really, any serious use. Furthermore, it has a number of performance problems that will cause the process to no longer work, especially if the number of monitored processes exceeds a relatively small number.

Work pool

Work pools are similar in concept to thread pools. There is some static allocation of worker threads that are able to execute general purpose work. Given some task, the thread or worker will run off, compute the work, and return the result. The queue portion arises from the need to still schedule work while the pool is fully consumed.

For the next example, let's go through the process of developing a work pool and job queue.

Typical of a work pool is to have some sort of scheduling process. For simplicity, we can use a FIFO-scheduler. It will simply compute work as it arrives; there is no special (re)ordering.

For this example, we will create it inside a project instead of a single file. Let's start by creating the project:

```
$ mix new workpool
* creating README.md
* creating .gitignore
* creating mix.exs
* creating config
* creating config/config.exs
* creating lib
* creating lib/workpool.ex
* creating test
* creating test/test_helper.exs
* creating test/workpool_test.exs

Your mix project was created successfully.
You can use mix to compile it, test it, and more:

    cd workpool
    mix test

Run `mix help` for more commands.
```

We will then start by creating the scheduler process inside the `./lib/workpool/` folder.

 Creating a folder with the same name as the root module is standard practice when creating submodules, for example, `Workpool.Scheduler`, of the root or base module.

So create the directory and let's start into creating the scheduler:

```
$ mkdir lib/workpool
$ touch lib/workpool/schduler.ex
```

We will create our typical internal loop that performs message handling. We will respond to several messages such as work queuing and the `:DOWN` messages to notify requesters of failure.

This version of the work pool will be unbounded; it will accept and perform as much work as it is given. We will later introduce an artificial limit and create some back pressure to not collapse the system.

For the internal loop, we do what we might expect. Wait and respond to messages with a `receive do` loop:

```
defp loop(state) do
  receive do
    {:queue, func, args, sender} ->
      {pid, _ref} = spawn_monitor(fn ->
        send sender, func.(args)
      end)
      processing = Dict.put(state.processing, pid, sender)
      loop(%{state | processing: processing})
    {:DOWN, _ref, :process, pid, :normal} ->
      loop(%{state | processing: Dict.delete(state.processing,
pid)})
    {:DOWN, _ref, :process, pid, reason} ->
      sender = Dict.get(state.processing, pid)
      send sender, {:failure, "pool worker died: #{inspect
reason}"}
      loop(%{state | processing: Dict.delete(state.processing,
pid)})
  end
end
```

When the scheduler receives a `:queue` message, it spawns a worker process that will apply the given function over the given arguments. The worker will also attempt to send the results back to the sender as is. Since the scheduler will have a monitor to the worker process, the scheduler is notified when the worker finishes or exits for a non-normal reason. In case the worker exits for normal reasons, the scheduler will simply remove the process from the processing dictionary; otherwise, the scheduler should notify the calling process about the failure and then remove it from the processing queue.

The `start_link` is the same as usual:

```
def start_link do
  spawn_link(fn -> loop(%{processing: HashDict.new()}) end)
end
```

Thus, the whole `Workpool.Scheduler` module consists of the following code:

```
defmodule Workpool.Scheduler do

  def start_link do
    spawn_link(fn -> loop(%{processing: HashDict.new()}) end)
  end

  defp loop(state) do
    receive do
      {:queue, func, args, sender} ->
        {pid, _ref} = spawn_monitor(fn ->
          send sender, func.(args)
        end)
        processing = Dict.put(state.processing, pid, sender)
        loop(%{state | processing: processing})
      {:DOWN, _ref, :process, pid, :normal} ->
        loop(%{state | processing: Dict.delete(state.processing,
pid)})
      {:DOWN, _ref, :process, pid, reason} ->
        sender = Dict.get(state.processing, pid)
        send sender, {:failure, "pool worker died: #{inspect
reason}"}
        loop(%{state | processing: Dict.delete(state.processing,
pid)})
    end
  end
end
```

We can then compile and load the project into an interactive session:

```
$ iex -S mix
Erlang/OTP 18 [erts-7.0] [source] [64-bit] [smp:12:12] [async-
threads:10] [hipe] [kernel-poll:false]


Compiled lib/workpool.ex
Compiled lib/workpool/scheduler.ex
Generated workpool app
Interactive Elixir (1.0.5) - press Ctrl+C to exit (type h() ENTER for
help)
iex(1)>
```

From the `iex` prompt, we can start up the scheduler and begin passing work to it:

```
iex(1)> scheduler = Workpool.Scheduler.start_link
#PID<0.101.0>
iex(2)> send scheduler, {:queue, fn(x) -> 2 * x * x end, 4, self}
{:queue, #Function<6.54118792/1 in :erl_eval.expr/5>, 4, #PID<0.99.0>}
iex(3)> flush
32
:ok
```

So far, it seems it is working as we would expect.

As we are using monitors instead of links, the scheduler shouldn't fail if an exception is raised inside a worker, child process:

```
iex(4)> send scheduler, {:queue, fn(_) -> raise "oops" end, [], self}

01:34:58.604 [error] Process #PID<0.108.0> raised an exception
** (RuntimeError) oops
    (workpool) lib/workpool/scheduler.ex:11: anonymous fn/3 in
Workpool.Scheduler.loop/1

{:queue, #Function<6.54118792/1 in :erl_eval.expr/5>, [], #PID<0.99.0>}

iex(5)> Process.alive?(scheduler)
true
```

And as we would expect, the worker process fails *and* the scheduler process is still alive.

This work pool scheduler is somewhat tedious to use. The consuming process has to know a few things about the scheduler, for example, its process ID. We can use process registration to help, but how would the consuming process ensure it's only starting a single scheduler or registering *over* an existing process?

A way this could be solved is to have the `Workpool` module do the start up and process registration. That way, it's in one place and all the consuming processes should be able to simply use the registered atom instead of having to know the PID reference.

To accomplish this, we need to add a function to the `Workpool` module, say, `start/0`:

```
def start do
  pid = Workpool.Scheduler.start_link
  true = Process.register(pid, :scheduler)
  :ok
end
```

This way, we can launch the scheduler from the `Workpool` module, and the consumers of the work pool do not need to know about the `Workpool.Scheduler` module. Let's see what it looks similar to now to interact with the `Workpool` module:

```
$ iex -S mix

Erlang/OTP 18 [erts-7.0] [source] [64-bit] [smp:12:12] [async-
threads:10] [hipe] [kernel-poll:false]


Compiled lib/workpool.ex

Compiled lib/workpool/scheduler.ex

Generated workpool app

Interactive Elixir (1.0.5) - press Ctrl+C to exit (type h() ENTER for
help)

iex(1)> Workpool.start

:ok
```

Now that the scheduler process is started, we should be able to send messages to it using the registered name:

```
iex(2)> send :scheduler, {:queue, fn(x) -> x * x end, 7, self}

{:queue, #Function<6.54118792/1 in :erl_eval.expr/5>, 7, #PID<0.84.0>}

iex(3)> flush

49

:ok
```

There is something else we should add to make this work pool better. Sending messages between processes can often be done incorrectly. There is so much variability in the tuple that is passed, and there is no good way for the sending process to know it made a mistake.

We can add some functions to the `Workpool` module that can be the public API for the scheduler. Then, consuming processes of the work pool don't need to know the message format, and they are more easily made aware of changes to the API. Since we really only have a single public message, we only need to add a `queue/2` function:

```
def queue(fun, args) do
  send :scheduler, {:queue, fun, args, self}
  :ok
end
```

This way, we can interact with the `Workpool` module via simply `start/0` and `queue/2`.

Here is the new final version of `Workpool`:

```
defmodule Workpool do
  def start do
    pid = Workpool.Scheduler.start_link
    true = Process.register(pid, :scheduler)
    :ok
  end

  def queue(fun, args) do
    send :scheduler, {:queue, fun, args, self}
    :ok
  end
end
```

Let's recompile and see this in action:

```
$ iex -S mix

...


iex(1)> Workpool.start
:ok
iex(2)> Workpool.queue(fn(x) -> x * x * 2 end, 4)
:ok
iex(3)> flush
32
:ok
```

This will be much easier to use for other end consumers. They will simply need to familiarize themselves with the `Workpool` module's API, and they would be set. Let's create a very basic module that uses the work pool and show, indeed, how easy it is now to use the work pool.

 This won't be part of the work pool project, but we will want to be able to load both the work pool project and this new module into the same `iex` session.

Let's create a module that computes a number of Fibonacci numbers, but uses the work pool to do this in parallel:

```
defmodule FibonacciWorkPool do
  def fib(fibonacci_digits) do
    fibonacci_digits |>
    Enum.map(fn(n) -> Workpool.queue(&fib_comp/1, n) end)
  end

  # Terribly slow version
  defp fib_comp(0), do: 0
  defp fib_comp(1), do: 1
  defp fib_comp(n), do: fib_comp(n-1) + fib_comp(n-2)
end
```

The main function is the `fib/1` function that takes an enumerable type and attempts to map it into the work pool scheduler using a very slow method of finding the Fibonacci number.

Let's load up the work pool, import this module, and see it in action:

```
$ iex -S mix
...

iex(1)> Workpool.start
:ok
```

We need the work pool going, but this could come *after* importing the `FibonacciWorkPool` module:

```
iex(2)> import_file "../fib_pool.exs"
{:module, FibonacciWorkPool,
 <<70, 79, 82, 49, 0, 0, 6, 172, 66, 69, 65, 77, 69, 120, 68, 99, 0,
0, 0, 125, 131, 104, 2, 100, 0, 14, 101, 108, 105, 120, 105, 114, 95,
100, 111, 99, 115, 95, 118, 49, 108, 0, 0, 0, 2, 104, 2, ...>>,
 {:fib_comp, 1}}
```

Now that the module is loaded, we can start asking it for multiple Fibonacci numbers, all to be delivered to the iex message queue:

```
iex(3)> FibonacciWorkPool.fib(5..35)
```

```
[:ok, :ok, :ok, :ok, :ok, :ok, :ok, :ok, :ok, :ok, :ok, :ok, :ok,
:ok, :ok, :ok,
 :ok, :ok, :ok, :ok, :ok, :ok, :ok, :ok, :ok, :ok, :ok, :ok, :ok,
:ok, :ok]
```

```
iex(4)> flush
```

```
5

8

13

21

34

89

55

144

233

377

610

987

2584

4181

1597

10946

17711

6765

46368

28657

75025

121393

196418

317811

514229

832040

1346269

2178309
```

```
3524578
5702887
9227465
:ok
```

Of course, small digits of the Fibonacci sequence are going to return almost immediately. Let's try with some bigger numbers:

```
iex(5)> FibonacciWorkPool.fib(39..45)
[:ok, :ok, :ok, :ok, :ok, :ok, :ok]
```

You should see your CPU start to cycle up for all of the separate computations. I waited about 10 to 30 seconds for the CPU to cycle down before proceeding:

```
iex(6)> flush
63245986
102334155
165580141
267914296
433494437
701408733
1134903170
:ok
```

The output being sent to a mailbox isn't ideal, but could be handled by more sophisticated work pool clients. But the *use* of the work pool was really only one line. The Fibonacci module had only to know *of* the `Workpool.queue/2` function to function. Using the Fibonacci module *without* starting the work pool would be a disaster. But under the current assumptions, it's not worth fixing.

The work pool is a great example of server-worker scheduling method that can be greatly expanded to solve real problems; however, in its current form, we have to deal with the Erlang/Elixir process API too much before we even get to a stable point. There should be a better way to implement everything we have so far and then some without a lot of extra effort.

Summary

This was a big chapter and we covered a lot of material. We started our discussion around the importance of concurrency constructs to be available in our languages to better utilize the current processors in the market and then we started deep into the process structure of the runtime and how we can use Elixir to create processes. We covered parallel computation versus concurrent computation, Erlang processes versus OS processes, actor-model, sending and receiving messages in Elixir, and spawning, linking, and monitoring processes in Elixir.

Finally, we covered a number of examples that use Elixir processes.

There's a lot of interesting things we can do with Erlang/Elixir processes and the concurrency they enable. However, there are a lot of disadvantages of using them in their raw form. As you might have noticed, we have duplicated a lot of work throughout the examples. We wrote a lot of similar functions for spawning the processes, the receive loops, message delivery failure, and so on. We also saw that monitoring and managing processes usually results in some duplication of effort. The work pool example started into a form of process supervision, but it's missing a few cases and is not entirely robust. Similarly, there's a lot of variability with the order and parent processes that start other processes, which can lead to false assumptions and failing invariants that would ultimately crash the system as a whole. Ideally, we could have a way to remove the duplication and variability without losing the ability to create rich and powerful processes.

7
OTP – A Poor Name for a Rich Framework

In the previous chapter, we started our journey down concurrent programming with Elixir, but we certainly wrote a lot of similar code and didn't really get very far. This is all about to change; enter OTP.

Open Telecom Platform (OTP) is a framework originally developed as part of Erlang in the early beginnings of Erlang, and its takeover of the telephone networks. It has grown rapidly outward into a general purpose library for creating Erlang and consequentially, Elixir applications.

OTP provides a set of basic ideas and principles for our processes that will guide us in the right direction. These include OTP applications, (process) supervision trees, server processes, event processes, and special processes.

Applications

Many topics surrounding Erlang/Elixir and OTP require us to be careful about our verbiage. We discussed before the difference between Erlang processes and OS processes. Similarly, we need to be careful about applications.

Outside of OTP, application is a very general term and we toss it around without much care. "There's an app for that," comes to mind often. In this less specific and constrained perspective, applications are general, not necessarily single purpose, programs that perform things for us. We have seen many different forms of applications take form over the years—desktop applications, web applications, and now mobile applications. For desktop applications, we can think of our word processors, web browsers, text editors, IDEs, games, and so on. For web applications, we can think of our social media sites, task tracking applications, games, office suites, and so on. The mobile app space contains similar applications to those already listed. The applications are mostly the same, differentiated only by platform.

With respect to OTP, applications are self-contained process trees that serve some purpose, or may even wrap several (OTP) applications together as a new (super) singular application. The question of *how* applications are defined, started, and managed is typically accomplished via process supervision trees, but this detail isn't necessary to understanding OTP applications in general.

The difference between applications and OTP applications is mostly contextual. However, the word can be scary to newcomers.

A great example of an OTP application that we have already used numerous times is `iex`. From all our examples, so far, running `Process.list/0` returns the current list of processes running:

```
iex(1)> Process.list
[#PID<0.0.0>, #PID<0.3.0>, #PID<0.6.0>, #PID<0.7.0>, #PID<0.9.0>,
#PID<0.10.0>,
 #PID<0.11.0>, #PID<0.12.0>, #PID<0.14.0>, #PID<0.15.0>,
#PID<0.16.0>,
 #PID<0.17.0>, #PID<0.18.0>, #PID<0.20.0>, #PID<0.21.0>,
#PID<0.22.0>,
 #PID<0.23.0>, #PID<0.24.0>, #PID<0.25.0>, #PID<0.26.0>,
#PID<0.27.0>,
 #PID<0.28.0>, #PID<0.29.0>, #PID<0.30.0>, #PID<0.38.0>,
#PID<0.39.0>,
 #PID<0.40.0>, #PID<0.41.0>, #PID<0.42.0>, #PID<0.43.0>,
#PID<0.45.0>,
 #PID<0.46.0>, #PID<0.47.0>, #PID<0.48.0>, #PID<0.51.0>,
#PID<0.52.0>,
 #PID<0.53.0>, #PID<0.54.0>, #PID<0.55.0>, #PID<0.56.0>,
#PID<0.57.0>,
 #PID<0.58.0>, #PID<0.60.0>]
```

These are all the different processes bundled up by the `iex` application, many of which are themselves OTP applications. For example, we can see the started, named applications when we launch an interactive session:

```
iex(2)> :application.which_applications
[{:stdlib, 'ERTS  CXC 138 10', '2.5'}, {:elixir, 'elixir', '1.0.5'},
 {:kernel, 'ERTS  CXC 138 10', '4.0'}, {:iex, 'iex', '1.0.5'},
 {:logger, 'logger', '1.0.5'}, {:compiler, 'ERTS  CXC 138 10',
'6.0'},
 {:syntax_tools, 'Syntax tools', '1.7'}, {:crypto, 'CRYPTO', '3.6'}]
```

The tuple returned by `:application.which_applications/0` is defined as `{Application, Description, Vsn}`, where `Application` is the name of the application, `Description` is either the application name in string form or an explanatory text of the application, and `Vsn` is the loaded version of the application (1).

What does it mean for an application to be loaded? The Erlang VM has a method for hot-swapping code, and therefore, being able to keep track of the loaded module version becomes more important. So, the "loaded" version is the currently in-memory version of the application (which is not necessarily the latest version).

Overall, the word application means what we would expect, a single entity for working with and manipulating a unit of code. The unit of code itself could be many different things—an API library for querying an HTTP endpoint, a distributed key-value store, `iex` itself, or whatever else you can imagine and develop.

Gen(eric) behaviours

OTP defines several generic behaviours we can use when creating Elixir applications. There is the `GenServer` behaviour, the `GenEvent` behaviour, and the `:gen_fsm` behaviour. All of these behaviours have their foundation in an even more general behaviour of OTP processes.

These behaviours remove some of the tedious work we had to do for handling messages and performing work that we encountered in the previous chapter.

We will start with our discussion on `GenServer`, and then move onto more specialized variants.

Gen(eric) servers

OTP gives us the basic blueprint for a process that receives messages, processes messages and sends a result back, like any server would.

Gen in `GenServer` really stands for generic or general because it provides the general details of such a process without constraining its users too much into an inflexible solution. For example, we saw that the main event loop of the processes we wrote in the previous chapter were all very similar in nature; the only real differences between each were the messages the process responded to and its handling of those messages. Most, if not all, other details were the same. *This* is what the `GenServer` behaviour provides for us.

For a quick example, let's recreate our key-value store from the previous chapter.

We will start with the skeleton code of any `GenServer` module:

```
defmodule KV do
  use GenServer

  def start_link(opts \\ []) do
    GenServer.start_link(__MODULE__, [], opts)
  end

  def init(_) do
    {:ok, HashDict.new}
  end

end
```

To create a `GenServer` process, we define a regular Elixir module. However, unlike other modules we've so far created, we have `use GenServer` at the beginning. This instructs Elixir that the module we are defining will use the `GenServer` behaviour.

Next, we define a few functions usually required to get things off the ground:

```
def start_link(opts \\[]) do
  GenServer.start_link(__MODULE__, [], opts)
end
```

The first function is similar to what we defined in the previous chapter, but instead of calling `Process.spawn` or `Process.spawn_link`, we use the helper function from the `GenServer` module to start up our process. This helper function will call our second function, `init/1`, as shown in the following code:

```
def init(_) do
  {:ok, HashDictnew}
end
```

The `init/1` function will be called to set up the state of the process and make sure the initial state is good. Most often, it will be the single line, `{:ok, state}`, where `state` is the internal state object of the process, initialized to the proper state. Since we are creating a simple key-value store, we can use the `HashDict` structure for our process state.

If the first atom of the tuple is anything other than `:ok`, the process will refuse to start. This is useful when upstream dependencies or other guarantees are unsatisfied and it is not desired to start under such circumstances.

This is enough code to get the server started and off the ground; however, it won't be very useful since we haven't defined a few other functions.

The `GenServer` processes have a few functions for handling messages — `handle_call/3` and `handle_cast/3`. These functions serve similar purposes, but have different behaviours. Moreover, these functions are never called directly by client code; they are called internally by the OTP framework. The OTP framework takes care of the internal main loop for each process, dispatching messages to our versions of `handle_call/3` and `handle_cast/3`.

Continuing our key-value example, let's define our `handle_call/3` function:

```
def handle_call({:put, key, value}, _from, dictionary) do
  {:reply, :ok, HashDict.put(dictionary, key, value)}
end

def handle_call({:get, key}, _from , dictionary) do
  {:reply, HashDict.get(dictionary, key), dictionary}
end
```

The first parameter of `handle_call/3` is the message tuple. Typically, we have an atom specifying the message type or action the server should perform, the second parameter (which we don't use in this example) is the calling process, and the third parameter is the internal data of the process, in this case, the dictionary we are storing data in.

The first pattern for `handle_call/3` matches against a triple of `{:put, key, value}`, where `key` is the key or identifier of the data being stored and `value` is the actual data being stored. The second pattern matches `{:get, key}`, where `key` is the identifier of the data to retrieve.

The returned triple is consumed by the OTP framework. The first element of the triple informs the OTP framework how to handle the response. The second element is the value to return to the calling process. The third is the internal state, modified or not, to be used the next time a message is received.

This is fairly similar to how our processes from the previous chapter worked, except the OTP framework takes care of a lot of the tedious plumbing required to get two processes communicating.

For completeness, here is the KV module so far:

```
defmodule KV do
  use GenServer

  def start_link(opts \\ []) do
    GenServer.start_link(__MODULE__, [], opts)
  end

  def init(_) do
    {:ok, HashDict.new}
  end

  def handle_call({:put, key, value}, _from, dictionary) do
    {:reply, :ok, HashDict.put(dictionary, key, value)}
  end

  def handle_call({:get, key}, _from, dictionary) do
    {:reply, HashDict.get(dictionary, key), dictionary}
  end
end
```

From here, we can actually try out the process in an interactive session:

```
iex(1)> import_file "kv.exs"
{:module, KV,
 <<70, 79, 82, 49, 0, 0, 12, 136, 66, 69, 65, 77, 69, 120, 68, 99, 0,
0, 2, 243, 131, 104, 2, 100, 0, 14, 101, 108, 105, 120, 105, 114, 95,
100, 111, 99, 115, 95, 118, 49, 108, 0, 0, 0, 2, 104, 2, ...>>,
 {:handle_call, 3}}
iex(2)> {:ok, kv_pid} = KV.start_link
{:ok, #PID<0.69.0>}
```

Notice, the `GenServer.start_link/3` function actually returns a tuple, `{:ok, pid}`. In the previous chapter, we only returned the PID, but here, we are returning a tag for the PID. This let's the calling or parent process know that the starting or child process started successfully.

Now, using the PID and the `GenServer.call/2` function, we can send our message to the key-value process:

```
iex(3)> GenServer.call(kv_pid, {:put, :a, 42})
:ok
```

We can also use the `GenServer.call/2` function to retrieve data from the key-value process as well:

```
iex(4)> GenServer.call(kv_pid, {:get, :a})
42
```

But, why should the client process depend on using the `GenServer.call/2` function? This should be something the KV module handles for the client. That is, we can add some helper functions to the KV module that will call and send the correct messages for clients:

```
def put(server, key, value) do
  GenServer.call(server, {:put, key, value})
end

def get(server, key) do
  GenServer.call(server, {:get, key})
end
```

These two functions are no different than what we ran previously in `iex`; we are just wrapping them up into the KV module.

Reloading and restarting the KV process, we can use the new functions:

```
iex(1)> import_file "kv.exs"
{:module, KV,
 <<70, 79, 82, 49, 0, 0, 12, 136, 66, 69, 65, 77, 69, 120, 68, 99, 0,
 0, 2, 243, 131, 104, 2, 100, 0, 14, 101, 108, 105, 120, 105, 114, 95,
 100, 111, 99, 115, 95, 118, 49, 108, 0, 0, 0, 2, 104, 2, ...>>,
 {:handle_call, 3}}
iex(2)> {:ok, kv_pid} = KV.start_link
{:ok, #PID<0.67.0>}
iex(3)> KV.put(kv_pid, :a, 42)
:ok
iex(4)> KV.get(kv_pid, :a)
42
```

The helper functions we create can be taken a step further; if we know there is only ever going to be one instance of the process, we can have the process registered as soon as it starts. To do this, we need to add a key-value pair to the `opts` list in `KV.start_link/1`; change the definition of `KV.start_link` to the following code:

```
def start_link(opts \\ []) do
  GenServer.start_link(__MODULE__, [], [name: __MODULE__] ++ opts)
end
```

That is, we pass the pair, `[name: __MODULE__]`, and whatever parent process passes to `GenServer.start_link/3`. By providing the `:name` attribute in `opts`, `GenServer. start_link/3` will register the process for us after it starts. This means we don't need to reference it by the PID returned. In fact, we can change `KV.put/3` and `KV.get/2` to be `KV.put/2` and `KV.get/1` with the following definitions:

```
def put(key, value) do
  GenServer.call(__MODULE__, {:put, key, value})
end

def get(key) do
  GenServer.call(__MODULE__, {:get, key})
end
```

After the process is registered, we can use the `__MODULE__` directive to reference the registered name of the module. That is, the new version of `KV` is the following:

```
defmodule KV do
  use GenServer

  def start_link(opts \\ []) do
    GenServer.start_link(__MODULE__, [], [name: __MODULE__] ++
opts)
  end

  def init(_) do
    {:ok, HashDict.new}
  end

  def put(key, value) do
    GenServer.call(__MODULE__, {:put, key, value})
  end

  def get(key) do
    GenServer.call(__MODULE__, {:get, key})
  end
```

```
    def handle_call({:put, key, value}, _from, dictionary) do
      {:reply, :ok, HashDict.put(dictionary, key, value)}
    end

    def handle_call({:get, key}, _from, dictionary) do
      {:reply, HashDict.get(dictionary, key), dictionary}
    end
  end
```

Using our new version of this module tends to be the same:

```
iex(1)> import_file "kv.exs"
{:module, KV,
 <<70, 79, 82, 49, 0, 0, 12, 152, 66, 69, 65, 77, 69, 120, 68, 99, 0,
 0, 2, 207, 131, 104, 2, 100, 0, 14, 101, 108, 105, 120, 105, 114, 95,
 100, 111, 99, 115, 95, 118, 49, 108, 0, 0, 0, 2, 104, 2, ...>>,
 {:handle_call, 3}}
iex(2)> KV.start_link
{:ok, #PID<0.76.0>}
iex(3)> KV.put(:b, 42)
:ok
iex(4)> KV.get(:b)
42
```

This time around, however, we do not need to know the PID of the server process. This may seem familiar to process registration in the previous chapter. In fact, what GenServer.start_link/3 and Process.register/2 are doing is, in effect, the same. To see this, remember from the previous chapter, we discussed an internal Elixir function, Process.registered/0, which returns the keys of all the registered, named applications. If we run this function from inside our current iex session, we will see that KV, our key-value server process, is among the members in the list:

```
iex(4)> Process.registered
[:init, :file_server_2, :user, :application_controller, KV,
:user_drv,
 :standard_error, :global_group, :elixir_counter, IEx.Supervisor,
 :elixir_config, :elixir_sup, Logger, :elixir_code_server, IEx.Config,
 :error_logger, :standard_error_sup, :kernel_safe_sup, :rex,
:erl_prim_loader,
 Logger.Supervisor, :inet_db, :kernel_sup, :code_server,
:global_name_server,
 Logger.Watcher]
```

Do not be fooled by the upper cased naming; every element of the list is an atom. Try `Process.registered |> Enum. at(n) |> is_atom`, where n is the index of KV. The result should be `true`.

We can also try the following command:

```
iex(5)> KV in Process.registered
true
```

This also definitively gives the desired result.

Asynchronous messaging

It may seem that we have lost asynchronous communication by switching to OTP and using the `GenServer` behaviour. That is, `GenServer.call/2` is a blocking, synchronous invocation, and the calling process must wait for the reply before continuing, effectively halting any form of parallelism that may have been exploited.

The `GenServer.call/2` function is not the end of the discussion though, there is still some hope for asynchrony yet.

There is another function available to us when creating `GenServer` processes— `GenServer.cast/2`. This function, instead of blocking, casts the message to the `GenServer` process and returns, practically, immediately.

Like `GenServer.call/2` requires `handle_call/3` to be defined, `GenServer.cast/2` requires a new function, `handle_cast/2`, to be defined. Luckily for us, this function too isn't much different though. Let's demonstrate with a very simplistic `PingPong` module:

```
defmodule PingPong do
  use GenServer

  def start_link(opts \\ []) do
    GenServer.start_link(__MODULE__, [], [name: __MODULE__] ++
opts)
  end

  def ping() do
    GenServer.cast(__MODULE__, {:ping, self()})
  end

  def handle_cast({:ping, from}, state) do
    send from, :pong
```

```
    {:noreply, state}
  end

end
```

First, we define the `PingPong` module and have it use the `GenServer` behaviour. The `start_link` and `ping` functions are helper functions for setting up and making the public API of the process easier. The `init/1` function only needs to be redefined when there is process state that must be initialized; otherwise, the default is fine.

In the `handle_cast/2` function, we match against a pattern or request of {`:ping, from`}, where `from` should be a PID. Upon receiving a {`:ping, from`} message, we send back the `:pong` message and return {`:noreply, state`}.

Unlike `handle_call/3` from earlier, we only return the success status of `:noreply` and the state. There is no direct return to the calling process; we have no channel to do so without using `send/2`, and using `send` requires a reference to the calling process.

Using our new `PingPong` module quite similar to before, we simply start and cast into it:

```
iex(1)> import_file "pingpong.exs"
{:module, PingPong,
 <<70, 79, 82, 49, 0, 0, 11, 48, 66, 69, 65, 77, 69, 120, 68, 99, 0,
0, 2, 124, 131, 104, 2, 100, 0, 14, 101, 108, 105, 120, 105, 114, 95,
100, 111, 99, 115, 95, 118, 49, 108, 0, 0, 0, 2, 104, 2, ...>>,
 {:handle_cast, 2}}
iex(2)> PingPong.start_link
{:ok, #PID<0.82.0>}
iex(3)> PingPong.ping
:ok
iex(4)> flush
:pong
:ok
```

We don't receive the `:pong` message when calling `PingPong.pong/0`; we will receive it when we call `flush/0` though. However, it should be noted that `PingPong.ping/0` still returns `:ok` from `GenServer.cast/2`. From the documentation of `GenServer.cast/2`:

> *"This function returns :ok immediately, regardless of whether the destination node or server does exists, unless the server is specified as an atom."*

Returning `:ok` is par for the course, but returning it immediately changes things. Since there is now inherent asynchrony happening, immediately calling `flush/0` after casting a message to the server process may not always return results. To demonstrate this, try adding `:timer.sleep 5000` into the `handle_cast/2` function .

 Testing `GenServer.cast/2` functions from a public API perspective can be highly frustrating and mildly tedious. We will cover some testing strategies around these functions shortly.

Gen(eric) events

Sending messages to a `GenServer` process can be thought to be similar to sending events. A tagged message to perform some action received and the `GenServer` process will compute some result or perform some action, based on the inputs of the message and current state of the process. However, performing complex logic around forwarding, dropping, filtering, and other such actions in the context of the `GenServer` behaviour is quite daunting.

The `GenEvent` behaviour handles many of the issues of developing an event-based process inside the context of OTP processes.

The `GenEvent` behaviour acts as an event dispatcher; it receives and forwards events to handlers. The handlers are in charge of performing actions on the received events. There are a number of applications of this model and process, there are even a few already in Elixir and OTP. For example, Elixir's `Logging` module is a `GenEvent` process, forwarding the log events to the console or any additional handler.

We can create our first `GenEvent` manager using the `GenEvent.start_link/0` function:

```
iex(1)> {:ok, event_manager} = GenEvent.start_link
{:ok, #PID<0.62.0>}
```

After we have created our managing process, we can use either `GenEvent.sync_notify/2` or `GenEvent.notify/2` to send events to the manager process:

```
iex(2)> GenEvent.sync_notify(event_manager, :foo)
:ok
iex(3)> GenEvent.notify(event_manager, :bar)
:ok
```

However, since the event manager has no handlers, the events are dropped. Let's define and add a basic forward handler. It will receive the event and send it to the parent process:

```
iex(4)> defmodule Forwarder do
...(4)>    use GenEvent
...(4)>    def handle_event(event, parent) do
...(4)>       send parent, event
...(4)>       {:ok, parent}
...(4)>    end
...(4)> end
{:module, Forwarder,
 <<70, 79, 82, 49, 0, 0, 9, 156, 66, 69, 65, 77, 69, 120, 68, 99, 0,
 0, 2, 10, 131, 104, 2, 100, 0, 14, 101, 108, 105, 120, 105, 114, 95,
 100, 111, 99, 115, 95, 118, 49, 108, 0, 0, 0, 2, 104, 2, ...>>,
 {:handle_event, 2}}
iex(5)> GenEvent.add_handler(event_manager, Forwarder, self())
:ok
iex(6)> GenEvent.sync_notify(event_manager, :ping)
:ok
iex(7)> flush
:ping
:ok
```

In the handler module, Forwarder, we define the handle_event/2 function for receiving events. This function takes the event and the current state variable of the process, sends the event to the process defined by parent, and then returns {:ok, parent} for the OTP main loop.

After defining the module, we add it to the handler we started earlier and send another event to the manager. This time, though, the event is dispatched to our handler. Our handler (Forwarder) receives the message and uses send/2 to send it to the parent process (the current IEx session). Thus, when we call flush/0, we see the :ping event message.

Without breaking the single responsibility principle, we can have more handlers do more things with the same events. For example, let's add another handler to the current example that prints the message to the console:

```
iex(8)> defmodule Echoer do
...(8)>    use GenEvent
```

```
...(8)>    def handle_event(event, []) do
...(8)>        IO.puts event
...(8)>        {:ok, []}
...(8)>    end
...(8)> end
{:module, Echoer,
 <<70, 79, 82, 49, 0, 0, 9, 156, 66, 69, 65, 77, 69, 120, 68, 99, 0,
0, 2, 10, 131, 104, 2, 100, 0, 14, 101, 108, 105, 120, 105, 114, 95,
100, 111, 99, 115, 95, 118, 49, 108, 0, 0, 0, 2, 104, 2, ...>>,
 {:handle_event, 2}}
```

Here, we define another handler that is very similar to the `Forwarder` from before. Instead, we call `IO.puts event` instead of `send parent, event`. We don't really need to keep track of any internal state, so we pass around an empty list.

After defining the handler, let's add it to the event manager and send an event to the manager:

```
iex(9)> GenEvent.add_handler(event_manager, Echoer, [])
:ok
iex(10)> GenEvent.sync_notify(event_manager, :hello)
hello
:ok
iex(11)> flush
:hello
:ok
```

Immediately, we see the message printed to the output of the console. Furthermore, we can flush the current process mailbox and see the message is there as well.

This also works with the asynchronous variant as well:

```
iex(12)> GenEvent.notify(event_manager, :world)
hello
:ok
iex(13)> flush
:hello
:ok
```

To better demonstrate the capabilities of asynchronously sending events, we will need to either perform more work or artificially pause one of the handlers. Try adding a `:timer.sleep` to the `Echoer` handler, and try both `GenEvent.sync_notify/2` and `GenEvent.notify/2`.

Special OTP processes

The OTP behaviours we have covered so far are often sufficient for a lot of the applications being developed. However, how do we get the benefits of supervision trees and the near-infinite level of traceability and debugging capabilities of the BEAM, and, most importantly, take control of the main event loop of the OTP process? If the task we are trying to solve does not fit into either of the OTP behaviours we have already covered, there is still a way to get a good number of benefits of OTP without using the given behaviours. These are referred to as special OTP processes in the Erlang world. There are a few requirements on the developer's part and as such, the use of special processes should be avoided if at all possible.

Unlike the processes we wrote in the previous chapter, these processes will conform to the OTP design principles and support the many tracing and debugging facilities inherent with the OTP processes and Erlang VM.

The definition of special process modules is very similar to that of the modules using the regular behaviours. They will have a `start_link` function, an `init` function, and a few system functions for handling specific OTP messages. As a simple example, let's create the `PingPong` module as a special process.

We will start with the `start_link` function:

```
def start_link(opts \\ []) do
  :proc_lib.start_link(__MODULE__, :init, [self(), opts])
end
```

So far, this isn't much different than what might be expected. We start and link the current module using the `init` function, passing the parent and `opts`. However, instead of using `spawn_link/3`, we are using `start_link/3` from the Erlang module, `proc_lib`. The difference between this function and `spawn_link/3` is that the former starts the process synchronously. Furthermore, as we will see, the resulting process must call `:proc_lib.init_ack/2` to signal the start of the process; if `:proc_lib.init_ack/2` is never called, the parent process will hang forever. There is a variation of `:proc_lib.start_link/4` that includes a `timeout` parameter; however, most often this can be handled by the supervisor process.

The init function is slightly more involved:

```
def init(parent, opts) do
  debug = :sys.debug_options([])
  Process.link(parent)
  :proc_lib.init_ack(parent, {:ok, self()})
  Process.register(self(), __MODULE__)
  state = HashDict.new
  loop(state, parent, debug)
end
```

We start by creating the debug object from the :sys module. This object will be used for retrieving debugging information; most often, the process will not use it directly.

Next, we create a link back to the parent process and call init_ack. This tells the parent process that child process is up and running. The tuple passed to init_ack is what is returned by the :proc_lib.start_link call from the start_link function. The call to init_ack should not happen until after all of the required dependencies and information for a successful start of the process are complete. That is, this function is how we tell the parent process that the child is successfully started or failed because of a :badarg error or missing dependency.

Next, optionally, we can register the process in the local nodes process table. The process can also have some more sophistication around process registration as well, such as, if the :name attribute is in the opts list, then register the process.

Finally, initialize the state dictionary and invoke the loop function passing the state dictionary, the parent process reference, and the debug object. The OTP design principles require that these are all held onto during the lifetime of the process.

 The loop function could really be named anything you want, I am just using loop for consistency with the previous chapter, and it's not the worst name to use for this context.

Next, we need to define the loop/3 function for our special process:

```
defp loop(state, parent, debug) do
  receive do
    {:ping, from} ->
      send from, :pong
    {:system, from, request} ->
      :sys.handle_system_msg(request, from, parent, __MODULE__,
debug, state)
  end
  loop(state, parent, debug)
end
```

When entering the `loop` function, the process will block, waiting for either a `:ping` message or a `:system` message. The `:ping` message is the message we care about receiving. The `:system` message, on the other hand, is an OTP message requirement. Luckily, we can leverage the Erlang `:sys` module to handle the `:system` messages. However, it also means we must define a few more functions — `system_continue/3`, `system_terminate/4`, and `system_get_state/1`. These functions are trivial to define and are really only a tedium for now:

```
def system_continue(parent, debug, state), do: loop(state, parent, debug)

def system_terminate(reason, _, _, _): do, exit(reason)

def system_get_state(state): do: {:ok, state}
```

These functions should never be called by users or clients, but they still need to be public for the OTP behaviours.

That covers the bare minimum required to get a special OTP process off the ground. Let's take it for a spin:

```
iex(1)> import_file "pingpong_sp.exs"
{:module, PingPong,
 <<70, 79, 82, 49, 0, 0, 11, 192, 66, 69, 65, 77, 69, 120, 68, 99, 0,
0, 1, 212, 131, 104, 2, 100, 0, 14, 101, 108, 105, 120, 105, 114, 95,
100, 111, 99, 115, 95, 118, 49, 108, 0, 0, 0, 2, 104, 2, ...>>,
 {:system_get_state, 1}}
iex(2)> PingPong.start_link
{:ok, #PID<0.79.0>}
iex(3)> send PingPong, {:ping, self()}
{:ping, #PID<0.60.0>}
iex(4)> flush
:pong
:ok
```

We are back to the API from the previous chapter; we lost our ability to use the `Gen*` functions for sending messages to our process. We can add a function to abstract away the `send/2` call:

```
def ping() do
  send __MODULE__, {:ping, self()}
  :ok
end
```

But, we've had a taste of `GenServer.call`. It would be nice if we had something along those lines.

We can use `receive`; let's try `ping/0` another way. Add the following function to our special process version of `PingPong`:

```
def ping() do
  send __MODULE__, {:ping, self()}
  receive do
    {:reply, response} ->
      response
  after 10000 ->
    {:error, :timeout}
  end
end
```

This code is similar to our first idea; however, it gives the result in a synchronous and blocking manner. We send the `:ping` message to the `PingPong` process and then wait for the `:reply` message. Upon receiving the `:reply` message, return the response. Additionally, if no `:reply` is returned in 10 seconds, return the `{:error, :timeout}` tuple.

Now, adjust the handling code for the `:ping` message:

```
defp loop(state, parent, debug) do
  receive do
    {:ping, from} ->
      send from, {:reply, :pong}
    {:system, from, request} ->
      :sys.handle_system_msg(request, from, parent, __MODULE__,
debug, state)
  end
  loop(state, parent, debug)
end
```

We are only adjusting the one `send/2` call, returning the `{:reply, :pong}` tuple. This is what the `receive` block here is expecting.

Now, loading up and starting the `PingPong` process, we should be able to simply call `ping` and receive the response as a return value:

```
iex(3)> PingPong.ping

:pong
```

Variable scope in the Gen* processes

When we create helper functions for our `Gen*` processes, we need to keep in mind the scope that these functions are running. Recall the key-value process from earlier. When we added the helper functions `put/2` and `get/1`, these functions are running under the context of the *calling* process, not the server process that will handle the message:

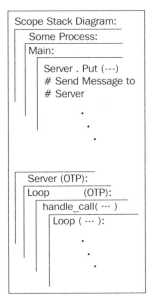

Figure 1: Scope stack diagram

This means that the helper functions themselves will never have access to the current state of the server, and thus, will not be able to do any extra logic with that respect.

Being in the calling scope is how we can, sometimes implicitly, grab the calling process identifier, or other known to exist variables. However, the helper functions should request the most (everything except calls to `self/0`) must-have variables as parameters instead of referencing the variables directly.

Back-pressure and load shedding

Throughout this chapter, we discussed many systems that used synchronous and asynchronous means of transport. The `GenServer` has `call` versus `cast`, and the `GenEvent` has `sync_notify` versus `notify`. In developing applications, it will be tempting to always use the asynchronous versions by default because they are faster, which can be true. Writing files to disk or writing data to the network *can* be very expensive; forcing upstream processes to wait for this process means clients or users may also experience that very same wait.

However, I don't support this temptation. Use the synchronous forms first and profile your system and processes. Then, if it is warranted, decide to use asynchronous methods. By using the synchronous variants, there is inherent back-pressure built into the system. This actually tends to be a good thing because it can keep the system from crashing by applying pressure on the source of input. Doing nothing tends to cause more catastrophic failures, queues spilling, and system resource contention; the system will apply its own back-pressure in the form of completely dropping everything.

Another approach is to use asynchronous behaviours, but have a mechanism to flip the API functions to synchronous behaviours when there are too many messages being sent. This is the exact approach used in Elixir's built-in `Logging` module.

Building back-pressure or load shedding into a system will be a huge benefit to building a truly scalable application. Without it, limits will be found the hard way, users will be angry, stock holders will be equally upset, and business can be lost. Choosing either back-pressure or load balancing (or both) will help mitigate these issues. There will still be upset users, but the number of upset users will be orders of magnitude smaller than *all* of them.

Furthermore, using good end-to-end design and idempotent APIs will largely hide the issues and failures of back-pressure and load-shedding from the users and clients.

Supervisors

We've mentioned process trees several times already, and it's time we discuss them in-depth.

The GNU/Linux- and Unix-based OSes are a great example of an existing process tree that can be studied and inspected. It has a root process, typically `init` with process ID 1, and it is the ancestor process of all the child processes. Each child process can itself create more child processes. The structure of this chain is a tree rooted at PID 1.

Process trees in Elixir/Erlang are not too dissimilar. There is a root process for the runtime and application controller. The applications loaded and started upon the startup of the VM are children of the application controller or immediate parent process.

However, OTP takes process trees to a new level with supervision trees. Supervision trees are similar to process trees except that they describe slightly different concepts. Process trees only describe the parent-child relationship between processes, whereas supervisor trees describe the class of parent-child supervisors for running processes *and* the strategies used to restart dead children:

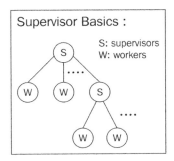

Figure 2: Supervisor basics

A simple example of a supervisor tree is a single supervisor monitoring a single process. The supervisor listens for events about the child process, and will take certain action on the receipt of certain events, the most basic of which is doing nothing. This is the basic premise of process supervision. A supervisor process starts and restarts a child process upon failure or an abnormal exit reason.

The supervisor is itself a process, so it is a natural extension that a supervisor monitor have other supervisors, and thus, the concept of a supervision tree arises. Furthermore, the supervisor can have different restart strategies for each monitored process.

Restart strategies describe how and what actions a supervisor should take when receiving notification of a dead child process. OTP describes four different strategies for use—one for one, one for all, rest for one, and simple one for one.

One for one describes what you might expect—restart the process that has died:

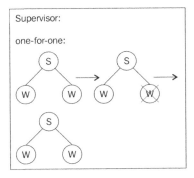

Figure 3: Supervisor one for one

One for all may also seem intuitive; this strategy tells the supervisor to restart *all* or every process when a single process fails:

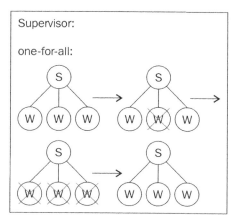

Figure 4: Supervisor one for all

Rest for one restarts all the child processes — from the failed to the last. For example, say we have four processes defined in a list, if process 2 dies, then process 3 and 4 will be killed and then process 2, 3, and 4 will be restarted:

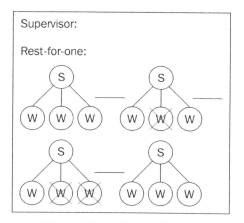

Figure 5: Supervisor rest for one

Simple one for one is a bit of a special case. It tends to be the most complex strategy of the four. The processes under a simple one for one supervisor are generally the same and aren't necessarily started statically, when the supervisor starts. There are also internal, structural differences between one for one and simple one for one. That is, one for one stores the child processes as a list, whereas simple one for one stores it as a dictionary making the simple one for one much faster with larger numbers of child processes.

Along with supervisor strategies, there are also restart options for child or worker processes. The default used restart option is :permanent, which means the process will *always* be restarted, even if the process is killed normally, for example, {:shutdown, :normal}. A common option used for simple one for one is :temporary—the process will *never* be restarted. This is often useful when the supervisor isn't the one process *starting* the processes, for example, connection pooling each process is associated with a connection. If the connection dies or it is reset, the supervisor monitoring the processes should not restart them. The third, final option for restarts is :transient, which means that the supervisor will only restart the process if it was exited abnormally. That is, if the process shutdown reason is anything other than :normal, :shutdown, or {:shutdown, term}, the supervisor will restart the process.

Creating supervisors in Elixir is very similar to creating other OTP behaviours. You need to define a module that uses the Supervisor behaviour and a few functions, and start it.

Let's create a simple supervisor for the KV process from before:

```
defmodule KV.Supervisor do
  use Supervisor

  def start_link do
    Supervisor.start_link(__MODULE__, :ok)
  end

  def init(:ok) do
    children = [worker(KV, [])]

    supervise(children, strategy: :one_for_one)
  end
end
```

As usual, there's a start_link function, which uses Supervisor.start_link to perform the synchronous starting and linking of the supervisor process to the current process. The init/1 function is where the supervising configuration is set. We define a list of children or monitored processes. These could be worker processes, or other supervisors.

 There's another helper function, supervisor/2, similar to worker/2. The difference is that supervisors have an infinite timeout value for shutdown, whereas workers default to 5 second timeouts.

Loading both modules into an IEx session, we can see the supervisor keep the KV process running, even after exits and failures:

```
iex(1)> import_file "kv.exs"
...
iex(2)> {:ok, sup} = KV.Supervisor.start_link
{:ok, #PID<0.71.0>}
iex(3)> Supervisor.which_children(sup)
[{KV, #PID<0.72.0>, :worker, [KV]}]
iex(4)> KV.put(:a, 42)
:ok
iex(5)> KV.get(:a)
42
```

The KV process is started after the supervisor starts and it works as we expect. But now, we can cause the KV process to exit and see that it restarts:

```
iex(6)> Process.whereis(KV) |> Process.exit :normal
true
iex(7)> KV.get(:a)
nil
```

There is no semblance of persistence with the KV process, but it is restarted by the KV.Supervisor. We can add persistence by adding more to the supervision tree.

Fail fast(er)

Why would we want process supervision? What is the benefit of using process supervision over exception handling?

Exception handling attempts to keep the process or thread alive by catching errors and having them propagate using a series of the try-catch blocks. This often will fail to raise the error to the appropriate level and, worse, it can leave the process or context in a very bad state, possibly masking more subtle, and farther reaching issues.

Failing fast and using process supervision, we can avoid the bad state issue entirely: if a process fails for any reason, restart it. Adding good logging around the supervisors and workers, error propagation to the correct party can be far easier.

Designing with supervisors

The concepts around process supervision are not necessarily complicated. The complexity usually arises in how to design applications using supervisors, what order to define the supervision tree, what level of the tree certain processes should be, and so on. This is not an easy problem, but it is not impossible.

There are some clues and other signs to look for that will guide the design. Look for process dependence. Does a process depend on another? The latter should be higher in the supervisor tree. Does a process depend on an entire process tree? The subtree should be defined before. Are there two processes that are co-dependent? Attempt to isolate them into their own supervisor tree and use `:one_for_all`.

Assumptions of the OTP process initialization

Along with the design of applications using supervisors, it's helpful to know or make explicit the assumptions being made when starting OTP processes. If a `GenServer` process on initializing makes a call to a database, the assumption is that this database will *always* be alive when this process starts. If it is not, then the process can't start. However, if the database can be expected to not always be available, the assumption of the defined OTP process will fail, and likely cause the entire application to fail because of the number of restarts will be exceeded. Therefore, the assumptions of what is available during initialization and startup of OTP processes must be known *a priori*.

Exercises

Read about OTP design principles at `http://www.erlang.org/doc/design_principles/des_princ.html`.

Summary

In this chapter, we discussed all the things OTP. Specifically, we covered OTP applications, process supervisors, the `Gen*` processes, and special OTP processes. We covered some examples using them and rewrote the examples from the previous chapter to show how much easier it is now.

Next, we will start distributing processes across nodes.

8
Distributed Elixir – Taking Concurrency to the Next Node

Generally, when we want to run code on different computers, we have to write special programs to handle loading code and sending data between nodes. This process is itself very error-prone and hard to get correct.

However, in Elixir and OTP, the hard work of getting code loaded on multiple machines and cooperating is done for us; the OTP framework will load code, connect nodes, and handle the task of distributing applications.

OTP will not do all the work, but it gives a good amount of tools to help guide us in the right direction and help us make the right choices.

Obligatory discussion about distributed computing

> *"Distributed computing is hard"*
>
> *– Everyone*

This quote, of course, is a bit hyperbolic. It's not necessarily the case that distributed computing is hard, it's mainly that there are far more edge cases and other assumptions we must shed before being able to proceed. This section won't attempt to be an exhaustive list of concepts and topics in distributed computing, but it will discuss what is most applicable to understanding OTP and developing distributed applications with Elixir.

Fallacies of distributed computing

Let's briefly discuss the 8 fallacies of distributed computing. By understanding the (false) assumptions of distributed computing, we can understand the assumptions made by Elixir and OTP, and how to leverage them.

The network is reliable

Often when designing distributed applications, developers will assume that the network will always be available and therefore, they will place themselves into strange and interesting failure modes. There are plenty of sources that debunk this myth; the network is, in fact, quite unreliable.

The network can fail for all kinds of reasons—cut wires, power outages, general hardware failure, hostile or malformed packets, and interdimensional timelords destroying critical components of the network.

Therefore, assuming that remote resources are always available will cause indeterministic failures: the process waiting for the resource could be waiting *forever*, certainly less than an ideal amount of time to wait.

Unfortunately, OTP and Elixir do not have any special features that solve this problem since it is often an application-specific decision of *how* to handle remote resource failures. However, we do gain scalability using the message passing model asynchronously; we handle remote failures the same as we handle local, inter-process failures. This way, the application can scale-out in both performance *and* design.

There is no latency

It's often hard to forget latency when developing applications in geographically separated environments. But latency on the same switch can even become an issue for particularly saturated switches, noisy applications, or when TCP incast shows its ugly face.

Worse, seemingly good distributed systems can actually make it easier to forget network calls cost time since it masks remote calls, making them virtually indistinguishable from local calls. The semantics of making all calls look the same is attractive since they do not require any extra effort to grow, but if they are later followed with the expectation of quick results, they will fail or hang.

The general semantics of isolated processes, timeouts, asynchronous messaging, and always expecting processes to fail is that OTP and Elixir can again guide us in the right direction. However, we must still keep a lookout for timeout thresholds being too low.

Bandwidth is infinite

Networks are generally fast (when they work) and are getting faster, but they are not infinitely fast. As there is an inherent cost of time to send packets, forgetting about packet size is another way to induce the cost of time or another way to cause applications to fail.

Fortunately again, the design and semantics of OTP and Elixir will help keep message size down. Another good trick for small messages is to send events instead of full objects. To borrow from the overused cliché of banking examples, instead of sending the balance (and account details) for updates, send the transaction details—deposit or credit and amount.

The network is secure

Assuming the network is secure is like assuming user input is safe, non-malicious. It's wrong! The degree to which applications break is inversely proportional to the assumption of sanity of user input.

Disappointingly, OTP failed to consider this assumption. When we discuss how to connect two running Erlang VMs together, we will see just how weak and poor the security is. Thus, it will be left to you to bake security into your applications.

Topology doesn't change

Hardware and servers fail, get recycled, and are upgraded. Hardware is added and removed; the topology of a cluster *will* be different from the moment it's turned on to the current time. There are a lot of factors that change a topology, but nonetheless, assuming it's always the same will cause applications to fail with strange unreachable resource errors or similar.

Fortunately, there are mechanisms in OTP that allow us to forget topology from the start. A process can be messaged regardless of which node it's running, and treating failures is, again, the same.

There is only one administrator

There isn't one administrator that operates the Internet. If an application depends on third-party remote resources, many administrators may be between the application and the resource(s). This can cause all sorts of problems, some of which, are covered in other assumptions. But failing to realize the maintenance windows of another application or resource can cause all sorts of failures.

Transport cost is zero

We have already noted some of the inherent costs of network calls, chiefly, time. The network may have latency and the data may be large; serializing and deserializing data itself takes time. However, transporting data has another cost—space (read money).

Copying data from disk to RAM certainly costs time, but copying data over a (metered) network costs money or incurs a bandwidth charge. Unnecessarily sending a large number of messages can not only increase the overhead of the application in terms of system resources, but can also incur the wrath of your operational cost.

The network is homogeneous

Every device, switch, and system that connects to, depends on, or is a member of an application that will *not* necessarily be the same, will *not* necessarily have the same capabilities, and will *not* necessarily behave the same as any other. The consequences of assuming the network is homogeneous are obvious—things will fail in expected and unexpected ways.

In terms of OTP, or programming in general, this means that the wire protocol is consistent and an open standard. Depending on closed standards can inherently yield this assumption and adding different implementations or languages will be problematic.

The OTP protocol is completely open and any node implementing the protocol can join the network, if it walks like a duck, quacks like a duck, it's a duck. This enables C interoperability or C-nodes.

 A C-node is just a C program that implements the OTP protocol and becomes a member node in an OTP cluster.

Fighting dragons blindfolded, equipped with a butter knife

Building distributed systems is hard, and with OTP and Elixir, it will still be hard. However, with OTP we might be able to peek through the blindfold and the butter knife might be a sword, but we will still be fighting dragons.

Understanding that there will be monsters and dragons lurking in the code, the assumptions, and the design of our applications will help us make the right decisions.

Of course, there are still many problems and challenges to overcome, but at least, we have some pretty awesome tools. Many of the issues become design decisions that will need to be made at the application layer. However, the most problematic issue will be how to deal with process and node failure and the network being unreliable.

Unfortunately, there is no way to determine if a process has failed or if the network is dropping. Thus, there is a choice—OTP could optimistically assume that the node is alive and continue to send messages, hoping the messages would eventually get through, or simply assume the node is dead and move forward (somehow).

Occasionally, it is in fact the network, and the process is simply behind; thus, choosing to assume the node is alive may be easier for resynchronizing. However, waiting to fail a node or process can delay normal failures with catastrophic consequences.

Choosing pessimistically avoids certain problems with assuming optimistically, but it also creates its own problems, namely, what should the application do when a node that was thought to be dead turns out to be alive and was only separated as a network partition? From the perspective of the other process, what should it do when it thinks *all* the other nodes are dead and they all come back alive?

CAP – choose two, and one will be partition tolerance

When a node or process dies, there are a few actions the application can choose to take, chiefly, to either become unavailable and gain strong consistency, or sacrifice strong consistency and stay available for the duration of failure.

If the application chooses to drop availability, the data will remain consistent. However, *no one* will be able to do anything because the service is unavailable. On the other hand, the service is still available and users are completely free to fully use the service; however, the data between nodes will drift, and reconciling this is non-trivial.

This choice that must be made is the result of a fundamental theorem of distributing computing call the CAP theorem, first proposed by Eric Brewer in 1998 and later proved in 2002. The essential result of the theorem is that from the triangle of choices for distributed systems, (strong, read linearly) **consistency (C)**, **availability (A)**, and network **partition tolerance (P)**, we can only choose two:

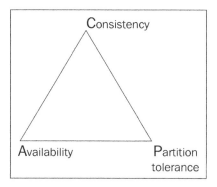

Figure 1: A CAP theorem triangle

In terms of the original CAP conjecture and the resulting proof, the definitions of consistency, availability, and partition tolerance are very specific.

That is, in terms of CAP, consistency is defined as linearized consistency. Linearized consistency is a very strong form of consistency, which requires all the events to properly follow the previous events and will be atomically isolated.

Availability is defined to be fully, successfully respondent; 500 errors do not count as a response. If a node is available, it must return and terminate successfully to all the requests.

Partition tolerance is, as it is terribly named, means that the system can tolerate the use of an asynchronous network where messages are delayed or dropped entirely. Usually, the distinction between a delayed message and a dropped message is immaterial as they are often indistinguishable by the system or application.

Therefore, using the preceding definitions, we can describe certain classes of systems — CP, AP, and CA.

A CP system is capable of maintaining consistency of its data during failure. This means that the system in question may become unavailable to certain requests, for example, reads and/or writes. Or, the system will only allow reads, but will refuse all writes, or some other variation of degraded availability. But the system will maintain consistency, always. And, if it uses the strict definitions of the CAP theorem, it means that the system will *always* be linearly consistent.

On the other hand, an AP system will be able to continue to respond to requests and serve data during a failure, although, the data returned or written may be stale or written against stale data. If the system is using the strict definitions of CAP, any form of consistency is no longer guaranteed. Writing against stale data is never good; thus, often the resolution for consistency is usually achieved by casual ordering (for example, vector clocks), application/user-level resolution procedures, or by relaxing the definition of consistency (or some combination of all of these).

Why you must choose partition tolerance

There's a reason one of the two is chosen for you. (Network) partition tolerance is fundamental to distributed applications, so much so that without it, making sensible distributed applications becomes overwhelmingly difficult, if not impossible, without it.

To see that partition tolerance must be included, imagine a system where there are three separate nodes and a partition separates the first two nodes from the third. If the system is claiming consistency *and* availability, *all* the nodes must be consistent and available.

Such a system may look as the one shown in the following diagram:

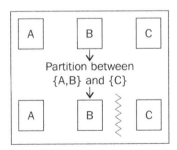

Figure 2: An ABC system

The third node, which is outside of the quorum, must ensure consistency *and* availability. Therefore, while clients are connecting to the third node, the third node must accept reads and writes, writing them consistently. However, there's a sort of impossibility here. Certainly, it could accept the read/write requests, servicing them as any single node would; however, when the partition heals, the two partitions will possibly have diverged from each other, making any decent form of consistency impossible to ensure:

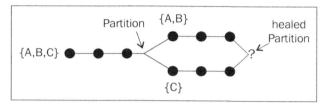

Figure 3: An ABC system state graph

Therefore, without relaxing the definitions of consistency and/or availability or providing application-level conflict resolution, there is no way to create a CA system.

Relaxing definitions

The definitions of consistency, availability, and partition tolerance with respect to CAP are very specific. Changing the definition of these terms removes us from the realm of CAP. Of course, this new realm isn't completely uncharted, but it definitely isn't CAP.

Relaxing the definitions of these terms is typically a choice made by the system or application developers and designers. The reasons for doing so are usually because the narrow definitions of CAP are too strict and are not always necessary for the modeling of the problem domain.

For example, bank transactions, the canonical example for demonstrating issues with distributed systems, in the real world are often modeled using a 24 hour period of indeterminate consistency, which will be reconciled at the end of the day (or whenever the reconciliation process runs). In this form, the system of transactions is consistent and available. Of course, it's not CAP, because the definition of consistent is quite obviously changed.

Another example of relaxing consistency are systems that are *eventually* consistent. This means exactly what it says. Such a system may accept many writes and eventually replicate those writes to the other nodes in the system. The latter group of nodes, in the mean time, can respond to reads and provide access to the now stale data.

Typically, such a system will use a leader node or nodes for writes, and have replicas or replica groups for each leader.

Similarly, another system can redefine available of an otherwise CP system to where non-quorum members can respond to reads but not writes. The data from the minority may be stale, but that is the accepted cost of the compromise.

All of these variations will provide a system that seems like it side-stepped and defeated CAP. Do not be fooled, this is not true. Marketing hype aside, CAP is so far a fundamental result of asynchronous networks that cannot be avoided if C stands for linearized consistency and A stands for successful responses to requests. Even changing the definitions, it's fairly easy to reason about some inherent limitations for creating truly robust distributed systems.

Another short discussion about networks

Before we go further, we should take a moment to talk about networking and more specifically, about network topologies.

Fortunately, OTP doesn't really require us to know a lot about the TCP/IP stack or the OSI model of networking. In fact, OTP abstracts away most of the difficulties with networking — remote calls are identical to local calls. Even if a raw TCP socket is desired, the default mode for the socket will be to marshal the data packets as messages to the controlling process. That is, the OTP process that owns the socket will be given regular messages as TCP data is received.

Topologies

There are several standard topology models that exist today. There is the line, bus, ring, star, tree, mesh, mesh ring, and crossbar topologies.

Knowing the topologies isn't entirely required for building distributed applications. The usefulness of knowing topologies really shows when attempting to optimize network traffic. Furthermore, knowing the layout of nodes can help tremendously when trying to decide communication strategies and other synchronization patterns in distributed code.

A line topology is defined by each node interconnected with its neighbors, in a linear fashion.

A bus topology is similar to line, except of the requirement of a message to be delivered *through* neighbors, it can travel directly to the recipient node however, the bus or the cable can receive extra noise and require frequent message negotiation and retransmission. Some variants of the bus topology are considered network hubs:

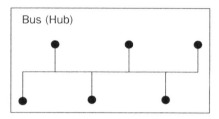

Let's take a look at the line topology diagram:

A star topology is similar to a line topology, except for a center node where all the nodes connect. This brings each node only one hop away from each other, but the center node receives an abundance of traffic:

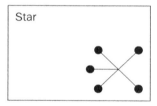

Tree topologies are similar to star topologies with embedded line topologies. More appropriately, tree topologies are recursive; however, this can confound the inherent hybrid approach in creating such a topology:

Backing up to the line topology, by adding one extra link or edge, the topology becomes a ring:

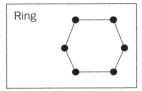

However, like the line topology, mesh topologies are limited by their corner to corner distances:

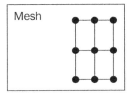

An improvement here is to add rings for the outer nodes:

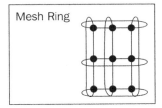

Of course, we can also have full networks, where every node is connected to each and every other node. However, this is typically very cost prohibitive in large numbers. A fully connected topology is called a crossbar or switch:

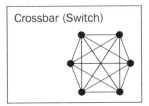

The crossbar topology is the topology used by OTP to connect nodes together. Every node has a direct address and path for sending messages to *any* other node, in one hop. This is the reason why it is not recommended to have OTP use connections across the Internet or to have a large number of nodes interconnected; the communication cost between nodes becomes pretty expensive and the underlying network will become quite saturated with just the OTP heartbeat traffic.

Distributed computing with Elixir

Now that we've had our obligatory introduction to distributed computing and networking, we can start to see how and what Elixir and OTP bring to the table for creating distributed applications. Again, Elixir and OTP won't solve the problems we've mentioned, but the design around Elixir and OTP will put us in a really good position for handling failures in our applications and systems.

OTP nodes

So far, I've used the term node pretty loosely. Certainly, nodes have many meanings in certain contexts. In computing, node could refer to an element in a tree, a graph, a network, a server, and so on. In terms of OTP, a node refers to an Erlang VM. There can be as many OTP nodes on a single computer as allowed by the resources of the machine. OTP nodes can be hosted across several machines in the same network. OTP nodes can even be geographically distributed, although it's not recommended.

The choices of how to distribute OTP nodes will usually be a choice of the application.

Node names

Using numbers for addressing servers is nice for computers, but isn't very nice for the humans using those computers. We see this most prominently with domain names and DNS. DNS takes a friendly name for a website or machine and returns the associated IP address.

Similarly, OTP and node addressing follows a similar principle. Nodes have long names and short names. The long name is typically the node identifier and the **fully qualified domain name (FQDN)** of the host. Node shortnames are similar, however, instead of the FQDN, the host identifier portion is simply the hostname. Let's see some examples:

```
iex(1)> Node.self
:nonode@nohost
```

The `Node` module offers some functions for working with OTP nodes and inspection. The `Node.self/0` function provides a means of seeing the current node's identifier atom (name). Starting `iex` without any options does not name the started node, essentially making it unaddressable. If we want an addressable name, pass either `--name` {long name} or `--sname` {short name} to `iex` when starting, and the started node will be addressable:

```
$ iex --name my_node@my_host
Erlang/OTP 18 [erts-7.0] [source] [64-bit] [smp:12:12] [async-threads:10]
[hipe] [kernel-poll:false]


Interactive Elixir (1.0.5) - press Ctrl+C to exit (type h() ENTER for
help)
iex(my_node@my_host)1>
```

Notice the prompt of IEx changes to include the node name identifier. Querying the node information is the same, but we should see the name has changed:

```
iex(my_node@my_host)1> Node.self :my_node@my_host.
```

Similarly, starting IEx with `--sname` provides a similar result:

```
$ iex --sname my_node
Erlang/OTP 18 [erts-7.0] [source] [64-bit] [smp:12:12] [async-threads:10]
[hipe] [kernel-poll:false]


Interactive Elixir (1.0.5) - press Ctrl+C to exit (type h() ENTER for
help)
iex(my_node@Eligos)1> Node.self

:my_node@Eligos
```

My hostname is `Eligos`, and your results will vary. The hostname section is derived from the machine.

As expected, the node starts up and the prompt is changed to include the new identifier information. Since we're using the short name, we are not required to provide the host information; it is inferred from the system. This, however, does not mean that it cannot be provided. For example, starting it again providing a host entry, we get a similar result:

```
$ iex --sname my_node@my_host
Erlang/OTP 18 [erts-7.0] [source] [64-bit] [smp:12:12] [async-threads:10]
[hipe] [kernel-poll:false]
```

```
Interactive Elixir (1.0.5) - press Ctrl+C to exit (type h() ENTER for
help)
iex(my_node@my_host)1> Node.self
:my_node@my_host
```

Connecting nodes

Of course, what good is providing a name if two or more nodes aren't connected?

Using another function from the Node module, Node.list/0, we can examine the list of the connected nodes:

```
iex(my_node@my_host)1> Node.list
[]
```

Well, as might be expected, when starting a new node, it will not be connected to another node. Thus, another node needs to be accessible and then the two will need to be connected.

Connecting two OTP nodes turns out to be fairly straightforward, and we won't need any special accounts or any special setup to demonstrate the connecting of multiple nodes together on a single machine.

Open up two terminals or shells. In one shell, start the IEx named node_one:

```
$ iex --sname node_one
```

In the other, start the IEx named node_two:

```
$ iex --sname node_two
```

Now that there are two nodes, and we need to connect them. To accomplish this, we will use the Node.connect/1 function, and the argument will be the atom of the node we wish to connect to:

```
iex(node_one@Eligos)1> Node.connect :node_two@Eligos
true
```

If all goes well, Node.connect/1 will return true and the two nodes will be connected. This can be verified by using Node.list/0:

```
iex(node_one@Eligos)2> Node.list
[:node_two@Eligos]


iex(node_two@Eligos)1> Node.list
[:node_one@Eligos]
```

Cookies and node security

The basic protection of connecting (or not connecting) two nodes in OTP is resolved by the Erlang cookie. This cookie file, `.erlang_cookie`, typically written to the home directory of the current user, is essentially a small set of characters that *acts* as a sort of password and authentication. There are several ways the file can be overwritten: IEx has a `--cookie` command-line argument that allows a cookie to be set at start up. There are also functions inside the `Node` module for inspecting and setting the cookie:

```
iex(node_one@Eligos)1> Node.get_cookie
:FNMKUGIDQMSIXFKHTTKC
iex(node_one@Eligos)2> Node.set_cookie :anewcookie
true
iex(node_one@Eligos)3> Node.get_cookie
:anewcookie
```

If we now attempt to have `node_two` connect in the current state, it will fail:

```
iex(node_two@Eligos)1> Node.connect :node_one@Eligos
false
```

And, a log message will appear in the `node_one` terminal:

```
iex(node_one@Eligos)4>
[error] ** Connection attempt from disallowed node :node_two@Eligos **
```

Changing the cookie on `node_two` to be similar as the cookie at `node_one` would resolve the issue and allow the two to connect.

Certainly, this mechanism isn't ideal in terms of security, and unfortunately, there doesn't seem to be any plans (currently) to improve this. Furthermore, as the assumption goes, be careful using this over public or not trusted networks, since the cookie negotiation is sent as clear, readable plain text.

Node ping pong

Now that we have two nodes connected together, we can create a larger version of ping pong:

```
iex(node_one@Eligos)3> pid = Node.spawn_link :node_two@Eligos, fn ->
...(node_one@Eligos)3> receive do
...(node_one@Eligos)3> {:ping, client} -> send client, :pong
...(node_one@Eligos)3> end
...(node_one@Eligos)3> end
#PID<8015.71.0>
```

The `Node.spawn_link` function is similar to the previous versions of `spawn_link` we've seen before; the difference, however, is that the `Node` version is able to start a process on a remote node. The remote process is indicated by the PID reference returned by `Node.spawn_link`. Decomposing the numbers, the first number, 8015, refers to the node number, and the rest are as we've seen previously:

```
iex(node_one@Eligos)4> send pid, {:ping, self}
{:ping, #PID<0.66.0>
iex(node_one@Eligos)5> flush
:pong
:ok
```

Sending a message to the process and flushing, we receive the `:pong` atom message back, as we expect.

Group leader

When writing inter-node Elixir applications, where does console output go? To which interactive session are log messages shown? In fact, this question isn't local to inter-node applications, but is also relevant with multiple processes.

The OTP I/O system uses the concept of **group leaders** to determine where certain output should be directed. This group leader is the process that handles the I/O tasks for a group of Erlang processes. Unless changed, the group leader is inherited by the parent process.

Continuing with the nodes from the previous section, if we use `IO.puts/1` in either terminal, the output will be directed to the current terminal:

```
iex(node_one@Eligos)1> IO.puts "hello world"
hello world
:ok
```

```
iex(node_two@Eligos)1> IO.puts "hello world"
hello world
:ok
```

However, if we spawn a process from node_one *on* node_two, the output of the `IO.puts` call will be directed to the standard output stream of node_one:

```
iex(node_one@Eligos)2> Node.spawn :node_two@Eligos, fn ->
...(node_one@Eligos)2> IO.puts "hello world" end
hello world
#PID<8015.75.0>
```

The output is directed here, but the process ran from the other node.

To make this more explicit, we will change the spawned process slightly:

```
iex(node_two@Eligos)3> Node.spawn :node_one@Eligos, fn ->
...(node_two@Eligos)3> IO.inspect Node.self end
#PID<8044.94.0>
:node_one@Eligos
```

From node_two, a process was started on node_one. Since this process is on node_one, Node.self/0 should report the correct node, and as expected, the output is, in fact, the atom for node_one.

Again, the output of these processes are redirected to the output of the group leader process. Therefore, although a process may be spawned on one node, and runs on that node, the output of any log messages or I/O output will be (re)directed to the group leader.

We can also use a process' group leader as an I/O process for writing from other nodes. Consider, for example, our two connected nodes, and that we want to change where output is directed using IO.puts/2.

First, we will need to get the group leader process reference to the other node. This can be done in several ways:

```
iex(node_two@Eligos)1> :global.register_name(:two, :erlang.group_leader)
:yes
```

This registers the process name between the nodes; we will go into depth on global registration in the next section.

Then, from node_one, we can retrieve the process ID for the group leader of node_two, and begin writing messages from node_one to the output of node_two:

```
iex(node_one@Eligos)2> two = :global.whereis_name :two
#PID<8896.33.0>
iex(node_one@Eligos)3> IO.puts(two, "Hello")
:ok
iex(node_one@Eligos)4> IO.puts(two, "World")
```

Notice that the output of node_one is just the result of IO.puts/2, but the output of node_two shows the text from IO.puts/2:

```
Hello
World
iex(node_two@Eligos)2>
```

Globally registered names

In the previous chapters, we registered processes such that they would become addressable by the atom instead of the PID reference. However, this isn't enough for inter-node communication. Registered processes are bound to the current node and are not shared outside. However, there is a mechanism for registering processes that *every* node apart of the interconnection can access.

If we spawn a process on one node, say, the ping pong process or a filter process, we may want to be able to use these processes from other nodes:

```
iex(node_one@Eligos)1> Node.connect :node_two@Eligos
iex(node_one@Eligos)2> pid = spawn_link fn() ->
...(node_one@Eligos)2> receive do
...(node_one@Eligos)2> {:ping, sender} -> send sender, :pong
...(node_one@Elgios)2> end
...(node_one@Eligos)2> end
iex(node_one@Eligos)3> :global.register_name(PingPong, pid)
:yes
```

On `node_one`, we start the simplistic ping pong receive loop. Afterwards, we use the `:global` Erlang module to globally register the process under the `PingPong` atom. Next, we can send messages from `node_two` to the ping pong process and receive results. However, global names can't be used as drop-in replacements for PID references. The PID will need to be looked up, using the `:global.whereis_name/1` function:

```
iex(node_two@Eligos)1> :global.whereis_name PingPong
#PID<8044.110.0>
iex(node_two@Eligos)2> :global.whereis_name(PingPong) |>
...(node_two@Eligos)2> send {:ping, self}
{:ping, #PID<0.66.0>}
iex(node_two@Eligos)3> flush
:pong
:ok
```

This allowed us to consume the ping pong process running on `node_one` from `node_two` with only atoms.

As another example of globally registered processes, we can create the filter service `GenServer` process that can be consumed from any node in the cluster.

We define our `FilterService` module as normal, similar to modules defined in the previous chapter:

```
defmodule FilterService do
  use GenServer

  def start_link(opts \\ []) do
    GenServer.start_link(__MODULE__, nil, [name: {:global, __
MODULE__}] ++
opts)
  end

  def init(_) do
    {:ok, %{}}
  end

  def filter(collection, predicate) do
    pid = :global.whereis_name __MODULE__
    GenServer.cast(pid, {:filter, collection, predicate, self})
  end

  def handle_cast({:filter, collection, predicate, sender}, state) do
    send sender, {:filter_results, collection |> Enum.
filter(predicate)}
    {:noreply, state}
  end

end
```

However, notice the difference in the `GenServer.start_link/3` options. Similar to how using the terms `[name: __MODULE__]` automatically registered the spawned process, using the modified version, `[name: {:global, __MODULE__}]`, automatically globally registers the process. Furthermore, the helper function, `FilterService.filter/2`, will do a lookup of the global process.

The module will need to be loaded on both nodes for the helper function to be of any use. But that is generally a small price to pay for having nice functions for calling into global processes.

As before, start two nodes, connect them, and load the filter service module:

```
iex(node_one@Eligos)1> Node.connect :node_two@Eligos
:true
iex(node_one@Eligos)2> import_file "filterservice.ex"
{:module, FilterService,
```

```
<<70, 79, 82, 49, 0, 0, 12, 120, 66, 69, 65, 77, 69, 120, 68, 99, 0, 0,
2,
174, 131, 104, 2, 100, 0, 14, 101, 108, 105, 120, 105, 114, 95, 100, 111,
99,
115, 95, 118, 49, 108, 0, 0, 0, 2, 104, 2, ...>>,
 {:handle_cast, 2}}
```

Similarly, on the other node:

```
iex(node_two@Eligos)1> import_file "filterservice.ex"
...
```

Choose either node and start the service:

```
iex(node_one@Eligos)3> {:ok, pid} = FilterService.start_link
{:ok, #PID<0.96.0>}
```

> Be sure to only start the process once and only on one node.
> Starting the process multiple times will result in an error
> because the name is already registered.

Now, we can test that the service works from both nodes:

```
iex(node_one@Eligos)4> FilterService.filter([1, 2, 3, 4, 5, 6], fn(x) ->
rem(x, 2) == 0 end)
:ok
iex(node_one@Eligos)5> flush
{:filter_results, [2, 4, 6]}
:ok
```

Similarly, on the other node:

```
iex(node_two@Eligos)2> FilterService.filter([7, 8, 9, 10, 11, 12], fn(x)
->
rem(x, 2) == 0 end)
:ok
iex(node_two@Eligos)3> flush
{:filter_results, [8, 10, 12]}
:ok
```

Although global processes aren't as convenient as locally registered processes, they are much easier to use than PID references shared through other means.

Summary

This chapter introduced the basic concepts and problems of distributed computing. OTP makes certain assumptions based on the concepts of distributed computing, some rightfully so, others falling prey to the fallacies of distributed computing.

We briefly discussed different network topologies and which topology is inherent with OTP. Knowing the different topologies is important for application design strategy, especially around message sizing, network optimization, and synchronization mechanisms.

Finally, we examined how Elixir and OTP can connect separate OTP nodes together and use them to cooperate processing with the nodes.

Metaprogramming – Doing More with Less

Doing more with less might be a strange concept at first blush, but anyone familiar with LISP macros will attest that metaprogramming is something special and certainly something that should be in every language.

Metaprogramming, as the name might imply, is the means to write code that writes code. Typically, macros are the means of metaprogramming and in Elixir, they are first class.

The term macro may be scary, especially, if your background with macros is C and its macro system. Elixir macros are *nothing* like C macros. Elixir macros define the language, and they enable some pretty awesome power. It all boils down to the following: "Any Elixir code can be represented with Elixir data structures."

Stop and think about this for a second.

What does this really mean? It means that any line of code in Elixir, any, can be represented using the most basic data structures of Elixir, namely, numbers, strings, tuples, and lists.

This chapter is going to explore how this concept enables the metaprogramming facilities available to all Elixir programmers.

Behaviours and protocols

Before we dive into the depths of metaprogramming, we need to discuss some related functionalities of Elixir that provide polymorphic features to the language. These are behaviours and protocols.

Briefly, behaviours provide similar functionality of interfaces from other languages such as Java and protocols provide a means for defining and dispatching function implementations for specific data structures.

Behaviours

Behaviours are not exclusive to Elixir; in fact, this is how Erlang implements the Gen* patterns. Behaviours are similar to interfaces in **object-oriented (OO)** languages. They specify a collection of functions that the module will expose. All the GenServer modules will have the handle_call, handle_cast, and handle_info functions.

 The spelling of behaviour in the core Elixir and Erlang API uses the British English spelling. However, Elixir's parser will allow either spelling.

Similar to interfaces in OO languages, the behaviour definition also helps the developers and users of behaviours know which functions *need* to be implemented for the proper usage of their modules. It's hard to create a useful GenServer module without your own handle_call and handle_cast.

Defining behaviours

Behaviours in Elixir are defined using regular modules and the defcallback macro.

A short introduction to typespecs

Elixir is a dynamic language, allowing for the types to be inferred at runtime. This is especially useful during development and exploration. However, to achieve this flexibility, compile-time type checks are left at the door. This means we can write functions like the following lines of code:

```
iex(1)> defmodule Foo do
...(1)>   def square(x), do: x * x
...(1)> end
```

And, this can be used as usual:

```
iex(2)> Foo.square(4)
16
iex(3)> Foo.square(4.4)
19.360000000000003
```

However, the compiler and runtime parser are unable to prevent invalid uses because there is no type check:

```
iex(4)> Foo.square(:foo)
** (ArithmeticError) bad argument in arithmetic expression
    iex:2: Foo.square/1
iex(5)> Foo.square("foo")
** (ArithmeticError) bad argument in arithmetic expression
    iex:2: Foo.square/1
```

Typespecs are used as a form of self-documenting attributes to the code. They can help prevent developers misusing certain interfaces. Unfortunately, they do not provide compile-time errors:

```
iex(6)> defmodule Foo do
...(6)>   @spec square(number) :: number
...(6)>   def square(x), do: x * x
...(6)> end
iex(7)> Foo.square(4)
16
iex(8)> Foo.square(4.4)
19.360000000000003
iex(9)> Foo.square(:foo)
** (ArithmeticError) bad argument in arithmetic expression
    iex:2: Foo.square/1
iex(10)> Foo.square("foo")
** (ArithmeticError) bad argument in arithmetic expression
    iex:2: Foo.square/1
```

Fortunately, there are tools such as Dialyzer (http://www.erlang.org/doc/man/dialyzer.html) that can check and validate the code annotated with typespecs. Dialyzer is a static-analysis tool for Erlang, and since Elixir is compiled to BEAM code, the bytecode of the Erlang VM, full support of Dialyzer is given essentially for free.

> The easiest way to use Dialyzer with Elixir projects is to use the Dialyxir Mix (https://github.com/jeremyjh/dialyxir) plugin.

The basic syntax for function typespecs is shown as follows:

```
@spec function_name(types_of_parameters) :: return_type
```

Typespecs are implemented as module attributes; thus, the `@spec` directive is declaring an attribute to the current module. The `function_name` declarative specifies *which* function the typespec is for, and the `function_name` declarative should match the actual function name. The parameter and return types are the main components of typespecs. The `::` symbol denotes the transition from function header and return type.

From the preceding example, we had the following typespec:

```
@spec square(number) :: number
```

Here, `square` is the function name, and `number` is the parameter and return type of the function. Another example of a typespec can be found from Elixir's standard library function, `round/1`:

```
@spec round(number) :: integer
```

This states that the `round` function takes anything that is a number and returns integers, where `number` is defined as either `float` or `interger`.

Typespecs are also used to define custom types. For example, let's presume we didn't have the `number` type from before; how would it be defined knowing what we know now? Short of knowing the full syntax, we are guessing something along the lines of:

```
number :: integer | float
```

This would be on point. The only missing part is the annotation:

```
@type number :: integer | float
```

The full list of types and typespecs can be found in Elixir's typespec (`http://elixir-lang.org/docs/stable/elixir/#!Kernel.Typespec.html`) documentation.

If you're familiar with BNF (`https://en.wikipedia.org/wiki/Backus%E2%80%93Naur_Form`) notation for defining languages, typespecs will feel similar.

Using – implementing – behaviours

Behaviour definitions provide implementors with compile-time checks for correctness and the syntax follows very similarly from typespecs.

The actual syntax uses the `defcallback` macro from the `Behaviour` module.

We will cover macros and their entirety later in this chapter.

Let's walk through a short example of a configuration file parser, where the configuration file could be in several different formats.

The `ConfigParser` behaviour could be defined with the following module:

```
defmodule ConfigParser do
  use Behaviour

  defcallback parse(String.t) :: any
  defcallback extensions() :: [String.t]

end
```

The behaviour is defined similar to how any other Elixir module is. It even uses the familiar `use some_other_module` directive at the beginning to import the `Behaviour` functions and macros. However, instead of defining actual functions, it defines two functions that will be exported by the implementors of this behaviour.

The first function, `parse/1`, takes a String as a parameter and returns an `any` type, where `any` is a catch-all for types; the returned type can be any valid Elixir type. The second function, `exentsions/0`, returns a list of strings.

Next, a supported configuration file format could be JSON, and thus, we would need a configuration parser that implements the behaviour. Again, this is simply another Elixir module:

```
defmodule JsonConfigParser do
  @behaviour ConfigParser

  def parse(str), do: str

  def extensions(), do: ["json"]
end
```

Similarly, a module is defined, but instead of `use`, it specifies a module attribute `@behaviour`. The module then goes to define implementations for the exported functions of the `ConfigParser` behaviour. Since the actual parsing of JSON data isn't really the important detail, it is being omitted.

If we go ahead and save these modules as `config_parser.ex` and `json_config_parser.ex`, respectively, we can compile them and *test* them out:

```
$ elixirc config_parser.ex
$ elixirc json_config_parser.ex
```

If no output is given, the modules have compiled successfully and without errors or warnings. To test it out, go ahead and launch IEx and `import` the latter module:

```
iex(1)> import JsonConfigParser
nil
iex(2)> JsonConfigParser.parse("foobar")
"foobar"
iex(3)> JsonConfigParser.extensions
["json"]
```

Now, let's say we would like to add support for YAML configuration files as well. We can add another module (and update the code that dispatches the parsers):

```
defmodule YamlConfigParser do
  @behaviour ConfigParser

  def prase(str), do: str

  def extensions(), do: ["yaml", "yml"]

end
```

And compile it using the following command:

```
$ elixirc yaml_config_parser.ex
yaml_config_parser.ex:1: warning: undefined behaviour function parse/1
(for behaviour ConfigParser)
```

Oops! It seems we mistyped the `prase/1` function and Elixir is complaining that we did not define the `parse/1` function. Correcting the issue, we will see that the warning goes away:

```
$ elixirc yaml_config_parser.ex
yaml_config_parser.ex:1: warning: redefining module YamlConfigParser
```

 Although it still complains, this warning is safe to ignore. In the previous run, the module still compiled into proper BEAM bytecode, however, Elixir complained about the missing definition for the behaviour.

We can similarly load up the `YamlConfigParser` module in `iex` and see that it works (the same) as expected:

```
iex(1)> import YamlConfigParser
nil
iex(2)> YamlConfigParser.parse("yaml!")
"yaml!"
iex(3)> YamlConfigParser.extensions
["yaml", "yml"]
```

Protocols

Protocols are Elixir's way of adding a splash of polymorphism to OTP. Protocols, in a sense, provides a means for generics in code. A specific function can be declared. However, the definition of such a function may be very specific to the types or records it is given. Thus, via a protocol, the function can be extended to new types that weren't defined, let alone considered, at the time of the original protocol.

 Protocols, in this context, are not related to "network protocols". This is an unfortunate abuse of terms.

Protocols are defined similarly to how modules are defined, except, unlike the behaviours from the previous section, a different directive is used to define protocols.

That is, instead of using `defmodule` to define a protocol, we use `defprotocol`.

Let's define a relatively simple protocol for testing **falsy** values.

We will define falsy to be, well, `false`, `nil`, the empty list, `[]`, `0`, and so on. Another semantic we need to choose `is_falsy?/1` return `true` for falsy things, or `false`. For this, since we are testing if something *is* falsy it should return `true` it is falsy. Another option would be to return `:yes` or `:no`.

The protocol itself can be defined as follows:

```
defprotocol Falsy do
  def is_falsy?(data)
end
```

For the implementations, another macro, `defimpl`, is used. The implementation will take the protocol being defined and the current type for the implementation.

Here is the implementation for atoms:

```
defimpl Falsy, for: Atom do
  def is_falsy?(false), do: true
  def is_falsy?(nil), do: true
  def is_falsy?(_), do: false
end
```

As mentioned in the preceding code, `false` and `nil` would be falsy. All other atoms are not.

And another implementation for integers:

```
defimpl Falsy, for: Integer do
  def is_falsy?(0), do: true
  def is_falsy?(_), do: false
end
```

Again, as decided in the preceding code, `0` is a falsy value, but all other integers are not.

There are a few more types to define:

```
defimpl Falsy, for: List do
  def is_falsy?([]), do: true
  def is_falsy?(_), do: false
end

defimpl Falsy, for: Map do
  def is_falsy?(map), do: map_size(map) == 0
end
```

For lists, we match against the empty list for falsy values, leaving the rest to be truthy.

Maps, on the other hand, are slightly different because `%{}` can't be used for pattern matching since it would match *every* map given. Thus, if the size of the map is 0, the map is falsy.

Now that we have defined falsy for a few types, we can go ahead and try the different types:

```
iex(1)> import_file "falsy.ex"
{:module, Falsy.Map,
 <<70, 79, 82, 49, 0, 0, 6, 136, 66, 69, 65, 77, 69, 120, 68, 99, 0, 0,
0, 174, 131, 104, 2, 100, 0, 14, 101, 108,
105, 120, 105, 114, 95, 100, 111, 99, 115, 95, 118, 49, 108, 0, 0, 0, 2,
104, 2, ...>>,
```

```
  {:__impl__, 1}}
iex(2)> Falsy.is_falsy?(false)
true
iex(3)> Falsy.is_falsy?(nil)
true
iex(4)> Falsy.is_falsy?(:yes)
false
```

As expected for the atoms, `false` and `nil` are falsy (`true` results), but `:yes` is not (the `false` result):

```
iex(5)> Falsy.is_falsy?(0)
true
iex(6)> Falsy.is_falsy?(42)
false
iex(7)> Falsy.is_falsy?([])
true
iex(8)> Falsy.is_falsy?([1, 2, 3, 4])
false
iex(9)> Falsy.is_falsy?(Map.new())
true
iex(10)> Falsy.is_falsy?(%{:a => 1})
false
```

Similarly, integers, lists, and maps are handled correctly.

However, what happens when a float value is passed, or any other type that is not explicitly defined?

```
iex(11)> Falsy.is_falsy?(0.0)
** (Protocol.UndefinedError) protocol Falsy not implemented for 0.0
    iex:1: Falsy.impl_for!/1
    iex:2: Falsy.is_falsy?/1
```

As might be expected, Elixir complains that there is no implementation for the given type. As a protocol developer, the decision can be made to leave **unknowns** unimplemented, to be handled downstream, or to provide a default. There are certainly pros and cons to both approaches, and this is a decision that will have to be made. The do nothing approach is to leave it undefined and *force* the decision on the consumer of the protocol.

Built-in protocols

There are several protocols built into the core of Elixir. These protocols, in fact, enable a large amount of some of the code we have already written.

Take `Enum.map/2` or `Enum.reduce`, for just two examples. Without the `Enumerable` protocol, these two functions would have a very difficult time being *actually* useful:

```
iex(1)> Enum.map [1, 2, 3, 4], fn(x) -> x * x end
[1, 4, 9, 16]
```

Or the reducer:

```
iex(2)> Enum.reducer(1..10, 0, fn(x, acc) -> x + acc end)
55
```

It is a similar case with the `Strings.Chars` protocol. Implementing this protocol for data types is essentially equivalent to implementing a `to_string` function typical of other languages.

```
iex(3)> to_string :hello
"hello"
```

Occasionally, the `String.Chars` protocol isn't sufficient to print **complex** datatypes:

```
iex(4)> tuple = {1, 2, 3}
{1, 2, 3}
iex(5)> "tuple #{tuple}"
** (Protocol.UndefinedError) protocol String.Chars not implemented for
{1, 2, 3}
    (elixir) lib/string/chars.ex:3: String.Chars.impl_for!/1
    (elixir) lib/string/chars.ex:17: String.Chars.to_string/1
```

In these cases, there is the `Inspect` protocol. The `Inspect` protocol enables a transformation of any datatype into a textual form. Thus, to print `tuple` from before, we can add a call to `inspect`:

```
iex(6)> "tuple #{inspect tuple}"
"tuple {1, 2, 3}"
```

IEx uses `inspect/1` and the `Inspect` protocol for printing results to the console. Notice, however, the printed output prefixed with # is no longer a valid Elixir input—the previous examples could be piped back *into* Elixir or Elixir's interpreter and would be valid Elixir code. For example, using `inspect` on a function reference yields invalid Elixir code:

```
iex(7)> inspect &(&1*&1)
"#Function<6.54118792/1 in :erl_eval.expr/5>"
```

There are some more functions of Elixir that allow us to get the code representation of our code, and they are known as **Abstract Syntax Tree (AST)**, and Elixir has great support for working with them.

Abstract syntax trees

ASTs are not just a concept of your programming language course. They are real and very useful in the real world.

Abstract syntax trees are the representation of our language compilers (or interpreters) used when parsing and translating written code into a new form, bytecode (for example, Elixir, Erlang, Python, and Java), machine code (for example, C/C++ and assembler), or another language (for example, Less, CoffeeScript, and so on). This, typically internal representation is where the majority of the language expression is broken down into its components for translation or evaluation.

Fortunately, for us, José Valim, and those before him with Erlang decided that the AST should be available to the programmer as first-class datatypes. That is, we can view, evaluate, and manipulate the AST of our code at compile time. This access is what enables metaprogramming. With access to the AST *and* the ability to manipulate it to suit our needs, we are able to write code that writes code.

To access the AST of any expression, we can use `quote`. It takes the expression or block provided and returns the AST Elixir representation. Let's examine a few examples of using `quote`:

```
iex(1)> quote do: 2 + 5
{:+, [context: Elixir, import: Kernel], [2, 5]}
```

The structure of Elixir's AST is always a tuple of three elements:

- The first element is an atom or another tuple
- The second element of the tuple is the context or available binds within the quoted expression
- The third element is the argument list to the function

In this example, our first element, `:+`, is the atom representation of the function to be evaluated; the second element of the tuple—the first list—is the imported environmental contexts; and finally, the third element of the tuple—the second list—is the arguments to the function.

Let's try a slightly more complicated example, the one that involves order of operations:

```
iex(2)> quote do: 2 + 4 * 6
{:+, [context: Elixir, import: Kernel],
 [2, {:*, [context: Elixir, import: Kernel], [4, 6]}]}
```

Here, the first element of the larger tuple is `:+` because it will be the *last* function called in the chain. The second argument to `:+` will be the result of evaluating `:*`.

Let's see the tree as an actual tree:

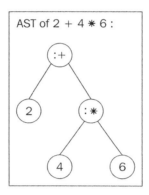

Notice, that **:+** is the root of the tree with children **2** and **:***. Most ASTs will be represented with prefix notation because it resolves the ambiguous case for operation order that is usually inherent with infix notations.

Let's examine some more complicated ASTs:

```
iex(3)> quote do: fn(x) -> x * x end
{:fn, [],
 [{:->, [],
   [[{:x, [], Elixir}],
    {:*, [context: Elixir, import: Kernel],
     [{:x, [], Elixir}, {:x, [], Elixir}]}]}]}
```

Here, the returned tuples represent the creation of an anonymous function.

Remember, *all* Elixir code can be represented using Elixir data structures.

This, of course, requires that there be a few core data structures to bootstrap the language together. Those types are atoms, numbers, Strings, lists (including keyword lists), and 2-pair tuples. Attempting to quote these types will result in themselves being returned:

```
iex(1)> quote do: :atom
:atom
iex(2)> quote do: 42
42
iex(3)> quote do: 19.9991
19.9991
iex(4)> quote do: "Hello, 世界»
«Hello, 世界»
iex(5)> quote do: [1, 2, 3, 4]
[1, 2, 3, 4]
iex(6)> quote do: [a: 1, b: 2]
[a: 1, b: 2]
iex(7)> quote do: {1, 2}
{1, 2}
```

The rest of the language can be realized with the previous data structures and a few special forms. This is where the macro system comes into play.

Our first macros

Now that we have the basics of abstract syntax trees, let's dive into macros, the heart of metaprogramming.

Macros, in the context of Elixir, are a means of deferring the evaluation of certain code. That is, instead immediately expanding an expression, say, when a value is passed, the expression will be passed in its quoted form to the macro. The macro would then be able to decide what it should do with the expressions passed.

This may become more clear when comparing macros to functions. For example, let's attempt to (re)create the if-else construct using a function:

```
defmodule MyIf do

  def if(condition, clauses) do
    do_clause = Keyword.get(clauses, :do, nil)
    else_clause = Keyword.get(clauses, :else, nil)
    case condition do
      val when val in [false, nil] ->
```

```
            else_clause
          _ -> do_clause
        end
      end

  end
```

After loading into `iex`, using `MyIf` may look something similar to the following lines of code:

```
iex(1)> c "myif.exs"
[MyIf]
iex(2)> MyIf.if 1 == 2, do: (IO.puts "1 == 2"), else: (IO.puts "1 != 2")
1 == 2
1 != 2
:ok
```

Since we have defined a function, the arguments passed to the function are evaluated *before* being passed to the function. Therefore, the value of both `do_clause` *and* `else_clause` are already set to `:ok`. Similarly, the `condition` value is already bound to `false`. Since `condition` is bound to `false`, the function returns the value for `else_clause`. This results in *both* `IO.puts/1` calls being executing and the function returning `:ok`. This is exact opposite of what an `if-else` expression should do. Let's fix it using a macro:

```
defmodule MyIf do

  defmacro if(condition, clauses) do
    do_clause = Keyword.get(clauses, :do, nil)
    else_clause = Keyword.get(clauses, :else, nil)
    quote do
      case unquote(condition) do
        val when val in [false, nil] ->
          unquote(else_clause)
        _ -> unquote(do_clause)
      end
    end
  end

end
```

Similar to how the function version is written, the macro extracts the `:do` and `:else` clauses (using `nil` if not found). Next, we return the result of quoting the `case` expression. Inside, the `case` expression, the passed condition is unquoted as to bind the passed value of the condition *into* the quoted block. Similarly, the `:do` and `:else` clauses are unquoted *into* the expression.

Then, using our macro may look similar to the following code:

```
defmodule Test do
  require MyIf

  MyIf.if 1 == 2 do
    IO.puts "1 == 2"
  else
    IO.puts "1 != 2"
  end
end
```

Save both modules into the same file and load them into an `iex` session:

```
iex(1)> c "myif_macro.exs"
1 != 2
[Test, MyIf]
```

As we expected, only the `else` clause was executed.

> The Elixir compiler needs to know *beforehand* the list of available macros as to know how to expand them. This is what the `require` directive at the beginning of the `Test` module does. It informs the Elixir compiler that the `MyIf` module is *required* to compile this module.

The result of a macro is an AST. The AST is then injected into module that uses it. That is, macros inject code.

Invoking `MyIf.if` inside the `Test` module yields changes in the `Test` module's AST that is then piped into the Elixir compiler.

We can inspect it by making a small change to the `MyIf.if` macro:

```
defmodule MyIf do

  defmacro if(condition, clauses) do
    do_clause = Keyword.get(clauses, :do, nil)
    else_clause = Keyword.get(clauses, :else, nil)
    ast = quote do
      case unquote(condition) do
        val when val in [false, nil] ->
          unquote(else_clause)
        _ -> unquote(do_clause)
      end
```

```
        end

    IO.puts Macro.to_string ast
    ast
  end

end
```

Instead of directly returning the result of the `quote` special form, we bind it to the variable, `ast`, and print it using `IO.puts/1` and `Macro.to_string/1`. Finally, the `ast` variable is returned to the caller so that it's properly consumed.

This way, any time the `MyIf.if` macro is used, the resulting AST will be printed to standard out before being injected.

 Note that `Macro.to_string/1` does not unquote any of the quoted expressions.

Let's look at another example for Elixir, `square`. The macro will take a single argument and return the square of the argument. The argument will most typically be a number, but could also be an expression of sorts, or be part of a bigger expression.

This macro is often shown in C/C++, as the following `#define` expression:

```
#define square(x)    x*x
```

 Don't worry if you don't know C or C++, we are only going to show basic arithmetic expressions of the language.

However, as some simple examples of this usage will show, this is entirely a non-starter for real use. For example, we may try something like this:

```
2/square(10)
```

And, this would expand to *2 / 10 * 10*, which is completely incorrect, and we may be tempted to resolve the issue by surrounding the expression in parentheses:

```
#define square(x) (x * x)
```

But this will still fail in the case of passing an expression to the macro:

```
square(1 + 1)
```

This would be expanded to *(1 + 1 * 1 + 1)*.

Again, we may be tempted to *solve* this problem by adding more parentheses:

```
#define square(x) ((x) * (x))
```

But this fails again with something like this:

```
x = 1
square(++x)
```

And, this would be expanded to *((++x) * (++x))*.

But what is the result of that expression? It's certainly no longer the square of x because x is inherently changed within the expression (read nasty variable mutation). Again, there are ways to solve this problem within the language, but more and even more subtle edge cases arise and this rabbit hole path of patching and finding more issues continues.

In Elixir, *none* of the preceding issues are a concern with even the naive version of the square macro:

```
defmodule Math do
  defmacro square(x) do
    quote do
      unquote(x) * unquote(x)
    end
  end
end
```

Loading this module into an iex session, we can see that all of the preceding mentioned cases do not result in issues.

```
iex(1)> c "math.exs"
[Math]
iex(2)> import Math
nil
iex(3)> square(10)
100
iex(4)> 2 / square(10)
0.02
iex(5)> square(1 + 1)
4
iex(6)> x = 2
iex(6)> square(x + 1)
9
```

The last example isn't exactly a direct mapping into the C/C++ version since the ++ operator of C languages doesn't exist (because it requires state and variable mutation).

All as we would expect an *actual* square function to behave. Now for a more interesting edge case, what if the expression involves sending a message to a process or printing text to the screen when expanded?

```
iex(6)> square((fn() -> IO.puts :square; 16 end).())
square
square
256
```

We still get the correct answer, as we might expect, however, :square is printed twice.

Looking back at the square macro, we define:

```
defmacro square(x) do
  quote do
    unquote(x) * unquote(x)
  end
end
```

We use unquote/1 twice. Thus, whatever expression for x gets evaluated twice. How can we solve this problem?

We could do it ourselves with something similar to the following code:

```
defmacro square(x) do
  quote do
    x_eval = unquote(x)
    x_eval * x_eval
  end
end
```

But this doesn't feel quite right.

We need another facility of Elixir's macro system, bind_quoted. Using bind_quoted is equivalent to doing the preceding variable assignment inside the quote block. It evaluates (read unqote) the provided arguments and holds onto their return values for use inside the quote block.

Using `bind_quoted` inside our `Math.square` macro looks something similar to the following code:

```
defmodule Math do
  defmacro square(x) do
    quote bind_quoted: [x: x] do
      x * x
    end
  end
end
```

Reloading this into an `iex` session, we can see this fixes our issue of invoking the `IO.puts` twice:

```
iex(1)> c "math.exs"
[Math]
iex(2)> import Math
nil
iex(3)> square((fn() -> IO.puts :square; 16 end).())
square
256
```

Another tool that we can use for inspecting that the `bind_quoted` option does what we expect is the `Macro.expand_once/2` function. This function takes an AST and the environment context and walks the given AST, expanding and unwrapping the top-level macro operations.

Thus, using this function on our current implementation of `Math.square` gives the following output:

```
iex(4)> Macro.expand_once(quote do square(5) end, __ENV__)
{:__block__, [],
 [{:=, [], [{:x, [counter: 4], Math}, 4]},
  {:*, [context: Math, import: Kernel],
   [{:x, [counter: 4], Math}, {:x, [counter: 4], Math}]}]}
```

> The `__ENV__` macro is a module level macro similar to `__MODULE__`, which we've used earlier. Information provided by `__ENV__`, `__MODULE__`, and others is available from `Macro.Env`. For more information visit `http://elixir-lang.org/docs/stable/elixir/Macro.Env.html`.

The expanded AST we receive from `Macro.expand_once` gives us a block that first assigns 4 to x, then returns the result of * with x and x, and this is exactly the expansion we expected.

Using `Macro.expand_once` on our more complicated variant (with `IO.puts`) results in a similarly structured AST, except with a lot more steps:

```
iex(5)> Macro.expand_once(
...(5)>      quote do square((fn() -> IO.puts :square; 16).()),
...(5)>      __ENV__)
{:__block__, [],
 [{:=, [],
   [{:x, [counter: 8], Math},
    {{:., [],
      [{:fn, [],
        [{:->, [],
          [[],
           {:__block__, [],
            [{{:., [],
               [{:__aliases__, [alias: false, counter: 8], [:IO]},
:puts]}, [],
               [:square]}, 16]}]}]}]}, [], []}]},
  {:*, [context: Math, import: Kernel],
   [{:x, [counter: 8], Math}, {:x, [counter: 8], Math}]}]}
```

Similar to the earlier example, the expanded AST yielded back is a block that first assigns the result of invoking the anonymous function to x that is denoted by the tuple with `:=` and the nested tuple and evaluation of the anonymous function is denoted by the tuple of `:.`. Finally, after x is assigned, the result would be the evaluation of `:*`, which includes parameters to x and x again.

The `Macro.expand_once/2` function is indispensable when trying to develop, debug, or simply understand the expansion and injection of code.

However, as you might be wondering, what about the binding of x? Does this effect the outer scope? Fortunately, the answer is that it doesn't. Attempting to use the bound x variable *outside* of the injected code will result in a compiler error or will return the value bound previously. That is, Elixir macros are hygienic.

Context and macro hygiene

Since macros are about injecting code, special care must be taken for the context, of both the caller and the context of the macro. The injected code of the macro cannot safely assume that certain variables will be available for it to consume. For example, let's look at a macro definition that attempts to access some variables of the caller context:

```
defmodule ContextInfo do
  defmacro grab_caller_context do
    quote do
      IO.puts x
    end
  end
end
```

Load up this module in `iex`:

```
iex(1)> c "context.exs"
[ContextInfo]
iex(2)> import ContextInfo
nil
iex(3)> x = 42
42
iex(4)> grab_caller_context
** (CompileError) iex:4: undefined function x/0
    expanding macro: ContextInfo.grab_caller_context/0
    iex:4: (file)
```

After importing and binding a variable, invoking the macro yields a compiler error, as we would expect, because the macro cannot implicitly access the caller's context.

Similarly, the macro cannot safely inject code that changes the context or environment of the caller. Let's add another macro to the `ContextInfo` module that attempts to change the value of x:

```
defmacro inject_context_change do
  quote do
    x = 0
    IO.puts x
  end
end
```

Loading it again into `iex`, we see something like the following output:

```
iex(1)> c "context.exs"
[ContectInfo]
iex(2)> import ContextInfo
nil
iex(3)> x = 42
42
iex(4)> inject_context_change
0
:ok
iex(5)> x
42
```

Again, the result of calling the macro does not change the context of the caller.

A more explicit example of macro context versus caller context is shown with the following two modules:

```
defmodule MacroContext do
  defmacro info do
    IO.puts "Macro context: (#{__MODULE__})"

    quote do
      IO.puts "Caller context: (#{__MODULE__})"

      def some_info do
        IO.puts """
        I am #{__MODULE__} and I come with the following:
        #{inspect __info__(:functions)}
        """
      end
    end
  end
end

defmodule MyModule do
  require MacroContext
  MacroContext.info
end
```

Loading the two modules into `iex`, we see the following output:

```
iex(1)> c "context2.exs"
Macro context: (Elixir.MacroContext)
Caller context: (Elixir.MyModule)
[MyModule, MacroContext]
```

Let's invoke the injected function:

```
iex(2)> MyModule.some_info
I am Elixir.MyModule and I come with the following:
[some_info: 0]


:ok
```

The first module defines a macro that before doing anything else, prints the current module name via the __MODULE__ macro. Inside the `quote` block, we print the caller's module name, again, via the __MODULE__ macro. Then, we inject a function that prints the module name and the available functions of the module.

The output of compiling the modules yields the output of the macro context (`IO. puts "Macro context ..."`) and the output of the caller context (`IO.puts "Caller context ..."`). Then, invoking the injected `some_info/1` function yields the rest.

How does the __MODULE__ macro show the correct module name for each context? This, it turns out, is the result of unhygienic macros, which is the topic of the next section.

Unhygienic macros – overriding context

Occasionally, part of writing good macros, overriding the context is required analogously to how dealing with state in programming is what results in useful programs.

To accomplish overriding the context, we need yet another macro facility from Elixir—`var!`. The `var!` macro is actually itself very versatile; it allows us to access members of the caller context *without* them being passed to the macro and allows the macro to modify the context of the caller.

Going back to some of our previous examples, let's try adding in `var!`:

```
defmodule ContextInfo do
  defmacro grab_caller_context do
    quote do
      IO.puts var!(x)
```

```
        end
      end
    end
```

After loading and compiling this new version of `ContextInfo` into an `iex` session, we see we can access the `x` variable of the caller context:

```
iex(1)> c "context.exs"
[ContextInfo]
iex(2)> require ContextInfo
nil
iex(3)> x = 42
42
iex(4)> ContextInfo.grab_caller_context
42
:ok
```

As expected, the macro was able to print the value of the bound variable, even though the variable was bound in the caller's context and not the macro.

Similarly, updating the `inject_context_change` macro from previous examples:

```
defmodule ContextInfo do
  defmacro inject_context_change do
    quote do
      var!(x) = 0
    end
  end
end
```

And loading the updated module into `iex`:

```
iex(1)> c "context.exs"
[ContextInfo]
iex(2)> require ContextInfo
nil
iex(3)> x = 42
42
iex(4)> ContextInfo.inject_context_change
0
iex(5)> x
0
```

The result of this modified macro is the ability to bind a new value for a variable bound in the calling context.

That is, using the var! macro allows macros to extract and inject values from or into the context of the caller, enabling unhygienic things to occur.

As a note of caution, this is, by definition, non-functional and introduces complexities into the macros (which are already complicated enough). However, like most things with programming and decisions, the choice to use an unhygienic macro must be weighed properly and not necessarily rejected outright. Is the macro's ability to change the caller's context absolutely necessary for the macro to work? Does it make sense? Is using a macro in this way even warranted to begin with? Consider these questions carefully.

Macro examples

Let's go through some more in-depth examples of using macros to accomplish some pretty cool things, things that are generally fairly difficult to accomplish in other languages.

Debugging and tracing

We'll start with a debugging/tracer module that will enable us to automatically trace the methods of our library.

 Of course, this is highly unnecessary since the Erlang VM itself is capable of adding this functionality for us without requiring anything from the developer.

As part of this example, we're going to dive into use and __using__. use as it turns out, is a relatively simple function that invokes the __using__ macro of the module passed. This, in turn, injects the code of the __using__ macro.

For example, let's say we've defined a basic module, UsingTest, as the following code:

```
defmodule UsingTest do
  defmacro __using__(_opts) do
    quote do
      IO.puts "I'm the __using__/1 of #{unquote(__MODULE__)}"
    end
  end
end
```

If we then define another, very simple module, say, MyUsingTest:

```
defmodule MyUsingTest do
  use UsingTest
end
```

Compiling them together should result in some output like the following printed to the screen:

```
iex(1)> c "usingtest.exs"
I'm the __using__ of Elixir.UsingTest
[TestMyUsing, UsingTest]
```

Since our goal is to add some tracing information to the invocation of the functions in our libraries, we need to redefine the def macro. That is, we will have a module, say, Tracer, with the following code:

```
defmodule Tracer do

  defmacro def(definition={name, _, args}, do: content) do
    quote do
      Kernel.def(unquote(definition)) do
        unquote(content)
      end
    end
  end

  defmacro __using__(_) do
    quote do
      import Kernel, except: [def: 2]
      import unquote(__MODULE__), only: [def: 2]
    end
  end

end
```

The first macro def/2 defines our new version of def that will be used by the modules using use Tracer.

However, all we have done is added a level of indirection to the definition of functions, we haven't done any tracing. Let's add some calls that perform these actions.

First, we are going to want a helper function for printing the arguments of the function. It will be a simple transform of the arguments to something printable:

```
def dump_args(args) do
  args |> Enum.map(&inspect/1) |> Enum.join(", ")
end
```

That is, loop the given arguments and map them through `inspect/1` function, then join them all together with commas.

Finally, we need to modify the `def` macro to use our new helper function and print the function name, arguments, and result:

```
defmacro def(definition={name, _, args}, do: content) do
  quote do
    Kernel.def(unquote(definition)) do
      IO.puts :stderr,
              ">>> Calling #{unquote(name)} with #{Tracer.dump_
args(unquote(args))}"
      result = unquote(content)
      IO.puts :stderr, "<<< Result: #{Macro.to_string result}"
      result
    end
  end
end
```

In this version, we inject a call to `IO.puts/2` to print the called function, its arguments, and its result.

The whole completed `Tracer` module looks similar to the following code:

```
defmodule Tracer do

  def dump_args(args) do
    args |> Enum.map(&inspect/1) |> Enum.join(", ")
  end

  defmacro def(definition={name, _, args}, do: content) do
    quote do
      Kernel.def(unquote(definition)) do
        IO.puts :stderr,
                ">>> Calling #{unquote(name)} with #{Tracer.dump_
args(unquote(args))}"
        result = unquote(content)
        IO.puts :stderr, "<<< Result: #{Macro.to_string result}"
        result
      end
    end
  end

  defmacro __using__(_) do
    quote do
      import Kernel, except: [def: 2]
```

```
        import unquote(__MODULE__), only: [def: 2]
    end
  end

end
```

Now, in another module, define a simple sort module and include a line at the top for using the `Tracer` module:

```
defmodule Quicksort do
  use Tracer

  def sort(list), do: _sort(list)

  defp _sort([]), do: []
  defp _sort(l = [h|_]) do
    (l |> Enum.filter(&(&1 < h)) |> _sort)
    ++ [h] ++
    (l |> Enum.filter(&(&1 > h)) |> _sort)
  end

end
```

We've probably seen this module a few times; the major difference is that we've only added the `use` expression at the top. This simple change allows us to see the function call of the top-level, `sort`:

```
% elixirc tracer.exs
% elixirc quicksort.exs
```

Loading the module into `iex`:

```
iex(1)> import Quicksort
nil
iex(2)> 1..10 |> Enum.reverse |> Quicksort.sort
>>> Calling sort with [10, 9, 8, 7, 6, 5, 4, 3, 2, 1]
<<< Result: [1, 2, 3, 4, 5, 6, 7, 8, 9, 10]
[1, 2, 3, 4, 5, 6, 7, 8, 9, 10]
```

Here, we see the output of the macro injecting its `IO.puts` calls for our function and we also see the result of the function itself.

Static data to functions

Since macros are expanded at compile-time, some interesting things can be done during this injection. This way, creating functions from near static data is not only a possibility, but something that is used regularly to support MIME type translations, or Unicode character data support.

For example, Elixir itself uses Unicode code points in a text file to create the functions related to String.upcase/1, String.downcase/1, and others for complete Unicode support. If a new code point is added tomorrow, the code itself does not have to change; the code point needs only to be added to the source text file, and the project recompiled.

Let's look at how Elixir defines the String.Unicode module, and specifically, how the String.downcase/1 function is *implemented*.

The Elixir source is available at https://github.com/elixir-lang/elixir.

Under the Elixir source tree, there is a folder for Unicode data points. Also, in this folder, is an Elixir source file, unicode.ex, which defines the String.Unicode module.

At the beginning of this module are a few list comprehensions and some uses of Enum.reduce/3:

```
data_path = Path.join(__DIR__, "UnicodeData.txt")

{codes, whitespace} = Enum.reduce File.stream!(data_path), {[], []},
fn(line, {cacc, wacc}) ->
  [codepoint, _name, _category,
   _class, bidi, _decomposition,
   _numeric_1, _numeric_2, _numeric_3,
   _bidi_mirror, _unicode_1, _iso,
   upper, lower, title] = :binary.split(line, ";", [:global])

title = :binary.part(title, 0, byte_size(title) - 1)

  cond do
    upper != "" or lower != "" or title != "" ->
      {[{to_binary.(codepoint),
         to_binary.(upper),
         to_binary.(lower),
         to_binary.(title)} | cacc],
       wacc}
```

```
      bidi in ["B", "S", "WS"] ->
        {cacc, [to_binary.(codepoint) | wacc]}
      true ->
        {cacc, wacc}
    end
  end
```

This reads the file, `UnicodeData.txt`, and streams each line through the provided anonymous function, in turn, breaking down each Unicode code point into a list of tuples.

Later, a list comprehension is used to define the `downcase/1` function:

```
def downcase(string), do: downcase(string, "")

for {codepoint, _upper, lower, _title} <- codes, lower && lower !=
codepoint do
  defp downcase(unquote(codepoint) <> rest, acc) do
    downcase(rest, acc <> unquote(lower))
  end
end

defp downcase(<<char, rest :: binary>>, acc) do
  downcase(rest, <<acc :: binary, char>>)
end

defp downcase("", acc), do: acc
```

The first line defines the public interface of the `String.Unicode.downcase/1` function, which returns the result of the privately-defined `downcase/2`.

Next, a list comprehension is used to unpack the list of codes and extract the lower case character of each. This is then used to generate a large number of the `downcase/2` functions that are capable of being individually matched.

If there's no match, it will match against the next version, `<<char, rest :: binary>>`, `acc`. Finally, the last function of the four provides the return value when processing the provided binary is complete. That is, it matches against the empty string, `""`, and returns the accumulator value, `acc`.

Four very similar functions are defined for `upcase/1`.

This example isn't necessarily using many macro features; however, the pattern of loading some static data from a file and generating functions for a module is a common enough pattern, which is useful to see.

Testing macros

Testing modular code is generally pretty easy and considered a good thing. Testing macros can be a little like testing black magic. At first blush, it's not always obvious how to even approach testing macros. However, one general rule can help steer the testing suite in the right direction: test the generated code, not the generation code. That is, test the *result* of the macro, not the macro's ability to generate code.

It's generally much harder to create a proper harness around macros than it is to generate a harness around the code generated by macros. For example, if we wrote a `while` macro, we could write a test for it using a block of code that *uses* the `while` expression:

```
defmodule WhileTest do
  use ExUnit.Case

  test "while loops while truthy" do
    pid = spawn(fn -> :thread.sleep(:infinity) end)
    send self, :one
    while Process.isAlive?(pid) do
      receive do
        :one -> send self, :two
        :two -> send self, :three
        :three ->
          Process.exit(pid)
          send self, :done
      end
    end
    assert_received :done
  end
```

Thus, if the assertion fails, we know that the termination of the loop is faulty. Some more tests could be added, but the idea is the same.

Similarly, for testing the generated functions, test the expected behaviour of the generated functions. In the case of the standard library, here are the tests for `String.upcase/1`:

```
test "upcase" do
  assert String.upcase("123 abcd 456 efg hij ( %$#) kl mnop @ qrst =
- _ uvwxyz") == "123 ABCD 456 EFG HIJ ( %$#)
KL MNOP @ QRST = - _ UVWXYZ"
  assert String.upcase("") == ""
  assert String.upcase("abcD") == "ABCD"
end
```

```
test "upcase utf8" do
  assert String.upcase("& % # àáâ ãäå 1 2 ç æ") == "& % # ÀÁÂ ÃÄÅ 1 2
Ç Æ"
  assert String.upcase("àáâãäåæçèéêëìíîïðñòóôõöøùúûüýþ") == "ÀÁÂÃÄÅÆÇÈ
ÉÊËÌÍÎÏÐÑÒÓÔÕÖØÙÚÛÜÝÞ"
end

test "upcase utf8 multibyte" do
  assert String.upcase("straße") == "STRASSE"
  assert String.upcase("áüÈß") == "ÁÜÈSS"
end
```

These, in themselves, don't seem to be sufficient for testing the `String.upcase/1` function. But knowing *how* `String.upcase/1` is implemented, this proves to be entirely sufficient.

It shouldn't be necessary to create a one-to-one testing of *all* the generated functions, but a large enough sample to know the generated functions are behaving correctly.

Remember that testing macros should be treated the same as testing the public interface of a module. Test the functions that are the result of the injected code. This changes it from a problem of testing code generation to a regular module testing problem.

Domain-specific languages

Macros have the ability to create small, embedded languages for solving specific problems. Occasionally, certain problems are not well expressed in the current language, however, they would be very easily expressible in a new, smaller, and more precise language.

Usually, creating a new language requires steps through lexers, parsers, and evaluators to even get the language off the ground. However, macros can extend the current language facilities to accomplish creating an embedded DSL.

A notable DSL example using Elixir and macros is the **Ecto project**. The Ecto project attempts to provide a similar language to SQL *in* Elixir for querying data stores. Instead of writing the SQL yourself and passing it to the database connector and letting it execute, the problem of querying data can be expressed in natural terms of Elixir, which, in turn, would be compiled to SQL and sent to the database.

For example, instead of having to write the following query to grab weather data from a table creatively named `weather`:

```
"select * from weather where prcp > 0" |> DB.Connector.query!
```

It could be expressed as:

```
query = from w in Weather,
         where: w.prcp > 0
         select: w
```

Furthermore, in this example, queries are now able to be checked at compile-time, whereas writing the SQL query into a string variant could only be checked once the query is executed.

Creating a DSL

Let's create a simple DSL for templating XML models. We may want to export our model data to XML so that it can be imported or loaded somewhere else or later.

Using a templating language might be acceptable, but it can sometimes be counter intuitive to express the models in this way. Similarly, using some of the already available libraries may require the model to be decorated or fit some arbitrary structure. However, we could achieve the same—exporting data to XML—with about 30 lines of code.

State of the macro

When creating a DSL for building up a string, we will need a way to save state. However, we've already seen some examples that allow us to save state, specifically, GenServers and the OTP framework, namely, the functions we wrote had a `state` parameter that the OTP framework would inject for us. We can use a similar idea, but another feature Elixir provides for doing this in a much more lightweight fashion—`Agents`.

That is, we can keep and manage state with Agent processes. In *Chapter 7, OTP – A Poor Name for a Rich Framework*, we wrote a key-value store process using `GenServer` and OTP. Let's rework that example using Agents instead. Let's start by exploring the Agent API.

```
iex(1)> {:ok, kv} = Agent.start_link &HashDict.new/0
{:ok, #PID<0.60.0>}
```

Like many OTP and Erlang processes, we call `Agent.start_link` to get things started. However, in the case of agents, we specify a function that initializes the state of the process; for our example, we use the `HashDict.new/0` function to create a new map.

```
iex(2)> Agent.get(kv, &(&1))
#HashDict<[]>
```

We can use the `Agent.get/2` function to retrieve the state from the agent. Similar to OTP examples, we specify the PID of the process or Agent, maintaining the data. Different from OTP though, we specify the function that will retrieve the data for us—in this case, it's the no-op lambda.

```
iex(3)> Agent.update(kv, &(HashDict.put(&1, :a, 2)))
:ok
```

Updating the state of an Agent is accomplished via the `Agent.update/2` function. Similar to the functions discussed earlier, we specify the PID and a function to perform the update. In this case, we simply use the `HashDict.put/3` function.

```
iex(4)> Agent.get(kv, &(&1))
#HashDict<[a: 2]>
iex(5)> Agent.get(kv, &(&1))  |> HashDict.get :a
2
iex(6)> Agent.get(kv, &(HashDict.get(&1, :a)))
2
```

Finally, using the `Agent.get/2` function, we can operate on our state data in a variety of ways.

Taking this small example a little further, we can completely rewrite the key-value example from *Chapter 7, OTP – A Poor Name for a Rich Framework*, with the following, very small module:

```
defmodule KV do

  def start_link do
    Agent.start_link(&HashDict.new/0, name: __MODULE__)
  end

  def get(key) do
    Agent.get(__MODULE__, &(HashDict.get(&1, key)))
  end

  def put(key, value) do
    Agent.update(__MODULE__, &(HashDict.put(&1, key, value)))
  end

end
```

Between the `iex` session and this module, we are using the `Process.register` feature available to us via the `start_link` functions. This is a full functioning KV store we can use instead of `Agent.put` and `Agent.get` manually:

```
iex(1)> c "kv_store.exs"
[KV]
iex(2)> KV.start_link
{:ok, #PID<0.60.0>}
iex(3)> KV.put(:a, 2)
:ok
iex(4)> KV.get(:a)
2
```

Returning to the XML DSL example, we need to define the DSL, specifically, the API of the DSL.

Let's break down what XML consists of:

- Arbitrary elements of a document; some may have attributes
- Elements may be nested; the same rules as in the preceding point apply
- Elements must be properly closed and properly nested

As such, the DSL we define could look similar to the following code:

```
xml do
  tag :model, name: "my model" do
    for i <- 0..5 do
      tag :attribute do
        text "some value #{i}"
      end
    end
  end
end
```

That is, we specify that the following is an XML block, we define a `model` tag with the attribute `name` with the value of `"my model"`, and we nest six `attribute` tags. The result of this block should look something like the following lines of code:

```
"<?xml version=\"1.0\"?>
<model name=\"my model\">
    <attribute>some value 0</attribute>
    <attribute>some value 1</attribute>
    <attribute>some value 2</attribute>
    <attribute>some value 3</attribute>
```

```
    <attribute>some value 4</attribute>
    <attribute>some value 5</attribute>
</model>"
```

 Formatted for readability.

Let's limit the scope slightly for our first iteration. We'll remove the ability to do attributes inside elements. Let's start with the helper functions for storing, updating, and retrieving the buffer for building the output:

```
def start_buffer(state), do: Agent.start_link(fn() -> state end)

def stop_buffer(buffer), do: Agent.stop(buffer)

def put_buffer(buffer, content), do: Agent.update(buffer, &[content | &1])

def render(buffer) do
  Agent.get(buffer, &(&1)) |>
  Enum.reverse |>
  Enum.join("")
end
```

We start by defining a function that starts and initializes the buffer and another to close the buffer once we are finished. Next, we have a function for updating or appending to the buffer. This is implemented using a basic stack, the anonymous function passed to `Agent.update` adds the new contents to the head of the list and concatenates it to the existing list. Finally, we have the `render` function that retrieves the buffer from the Agent, reverses the elements, and joins all the elements together. The reversal is required, since we are inserting the elements to the top of the list.

Next, we need to define a few macros, namely, the `xml`, `tag`, and `text` macros:

```
defmacro xml(do: block) do
  quote do
    {:ok, var!(buffer, Xml)} = start_buffer(["<?xml
version=\"1.0\"?>"])
    unquote(block)
    result = render(var!(buffer, Xml))
    :ok = stop_buffer(var!(buffer, Xml))
    result
  end
end
```

```
defmacro tag(name, do: inner) do
  quote do
    put_buffer var!(buffer, Xml), "<#{unquote(name)}>"
    unquote(inner)
    put_buffer var!(buffer, Xml), "</#{unquote(name)}>"
  end
end

defmacro text(string) do
  quote do: put_buffer(var!(buffer, Xml), to_string(unquote(string)))
end
```

Starting with the xml macro, inside the quote block, we start and initialize the buffer, inserting the XML header information into the state of the buffer. Next, we unquote the provided block. This block will likely contain the internal tag elements that will later be expanded. Once the block is done being expanded, we render the result, stop the buffer, and return the result. This macro is essentially the general strategy of rendering the XML code to follow.

Next, the tag macro inserts the start and end of the provided element into the buffer. However, before the end element tag is inserted, the inner block is expanded; this is how nesting will be achieved.

Finally, the text macro, simply expands inner element text and inserts it into the buffer.

Notice the use of var!/2. In this case, we need an unhygienic variable so that each macro can get the buffer variable, but we don't want the variable inserted into the caller's context, so we specify the Xml module as to insert the variable into the Xml module's context instead.

Here is the full Xml module:

```
defmodule Xml do

  def start_buffer(state), do: Agent.start_link(fn -> state end)

  def stop_buffer(buffer), do: Agent.stop(buffer)

  def put_buffer(buffer, content), do: Agent.update(buffer, &[content | &1])

  def render(buffer) do
    Agent.get(buffer, &(&1))
    |> Enum.reverse
    |> Enum.join("")
```

```
    end

    defmacro xml(do: block) do
      quote do
        {:ok, var!(buffer, Xml)} = start_buffer([])
        put_buffer var!(buffer, Xml), "<?xml version=\"1.0\"?>"
        unquote(block)
        result = render(var!(buffer, Xml))
        :ok = stop_buffer(var!(buffer, Xml))
        result
      end
    end

    defmacro tag(name, do: inner) do
      quote do
        put_buffer var!(buffer, Xml), "<#{unquote(name)}>"
        unquote(inner)
        put_buffer var!(buffer, Xml), "</#{unquote(name)}>"
      end
    end

    defmacro text(string) do
      quote do: put_buffer(var!(buffer, Xml), to_
string(unquote(string)))
    end

end
```

Then, we can create a `Template` module, which imports the `Xml` module and creates the preceding XML:

```
defmodule Template do
  import Xml

  def render do
    xml do
      tag :model do
        for i <- 0..5 do
          tag :attribute do
            text "some value #{i}"
          end
        end
      end
    end
  end

end
```

Finally, inside `iex`, we can try it out:

```
iex(1)> c "xml.exs"
[Xml]
iex(2)> c "template.exs"
[Template]
iex(3)> Template.render
"<?xml version=\"1.0\"?><model><attribute>some value 0</
attribute><attribute>some value 1</attribute><attribute>some value
2</attribute><attribute>some value 3</attribute><attribute>some value
4</attribute><attribute>some value 5</attribute></model>"
```

Now that we have a basic version working, let's add the ability to specify attributes to the elements.

First, let's add a small helper function to create the opening tag for each element. If a non-empty list of attributes is provided, let's add those as well:

```
def open_tag(name, []), do: "<#{name}>"
def open_tag(name, attrs) do
  attr_text = for {k, v} <- attrs, into: "", do: " #{k}=\"#{v}\""
  "<#{name}#{attr_text}>"
end
```

The job of this function is easy if no attributes are passed. However, if some attributes are passed, they should be looped over and accumulated into a string in the proper $k=\backslash "v\backslash "$ form, then added as part of the opening tag.

Now let's modify the `tag` module to accept attributes as an argument and use our new `open_tag` function for creating each element:

```
defmacro tag(name, attrs \\ [], do: inner) do
  quote do
    put_buffer var!(buffer, Xml), open_tag(unquote_splicing([name,
attrs]))
    unquote(inner)
    put_buffer var!(buffer, Xml), "</#{unquote(name)}>"
  end
end
```

Here, instead of simply opening the tag before unquoting the `inner` block, we use our new `open_tag/2` function to create the correct opening element tag, passing the name and attributes.

Notice that we use the convenience macro, `unquote_splicing`, to unquote both `name` and `attrs` before passing them as arguments to `open_tag/2`. That is, using `unquote_splicing` is the same as using a series of calls to `unquote`, for example. These are equivalent:

```
open_tag(unquote_splicing([name, attrs]))

open_tag(unquote(name), unquote(attrs))
```

Now that the `tag` macro is updated, we can update the `template` module to use it to add, say, a name attribute to the `model` element:

```
xml do
  tag :model, name: "my_model" do
    for i <- 0..5 do
      tag :attribute do
        text "some value #{i}"
      end
    end
  end
end
```

Compiling and loading the `Xml` and `Template` modules into an `iex` session, we can see that it now works as we expect:

```
iex(1)> c "xml.exs"
[Xml]
iex(2)> c "template.exs"
[Template]
iex(3)> Template.render
"<?xml version=\"1.0\"?><model name=\"my_model\"><attribute>some value
0</attribute><attribute>some value 1</attribute><attribute>some value
2</attribute><attribute>some value 3</attribute><attribute>some value
4</attribute><attribute>some value 5</attribute></model>"
```

With this, we can create models, records, or other arbitrary data structures and walk the data structure the same way that processing it would be to create an XML export of the data without having to add extra decorations or model contortions.

With great power...

Although, we've spent an entire chapter on macros and how awesome they are, a word of caution is required. Seldom use macros. That's worth repeating: _seldom_ use macros! Macros have the very real possibility of creating enormous complexity and technical debt—they have the ability to change the core semantics of the language. This can result in very difficult code to read and reason about. Thus, reaching for the macro system should be taken with a great amount of thought. Ask questions and poke the problem, really determine whether using macros is a good choice or not. Several questions may be:

- Is the problem tractable via macros or can the problem be easily expressed via macros? More so than *not* using macros?

- Is there significant overhead on the caller of using macros?

If either of these are answered negatively, it's likely that choosing macros is a bad move.

If both are answered positively, go forth and incur the complexity at the benefit of an elegant solution that may be impossible to express in other languages without the use of macros and metaprogramming.

Furthermore, when considering implementing a DSL, the preceding questions *really* need to be considered. Does the DSL *actually* create a simpler solution? Does the overhead of learning another small language outweigh the technical complexity cost associated with creating the DSL itself?

Exercises

Read:

- The Enumerable protocol (https://github.com/elixir-lang/elixir/blob/v1.0.5/lib/elixir/lib/enum.ex) in the Elixir source

- The typespec documentation (http://elixir-lang.org/docs/stable/elixir/#!Kernel.Typespec.html)

Do:

- Write your own unless macro. You may use either your if from the chapter or the standard library if:

    ○ Does using the standard library, if, produce a deeper AST than using case directly?

- Write your own `while` macro:
  - ○ Use the test `WhileTest` module to make sure it functions correctly.
  - ○ Add a test case for a `break` statement. (Hint: It will look similar to the test case provided.) Now add `break` to your macro.

Summary

In this chapter, we discussed a number of topics concerning Elixir and metaprogramming.

Typespecs are used as a means for documenting code (with code) such that other programmers (and ourselves) will know at a glance the expected types of certain functions. Typespecs are also a great tool for annotating code, functions, and modules for static analysis, and for finding type issues or other bugs typically unavailable to dynamically-typed languages.

Behaviours can be thought of akin to interfaces from OO languages. They are a means to define modules that *will* have a set of public functions with specific arity. If the modules adopting a behaviour do not define any or all of the functions from the behaviour, Elixir will raise a compiler warning.

Protocols are a means of performing high-level pattern matching and function dispatching for certain **actions**. For example, translating types into **printable** strings requires implementation of the `String.Chars` protocol for the specific type. This allows for the polymorphic call to functions such as `to_string/1` while abstracting (read disassociating) the detail of how each type needs to be translated to binaries.

Moreover, we chiefly discussed Elixir macros and how they enable metaprogramming.

Along the lines of macros, we covered a few examples of macros, some of which come from the standard library of Elixir, and others were used as examples of small problems that can be solved using macros.

Finally, although macros and metaprogramming can be very, very powerful and exciting, we also discussed how macros can be detrimental to a project and can incur technical debt if used improperly. Remember that macros shouldn't be used if a function would be sufficient.

Going forward

Our journey through the depths of Elixir have come to an end. Throughout our tour, we covered many topics from the syntax and types to the macro system defining the language. We covered the actor model and pipeline programming to initial discussions of distributed programming to distributed Elixir programming and OTP. All of the topics we covered are with the explicit goal of teaching Elixir and how to build robust, distributed applications using Elixir.

Now is the time to begin a new exploration of Elixir, to learn more of the language, its capabilities, of the potential, and to realize that potential.

Of course, going alone is difficult and dangerous: take the lessons you have learned so far and some extra resources with you:

- Elixir's getting started guide (`http://elixir-lang.org/getting-started/introduction.html`)
- Elixir's core documentation (`http://elixir-lang.org/docs/stable/elixir/Kernel.html`)
- The Elixir mailing list (`https://groups.google.com/forum/#!forum/elixir-lang-talk`)
- The `#elixir-lang` on freenode IRC (`http://irc.lc/freenode/elixir-lang`)
- Many others available on the Elixir homepage (`http://elixir-lang.org/`)

I hope the experience of learning Elixir has been a delightful one. As with any new language, it may not be immediately applicable nor feasible for your next projects—although I hope you will consider it—the concepts remain applicable in any language.

Mix together new potions, create new concoctions, and build robust applications.

Index

mix.exs 63
project, compiling 66
project, testing 66
README.md 65
test 65
structures 86, 87
supervisors
about 186-190
assumptions, of OTP process
initialization 191
designing with 191
fail fast(er) 190

T

tail recursion 54
topologies
bus topology 202
line topology 201
star topology 202
tuples
about 27
versus lists 28
types
about 16
atoms 19
binaries 28
binary 18
booleans 20-22
exponent floats 18
hexadecimal 18
(linked) lists 25
numerical types 17
octal 18
strings 23, 24
tuples 27

U

underscore
using 34

W

Windows
Elixir, installing on 7
work pools 155-164

Y

yum package manager tool 5

Thank you for buying
Learning Elixir

About Packt Publishing

Packt, pronounced 'packed', published its first book, *Mastering phpMyAdmin for Effective MySQL Management*, in April 2004, and subsequently continued to specialize in publishing highly focused books on specific technologies and solutions.

Our books and publications share the experiences of your fellow IT professionals in adapting and customizing today's systems, applications, and frameworks. Our solution-based books give you the knowledge and power to customize the software and technologies you're using to get the job done. Packt books are more specific and less general than the IT books you have seen in the past. Our unique business model allows us to bring you more focused information, giving you more of what you need to know, and less of what you don't.

Packt is a modern yet unique publishing company that focuses on producing quality, cutting-edge books for communities of developers, administrators, and newbies alike. For more information, please visit our website at www.packtpub.com.

About Packt Open Source

In 2010, Packt launched two new brands, Packt Open Source and Packt Enterprise, in order to continue its focus on specialization. This book is part of the Packt Open Source brand, home to books published on software built around open source licenses, and offering information to anybody from advanced developers to budding web designers. The Open Source brand also runs Packt's Open Source Royalty Scheme, by which Packt gives a royalty to each open source project about whose software a book is sold.

Writing for Packt

We welcome all inquiries from people who are interested in authoring. Book proposals should be sent to author@packtpub.com. If your book idea is still at an early stage and you would like to discuss it first before writing a formal book proposal, then please contact us; one of our commissioning editors will get in touch with you.

We're not just looking for published authors; if you have strong technical skills but no writing experience, our experienced editors can help you develop a writing career, or simply get some additional reward for your expertise.

PHP and MongoDB Web Development Beginner's Guide

ISBN: 978-1-84951-362-3   Paperback: 292 pages

Combine the power of PHP and MongoDB to build dynamic web 2.0 applications

1. Learn to build PHP-powered dynamic web applications using MongoDB as the data backend.

2. Handle user sessions, store real-time site analytics, build location-aware web apps, and much more, all using MongoDB and PHP.

3. Full of step-by-step instructions and practical examples, along with challenges to test and improve your knowledge.

Instant RubyMine Assimilation

ISBN: 978-1-84969-876-4   Paperback: 66 pages

Utilize the RubyMine IDE to develop your own Ruby on Rails applications

1. Learn something new in an Instant! A short, fast, focused guide delivering immediate results.

2. Incorporate features of RubyMine into your everyday Ruby and Ruby on Rails development workflow.

3. Learn about the integrated testing and debugging tools to make your coding bulletproof and productive.

Please check **www.PacktPub.com** for information on our titles

Made in the USA
Monee, IL
05 March 2021